A WORLD LIKE OUR OWN

A WORLD

Photographs by Russ Kinne

LIKE OUR OWN

MAN AND NATURE IN MADAGASCAR

ALISON JOLLY

NEW HAVEN AND LONDON
YALE UNIVERSITY PRESS
1980

The translation of the excerpt from Dox Razakandraina's poem "Red Island" on page 125 is from F. Labatut and R. Raharinarivonirina, *Etude historique* (Paris: Éditions Fernand Nathan, 1969). Ramasindraibe Salomon Elie, in the name of the heirs of Dox Razakandraina, graciously granted us permission to use this quotation from his father's work.

"God's First Defeat: A Tsimihety Legend" (pp. 237–38) is translated from Rabearison, *Contes et Légendes de Madagascar* (Imprimerie Luthérienne de Tananarive, 1967).

DESIGNED BY CHRISTOPHER HARRIS
AND SET IN VIP TRUMP TYPE BY
THE COMPOSING ROOM OF MICHIGAN, INC.
PRINTED IN THE UNITED STATES OF AMERICA BY
THE MURRAY PRINTING CO., WESTFORD, MASSACHUSETTS.

LIBRARY OF CONGRESS CATALOGING IN PUBLICATION DATA

JOLLY, ALISON.
  A WORLD LIKE OUR OWN.

  BIBLIOGRAPHY: P.
  INCLUDES INDEX.
  1. NATURE CONSERVATION—MADAGASCAR. 2. MAN—
INFLUENCE ON NATURE—MADAGASCAR. 3. NATURAL
HISTORY—MADAGASCAR. I. TITLE.
QH77.M28J64   304.2'0969'1   80-11871
ISBN 0-300-02478-9

For Richard
who said, "Tell the whole story—ecology with people,
not just your animals"

Our land, compared with what it was,
is like the skeleton of a body wasted
by disease. The plump soft parts
have vanished, and all that remains
is the bare carcass.

Plato, *Critias*
quoted in Eckholm 1976*a*

The zebu licks bare stone, and dies in
the place he loves.

Malagasy proverb

CONTENTS

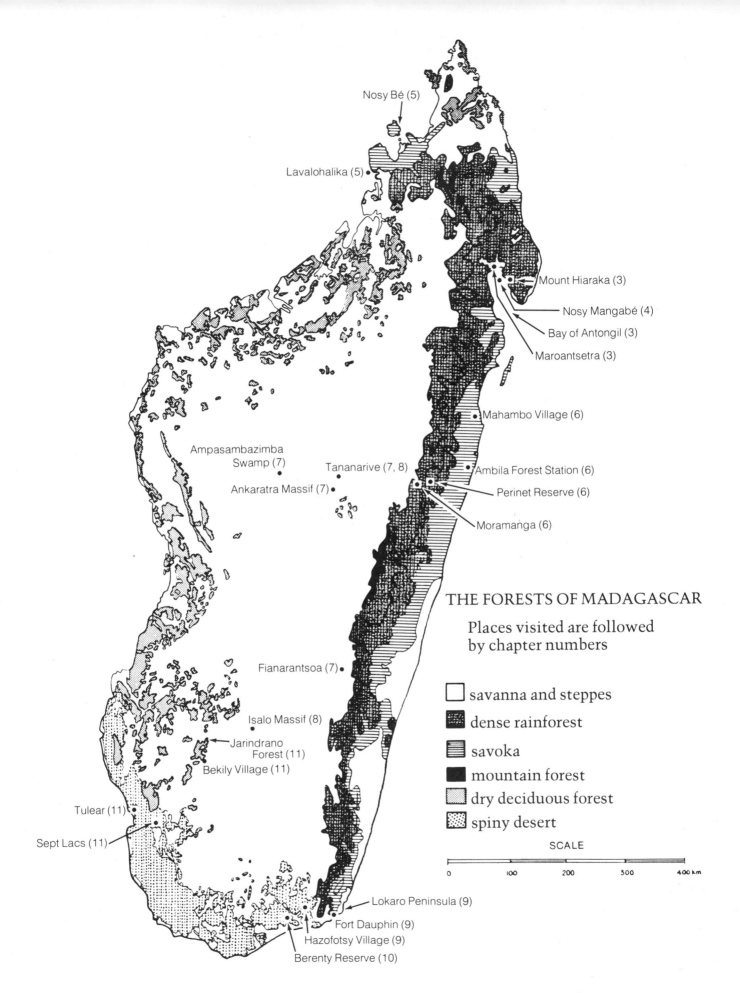

Nosy Bé (5)

Lavalohalika (5)

Mount Hiaraka (3)

Nosy Mangabé (4)

Bay of Antongil (3)

Maroantsetra (3)

Mahambo Village (6)

Ampasambazimba
Swamp (7)

Tananarive (7, 8)

Ambila Forest Station (6)

Ankaratra Massif (7)

Perinet Reserve (6)

Moramanga (6)

THE FORESTS OF MADAGASCAR

Places visited are followed
by chapter numbers

☐ savanna and steppes

▦ dense rainforest

▤ savoka

■ mountain forest

▥ dry deciduous forest

▨ spiny desert

SCALE

0   100   200   300   400 km

Fianarantsoa (7)

Isalo Massif (8)

Jarindrano
Forest (11)

Bekily Village (11)

Tulear (11)

Sept Lacs (11)

Lokaro Peninsula (9)

Fort Dauphin (9)

Hazofotsy Village (9)

Berenty Reserve (10)

Adapted from Humbert and Cours-Darne 1965

INTRODUCTION

Madagascar is an island, a continent, a world.

To its plants and animals Madagascar is a world, complete in itself. Ninety percent of Malagasy forest species are unique, found nowhere else on earth. The aye-aye with its bat ears, rodent teeth, and single skeletal finger, the piebald indri whose song resounds over 5 square kilometres of rainforest, and the 40 other races of Malagasy lemurs comprise a separate branch of the primate line. They are a clue to the moment when our own ancestors began to specialize in monkey sociability and monkey cleverness. The red fossa with its square cat's jaws and retractile claws is an aberrant mongoose, a similar clue to the evolution and adaptability of the carnivores. Five families of mammals, six families of plants, and four of birds exist only here, including the staghorn spikes of the Didierea euphorbs and the top-heavy, beak-heavy helmet bird. Only a tiny number of the thousands of Malagasy species have spread outside the island, and most of us have forgotten their origin: the flamboyant tree which marches down city boulevards from Lusaka to Miami, the periwinkle which checks childhood leukemia, the pearly stephanotis of brides' bouquets.

No list of single species is adequate, however, to convey Madagascar's scientific importance. It broke free from Africa about 100 million years ago; its latest founding stocks are 50 or 60 million years old. These pioneers have radiated in isolation to take their own path as bizarre specialists or living fossils. Because they have evolved together they have formed parallel biological communities—that alternative sphere dreamed of by science fiction writers and scientists. The world of Madagascar tells us which rules would still hold true if time had once broken its banks and flowed to the present down a different channel. A biologist from space, or even from Earth two centuries hence, could not believe or forgive us if we indifferently destroy the Malagasy habitats and let a major experiment of evolution dwindle away to nothingness.

To its people, Madagascar is a continent. It is 1,606 km long, the distance from

Boston to Atlanta or from London to Naples. It has fever-ridden jungles, granite mountains towering out of the prairie, and parching sand of the spiny desert. It is a nation whose twenty tribes speak one language and share one fundamental culture, though their ways of life are as different as city, desert, rainforest. Above all, it shares the dilemmas of all the rest of mankind: the economic pressures of life in the 20th century and the tightening outer limits of a fragile environment.

For many of its people, Madagascar still seems a new continent, a frontier. The first Malagasy sailed their outrigger canoes from Indonesia about 1,500 years ago. They discovered a lost world of fauna and flora, complete with chimpanzee-sized lemurs and Aepyornis, the elephant bird. Since that time people have cleared 80% of the face of the land. In places they have created intensive agriculture; in places they have destroyed the soil itself. The Malagasy are now approaching a time of crisis, when their last forests, their last frontiers, may disappear. With the forests will go not only the unique plants and animals but much of the traditional basis of human life.

To the rest of us, Madagascar is an island. Some may know it as the port of dhows, the haunt of slavers and pirates, and fief of French administrators, or, today, as a Third World nation affirming its independence and pride. However, for most of us it is simply a splotch on a map. In our mind's eye we see the opaque, flat blue of printer's ink. Only vaguely can we look through the page to the shimmering cerulean of tropic sea, or let the black boundary line dissolve into the circling fringe of surf on coral reef, surf on white sand, ripples lapping the muddy roots of mangrove trees.

Perhaps because we see it as an island, remote from us and beautiful, we can learn from Madagascar. This book is about the Malagasy environment—plants, animals, and people. It is about the natural communities, fascinating because of their long isolation, and the human beings who cannot live in isolation. It is about the conflict between the short-term urgency of rice for today and the long-term hope of rice for tomorrow. It is about the quality of life for the Malagasy if they choose to save or to destroy their natural heritage.

The World Wildlife Fund sent me to the Malagasy Republic for five months, with Russ Kinne, wildlife photographer, there during half that time. Our charge was to produce a book which would convey the scientific excitement of Madagascar. The problem has been to choose what is most significant from the riches of an island-world.

Three themes run through the book. First, I have tried to describe whole biological communities: rainforest, dry forest, spiny desert, mangrove, and even a fossil swamp of extinct giant lemurs. To me the interactions of species are more interesting than their individual peculiarities, and the importance of Madagascar is that it shows us the "ecological theatre and evolutionary play"* with a different cast of characters.

Second, in each environment I describe the human pattern of life. Peasants adapt their agriculture to varying habitats like any other creature which needs rain and soil and plants to live. Too often, even against their will, the human patterns include irreparable felling, overgrazing, forest fires—whichever form of destruction most

*Hutchinson 1965.

quickly undermines the environment. Mining the environment to stay alive is hardly confined to Madagascar; it is a central problem of the 20th century in rich countries and poor alike. Therefore, the particular villages and villagers I quote are only spokesmen for millions of others like themselves throughout the tropical world.

Third, this was a journey, with its incidents and accidents. We planned to look for the best-known species and to sample each major forest type. In the end which bird erupted from the bushes, and which lemur click-grunted from a tree, was not under our control. I have left the journey as a journal because it happened that way. In a place where nearly every species is unique, all are worth describing.

The details of our travels depended largely on the interests of Malagasy colleagues. We are deeply grateful that the scientific community of Madagascar became personally involved in this book. Georges Randrianasolo, coauthor of the *Birds of Madagascar* and Director of the Zoological Park, traveled with us in the eastern rainforest. Not surprisingly, this forest was full of birds which Georges pointed out. Guy Ramanantsoa, associate professor of forestry, expert on chameleons and on the folklore of wildlife, took us to the northwestern island of sacred lemurs. There, with Guy as interpreter, the islanders spoke in flowery oratory or ribald proverb about their belief in reincarnated spirits and the way lemurs guard the tombs of their ancestors. Marguerite Razarihelisoa, professor of zoology, showed us one of her amphibian study sites in montane forest, where tadpoles swim along the cloud-soaked moss. Ernest Ranjatson, a forester, accompanied us to the southern spiny desert. He listed names of its barbed, bloated flora in Malagasy, French, and Latin, as well as medicinal uses for the plants' defensive chemicals. I turned the tables a little by showing Guy and Marguerite around my own research site near the Mandrare River. There we could see how the social behavior of ringtailed lemurs and white sifaka relates to population control, as well as to the evolution of intelligence. We walked and swam over the barrier reef of Tulear with Hanairivo Rabesandratana, Director of the Marine Research Station, while he inspected coral boulders for poisonous cone shells. Finally, we camped in the deciduous woodland of the west with Rachel Rabesandratana, teacher and botanist, amid the cataclysm of deliberately set forest fire.

Many others from Tananarive helped us, in particular Dr. Étienne Rakotomaria, Director of the Direction de Recherche Scientifique et Technique, J. M. Andrianampianina, Ingenieur-en-chef of the Department des Eaux et Forêts, Dr. Razafindrambao, Director of the Institute of Medicinal Plants, and Roger Ramanantoanison of the Planning Office, economist caught willy-nilly in pursuit of wildlife.

Because we traveled with Malagasy colleagues we were received as friends in villages, with traditional warmth and hospitality. Villagers in all parts of the island told us why and how they themselves felled forest, set fires, harpooned turtles, ate lemurs—all technically illegal, all a part of their lives. I have tried therefore to let people of opposing viewpoints speak for themselves as the journey unfolds. This is the novelists' way of reaching a conclusion, not the scientists', but the argument seems far too important to leave to faceless statistics.

Madagascar is a microcosm of the planet. Just as the alternative world of Malagasy plants and animals reveals to us what forces shape the patterns of biology, so the human conflicts illuminate our own dilemmas. In the end, the question "Is the conservation of nature worthwhile in Madagascar?" becomes simply "Is conservation worthwhile?" and the greater question, "If we destroy nature, can we save humanity?"

PART 1

THE EVOLUTION OF AN ALTERNATE WORLD

1

ONLY HERE

THE WOUNDED SIFAKA

Imagine a forest of no shade. Interlaced whips of thorns claw at your arms as you push through. Thirty-foot clubbed trunks tower against the sky, studded with helical rows of spikes. Harpoon-hook burrs embed themselves in clothing and flesh; triple-pronged spines of a leafless tree defend the bitter liquid inside the bole. Coralliform shrubs offer a hope of green in their bloated fingers, but the fingers break to drip white latex which sears the skin and blinds the eye.

This is the spiny desert of Madagascar. The defensive warfare of near-desert vegetation is universal. You can see similar patterns of clawing thorns in the cactus forests of Mexico, the Karamoja scrub of East Africa. You will not, however, see the same plants. Ninety-five percent of all the species in this forest have evolved in Madagascar and grow only here in all the world.

We stopped our Land Rover to eat by the side of the main road, a corrugated track stretching 600 km northward to Tananarive, on Madagascar's high plateau. The spiny desert rose around us, each single plant or animal a biological treasure.

Three Antandroy strode toward us from the forest. They dragged a half-choked sifaka by a vine around its neck, holding it well away from them with the butt of their spears. The animal's arm dangled loose below the elbow, a jagged end of tibia protruding. Blood oozed down the white fur, stickily clotting on the bare hand with its thumb and fingernails. The sifaka gasped through a muzzle smashed by a flung stone.

I flew at the youngest tribesman, who stood smiling, offering me the end of the vine. Might we give them a few francs for such a present? I put my hands around his neck, to his own amazement and the laughter of his two companions. The minute, conical straw hat, which was all his clothing besides loincloth, bracelet, and spear, wobbled on his tufted hair. That made the point without words. Then phrases of

3

OPPOSITE: *Alluaudia procera.*

Malagasy burst out which I had not realized I knew, having always chatted with friends and colleagues in postcolonial French.

"This is an Antandroy sifaka. It lives only here. There are no sifaka on the plateau near Tananarive. No sifaka in France. No sifaka in America. Only here."

Now they were all amazed. We squatted around the sifaka, the men well out of reach of its upper canines as I loosened the choking vine. The one older man motioned solicitously to be careful and then repeated, querying, "Only here? Only Antandroy?"

One of my children fetched a jerrycan of water from the vehicle and spooned drops between the sifaka's jaws, over the toothcomb made of the lower canines and incisors. The toothcomb is a social organ evolved to groom the downy pelage of other sifaka when they sit together warming in the first sun-rays of morning, or when mating, when mothering, after quarrels, in play, when rising, when going to sleep.

Sifaka are primates like ourselves, but they have been isolated on Madagascar since the Eocene age. Like ourselves, they are social. The structure of sifaka groups, like the social life of other Malagasy lemurs, gives us clues to the wellsprings of society in the primate line. Sifaka social organization provides an insight into the beginnings of care and cooperation among our own earliest ancestors.

Another child brought books—my own text on primate behavior, open to a picture of the sifaka as it should be—jumping hindlegs extended straight back in line with its body, to propel it 6 m against the blue sky in a curve taut as ballet.[1]

"American book." I showed them. "American book; Antandroy sifaka. Killing sifaka is taboo for Antandroy (the older man frowned agreement) and forbidden by the police (the two younger ones sniggered)."

The elder asked in wonder, "Only here, but American book? Not even on the plateau, among the Merina tribe?"

"No. There are Sakalava sifaka in the far north, black here and here." (I did not know the words to say that northern sifaka bear maroon eagle-wing capes on arms and legs.) "Betisimisaraka sifaka in the east are gray on the back, with golden-orange limbs" (again, how to say there are two species and nine races of sifaka in the remaining Malagasy forests? They are as different as blueish black to white, gold, maroon. They depend on eyesight, not just scent, so their markings distinguish races and individuals to each other's eyes as they do to ours). "This sifaka, white with black head, only here in the south, only yours."

We rose. The youngest adjusted his hat, then put out his hand, with silver bracelet shining against his dark skin. "A few francs anyway?" The elder turned to him, angry. The young man dropped his hand, scratched his buttock, grinned. It was worth trying. He knew and I knew that one family's camping gear in the back of our Land Rover cost more than all the houses and household goods of his village. The binoculars around my neck were worth the equivalent of five zebu cattle: the bride price of a wife. A few francs, an empty bottle, a film canister he could use to hold salt had incomparably different meaning in his world or mine.

The sifaka sat on the ground between us, its eyes glazing, not merely with shock but with the apathy of all its kind when captured. You will not see a sifaka in zoos of

OPPOSITE: Antandroy sifaka (*Propithecus verreauxi verreauxi*), showing jagged cap line that allows individual identification.

Europe or America; only in the wild or the national park of Tananarive. Captive sifaka simply look down and never look up again.

I shook my head. "No money for killing a sifaka." I returned to the Land Rover, space capsule from another world. It would take me back to that world where people can afford not merely a few francs but the luxury of knowledge, where schools and books and television can reveal the leaping sifaka at the end of the earth.

The elder raised his spear in farewell, repeating what no one had ever said to him before. "Our own sifaka; only here."

MALAGASY NATURE, WORLD HERITAGE

Georges Randrianasolo slapped his briefcase on the desk. "Do you know what I use for visual aids in my university lectures? Do you want to see the only pictures of lemurs you can buy in Tananarive?" He clicked open the forward pockets and pulled out—two boxes of matches. On one was a female *Lemur macaco*, golden against green leaves, a white sunburst of whiskers around her face. A heavy piebald *Lemur variegatus* clung to cage wire on the other box.

"The forestry department took these photographs just outside this office, here in the zoo. Then they persuaded the match company to print them up for tourists. These boxes cost 25 francs (13 cents) each. No peasant would pay for one. And that is all we have. Even the *Birds of Madagascar*[2] is not sold here. We have no foreign exchange for luxuries like a bird guide, and of course the French send us none free. I believe people need pictures to understand wildlife. How can you expect anyone to care for animals and forests they have never seen? So I lecture with matchboxes, and the color plates of my own copy of my own book!"

Dr. Étienne Rakotomaria turned from the flamboyant zoo director. "It is not simply a question of conservation education, but of the entire defense of the forest, and forest reserves. Perhaps Mr. Andrianampianina, who is chief engineer of the forestry service, can tell you how foreign conservation interests look from here."

The forest engineer was a tiny man, even for a plateau Malagasy, with close-clipped white hair. He unfolded a sheet of paper and read out a list from it in his equally controlled and gentle voice.[3]

He listed, by date and amount, requests for assistance which the Malagasy have made to foreign conservation bodies over the past five years. Then he listed the funds granted: of the order of half a cement house for one forest guard.

The disappointment is particularly bitter because the International Union for the Conservation of Nature held a landmark conference in Tananarive in 1970. Everyone came: heads or very distinguished representatives of WWF, FAO, UNESCO, ORSTOM, and several alphabets' worth of further initials. Every Malagasy official concerned with the protection of nature and many Malagasy politicians also attended. Scientists from other continents converged. We all took the chance to add to research already done or to initiate new projects in the field. Who would not, given the opportunity to reach Madagascar at all? Foreign delegates who could not strike out to follow their own research had postconference tours laid on, for at least a capsule view of the Malagasy wilds.

It was a great success. Scientists expertly summarized the imminent dangers to the Malagasy forests; officials exhorted one another to act. The august assemblage was moved when one forester told of his life attempting to watch, alone, over the 605 km^2 reserve of Ankarafantsika. He simply cannot cover the ground, because he has no transport. There was a bicycle once, but it broke.

The 1970 conference ended with a list of printed resolutions and a longer list of verbal promises.[4] Essentially nothing has come of it all.

Why? The government changed from one that still had French civil servants in every office to one that is visibly Malagasy. Communications lapsed and so did foreigners' confidence. The mesh of the old boy net unraveled. Meanwhile, the Malagasy themselves were gaining confidence.

Why, they asked, do missions from other countries not stop, visit, and lecture at the University of Tananarive as a matter of course? You would not expect a party of Russian scientists to turn up in Texas, train their binoculars on the whooping cranes, and never so much as nod at American colleagues or officials. You do not find betelephotoed Texans in Szechuan ogling pandas without permission of the Chinese. Why should foreign scientists come to Madagascar and often act as though Malagasy do not exist?

And why has there been no progress since 1970 on the largest questions—aid for forest reserves, aid for education? Dr. Rakotomaria, Director of Scientific Research, summed up that meeting of biologists:

"We have touched on three problems—forest reserves, education, and the role of foreign scientists. In all three spheres we have seen international organizations negotiate with Frenchmen in the name of Madagascar but systematically exclude the Malagasy from our own concerns. Of course much of this is historically understandable, and of course there have been some Frenchmen of personal devotion to our country. In the future, however, you will find that negotiations must take place only with our government's representatives. Scientists will only be allowed to work here if they arrange reciprocal benefits for Malagasy colleagues. The people in this room know that Malagasy nature is a world heritage. We are not sure that others realize it is our heritage."

The status of foreign scientists is a small and short-term problem: whether the Malagasy Republic gains from people whose careers lie in other countries. Education is a large and long-term problem: how to produce a curriculum which concerns Malagasy nature as well as their own politics, economics, and history. (Children still recite set pieces about European rabbits under snow-covered pines.) Guarding the forests and the very existence of the Malagasy species is the largest problem of all, for it is intertwined with day-to-day economic needs of the Malagasy people.

The plants and animals are unique, but the human dilemmas of the Malagasy Republic are universal. Malagasy react to their environment like any other people. They slash and burn wet forest, they fire dry grassland, like peasants on any tropical continent. Their agriculture runs parallel to that of other peasants; their economy is not parallel but intermeshed with that of all other nations, rich and poor.

Conservation of Malagasy forest is no simple question of discovering another

world's wilderness. It is, instead, the complex question of finding ways that a Third World nation can preserve the heritage of its people.

Foreigners, including scientists, still find it hard to understand that all the wild places are inhabited. Many of us would like to forget the economic and political bonds mankind has locked around the body of nature. We reach for a picture book to escape into wilderness—to a trackless land where the sifaka soars against the sky, the aye-aye probes with its skeleton finger, and the black-and-white indri sings. We escape with the author, the photographer, the explorer into a wilderness, but it is networked with tracks. And always we are led by a guide for whom one track is the pathway home.

OPPOSITE: Face of Sakalava sifaka (*Propithecus verreauxi coquerili*), named for its call ("shi FAKH"). They gaze with monkey-like, binocular vision above the long muzzle.

ABOVE: Leaping sifaka (*P.v.v.*) (Berenty Preserve). Arms above head give balance when leaping, or bouncing bipedally on the ground.

2

AN ALTERNATE WORLD

Every science fiction writer tries his own version of the tale of alternate worlds. At some moment in the past, time parted. An earthquake stranded the lost world of dinosaurs on South America's Roraima plateau; or the death of a butterfly distorted evolution and history. Sometimes the hero, by a lateral-time machine or by concentrated focusing of his mental powers can make our own world shimmer and disappear, to recapture the heroine who has been kidnapped into an alternate time-stream.

Madagascar is just such a world, reached by the more prosaic means of jet, dhow, pirogue. It has evolved its own flora and fauna, on its own plan, into climax communities of rainforest, deciduous woodland, spiny desert. These communities exist in parallel with those in the tropics of Africa, Asia, South America to show us what happens when time has broken its banks and flowed to the present down a different channel.

One hundred million years ago a fragment of continent wrenched loose from the side of Africa. Its granite hulk carried ancestral flowering plants, boa constrictors, half-evolve frogs, and a flightless bird, the gigantic cousin of the ostrich. Disputing scientists have given it points of departure all up and down the African coast, from Somalia to Mozambique.[1] Only in 1975 do we seem to have a clinching bit of evidence that traces the island to a home port in the dip of the East African coastline, off present-day Kenya and Tanzania, well to the north of its present position.

The geologists Embleton and McElhinny collected samples of red and brown Isalo sandstones in northern Madagascar and at the out-jutting Col des Tapia in the southwest.[2] They cooked their samples in ovens at 600°C, which removes the random magnetization induced by lightning flashes. (Lightning kills several dozen people a year in Madagascar. In the southwest, near the Col des Tapia, all men, women, and children wear silver bracelets, said to guard from thunderbolts.) With the recent magnetization

10

cleaned from their samples, Embleton and McElhinny analyzed the ancient direction of magnetization: it matches that of Triassic and Jurassic beds that you drive over on the Kenyan tourist way from Nairobi to Mombassa. These beds, called the "Maji ya chumvi," the "salt-lake" beds, have the same fossils as equivalent Malagasy levels, in alternate land-laid and marine layers, as well as the same magnetic direction toward the ancient South Pole.[3] Such sedimentary layers lie only on the western slope of Madagascar. The center and east of the island form a granite shield, some of which dates to 3,020 million years—perhaps the oldest rocks on the face of the earth.[4]

Presumably the plants and animals of Madagascar were like those of the rest of East Africa until the Upper Cretaceous, some 100 to 65 million years ago. Then continental drift detached the island-continent, a granite raft among the complex ridges, trenches, and thermal vortices of the Indian Ocean floor.

Alfred Wegener first recognized "continental drift" in 1920 simply from looking at the jigsaw puzzle fit of Africa and South America across the South Atlantic.[5] Wegener was sure the southern continents were once joined, then had plowed their way apart like steamships across the oceans. Later geologists could imagine no driving mechanism and could certainly see no evidence of the rumpling up of rock that should occur at the "ship's" bow or in its wake, so after early enthusiasm, for several decades they ignored Wegener's ideas. Now, in the last ten years they have discovered that whole fragments of the ocean bottom move, welling up at the midoceanic ridges and sucked under again at the trenches. In this view, continents are irrelevant bits of flotsam, lighter granite that floated to the surface long ago. They shift about passively like scum over a working beer-vat as the basalt of the earth's mantle simmers beneath.[6]

Originally all the continental rocks formed one expanse. About 180 million years ago, the North Atlantic began to open and Eurasia separated from Africa. Direct migration of animals ceased between north and south. This left the present-day southern continents, with peninsular India as well, joined together as the gigantic land mass of Gondwanaland.

The eastern Indian Ocean split open about 150 million years ago. Peninsular India started northward toward the rest of Asia, although it did not arrive for 100 million years, and then crashed with a force that is still crumpling up the Himalayas.

South America, Africa, Antarctica, and Australia remained linked much longer. Many of their flowering plants evolved by the Upper Cretaceous and dispersed by land. The group of flightless birds evolved in South America, then simply walked to their respective modern haunts; moas and kiwis to New Zealand, emus to Australia, ostriches to Africa, rheas in circles where they began. Aepyornis, the elephant bird, strode into Madagascar and was carried off into the ocean as a passenger on a continent-sized raft. Aepyornis did, in passing, leave a few eggshells in the Canary Islands.[7]

The separation of Madagascar only 100 million years ago or less would explain a great many such biological puzzles. Most of Madagascar's plants and animals clearly came from Africa. However six plant families or subfamilies occur only in South America and Madagascar, as well as several genera, including the traveler's palm,

Ravenala, and a close South American relative.[8] A few groups of insects show the same distribution, and more dramatically, so do the boa constrictors. A fossil boa has been found in Egypt, but there are no boas in Africa today—only pythons. (To my delight, one set of animals which never reached Madagascar at all are the later-evolved venomous snakes.)[9]

It is very difficult to explain plants and animals jet-setting between South America and Madagascar by windblown seeds, or drifting all the way past the Cape of Good Hope on logs if they did not come to land and establish a foothold anywhere else in the tropical world. On the other hand, it is reasonable to picture the boas and their ilk slithering directly across Africa toward Madagascar and then becoming extinct in Africa.

The doyen of rainforest botanists, Paul W. Richards, believes that a large number of plants and animals may be recently extinct in Africa.[10] African forest is in several ways the "odd man out" in comparison with South America, Southeast Asia, and even Madagascar. For instance, Africa has a great dearth of palms and epiphytes, that is, the plants which grow on other plants such as many orchids. Besides, Africa grows a far smaller variety of tree species per stand of forest. Madagascar, in palms, epiphytes, and sheer number of species, has in some ways a more balanced forest flora than Africa itself and may have preserved species that could not survive in Africa.

There are four possible reasons for the difference. First, the interior of the huge land mass of Gondwana was probably very dry, with a harsh midcontinental climate. Many species probably flourished on the more favored periphery in present-day South America and Madagascar.[11] Second, all rainforest in Africa has at least one or two relatively dry months. Even a ten-day period without rain means serious water loss for the lowland forest trees of Southeast Asia and perhaps in the wettest parts of Madagascar.[12] Third, the climatic changes of the Pleistocene, the recent period which includes the ice ages, may have hit Africa very hard. It reduced rainforest to relatively few refugees of adaptable species which later recolonized as the climate, from their damp point of view, improved. Finally, there was man. Our species evolved in Africa in the Pliocene and Pleistocene. We have not been an accommodating form of life even early in our career. We apparently inaugurated our status as a big game hunter by demolishing many of Africa's giant species of mammals,[13] and Richards argues that later agricultural man may have so persistently cleared Africa that it has no true virgin forest left.

Thus, the basis of Madagascar's fauna and flora is the living creatures of Gondwanaland, preserved here from the early Cretaceous era. The story, however, by no means ends with the split from Africa. Even if that split came as late as the end of the Cretaceous 65 million years ago, some of Madagascar's present fauna had not yet evolved.

Here appears the importance of that fit to East Africa, well to the north. For the first few million years after splitting, Madagascar made southward as well as eastward. The Mozambique Channel probably took tens of millions of years to approach its present width of 350 km and depth of 3,000 m. It is now a formidable barrier to land animals, but it remained within reach of invasions from the African coast up to the end of the Eocene "only" 40 million years ago.[14]

OPPOSITE: Gondwanaland granite outcrops in central Madagascar.

Feeding goats, on 3 billion-year-old pink granite (Mananara River).

Now we move from the grandiose rafting of continents to the comic or pathetic—to real rafts of floating tree trunks or tangled branches—where a pop-eyed ancestral lemur clung with all its hands onto the wave-washed twigs.

All southern Africa is seasonal. The wet summer of October to February alternates with the drought of southern winter. The Zambezi floods vast plains in its season. At high water you cannot even see past the spray halfway to the bottom of Victoria Falls. Downstream the floodwaters of the Zambezi and Ruvuma rivers roll brown mud miles out to sea, bearing whole uprooted trees, perfect boats for the ancestors of Malagasy lemurs and tenrecs and fossas.[15]

Many of the Malagasy animals might plausibly have rafted across water. Its current denizens are just the sort of tree-loving animals who could have accidentally cruised down the Zambezi on a log. Most of these ocean voyagers were African, but some have come from even farther afield. Blocks of pumice from Krakatoa's explosion in 1883 floated up on Malagasy shores six months after the eruption: seeds or spores that could survive drifting so long have rafted here from Asia. Finally, there are the true travelers, those which have colonized the shores of oceanic islands as well as the small continent of Madagascar, such as coconut palms and *Rhipsalis,* the only Malagasy cactus, which grows alongside orchids on the bark of beachside trees, or *Nepenthes madagascariensis,* the local version of Southeast Asian pitcher plants.

Madagascar, then, is not just any alternate world, imagined at random. It is a museum of plants and animals, preserved by the drifting of continents or by skill and luck at long-distance dispersal over water. Whichever the origin for any given group, they have also been preserved by the luck of a fairly equable Pleistocene climate and by the remarkable luck of having had relatively little to do with people, at least before the first settlers came 1,500 years ago.

RICHES FROM POVERTY

When they reached here, the plant and animal colonists found not one habitat but many. Madagascar is the fourth largest island in the world, after Greenland, New Guinea, and Borneo.[16] It rises sharply on the eastern side in great scarped steps. Although the highest point of the island-continent is only 2,800 m, the eastern escarpment blocks the trade winds of the Indian Ocean. The east coast or windward domain, therefore, is clothed in the sort of forest that thrives under a rainfall of 1,500 to over 3,500 mm a year.[17]

The western, leeward side of the island has a gradient of progressively decreasing rainfall from north to south. The north part, or Sambirano, receives scarcely less rain than the east, although with a dry season of several months instead of continuous sog, so it bears a hardier version of the windward rainforest.

The midregion of the west, from Majunga to Tulear, bears dry deciduous woodland, mostly very susceptible to fire. The far south, with less than 400 mm of rain and that rain falling only from November to February, grows the spiny desert.

With this large area, disjointed terrain, and variety of climate, it is small wonder that plants and animals have speciated explosively. In many branches of living things

Madagascar shows a strange combination of richness and poverty—vast radiation from the few ancient founding stocks.

There is, for instance, only one kind of baobab in all of continental Africa—Madagascar boasts nine. Six plant families are endemic including the Chlenaceae, a group of lovely flowering trees. The oddest are the Didiereaceae, cactus-like growths of the southern desert, whose thorn-studded fingers (in *Alluaudia*) tower 9 m upward against the sky, or (in *Didierea trolli*) twist sideways like staghorn coral. Many more plant groups are highly endemic: for instance, only 1 of Madagascar's 97 species of ebony grows outside the island, and all but 2 of the 130 palm species are unique to Madagascar.[18]

Among the invertebrates, one finds the same complexity and peculiarity wherever they have been studied—the French have left a wealth of monographs. Millot lists as endemic 942 of the 1,024 recorded species of carabid beetles, all 210 species of Melolonthinae, a subfamily of the scarab beetles, and so forth right down to the Malagasy nematode worms.[19] Andé Peyriéras tells of his own work on the scaritines, a family of earth beetles, supposedly very rare. In the first five years that he took an interest in the beasts he found or was brought ten specimens. Then, by chance, he found one at its burrow and learned to recognize the characteristic tunnel mouths, with little trails leading off through the leaf litter. In the following five years he saw them everywhere and found not just more specimens but eighteen new species.[20] Much else probably remains to be noticed here.

The vertebrates are better known. None of the African or Indo-Malayan freshwater fishes reached Madagascar. All local fishes are derived secondarily from fish which could tolerate saltwater. Eight genera and 39 species are endemic, which is one-third of the species that have penetrated the streams and lakes. All the local cichlids are unique to Madagascar.[21] There are 40 endemic reptile genera, including two-thirds of the world's chameleons, and the smallest land vertebrate, which is a chameleon called *Brookesia minima*.[22] Of the 235 reptile species 225 are endemic: geckos, skinks, and chameleons, tortoises and colubrid snakes, which all have "normal" relatives in Africa. The boid snakes and two genera of iguanid lizard, however, are related only to the boas and iguanas of South America. They provide one of the arguments for Gondwanaland, although in some respects the Malagasy forms are so primitive anatomically that they could be considered survivors of almost any earlier distribution, including a worldwide one.[23]

About 155 species of frogs live in Madagascar but no toads, newts, salamanders, or hylid frogs. Amphibians cannot cross saltwater—they would dry out through their porous skin—so it is not surprising that all the Malagasy species evolved on the island.[24]

Even birds, which could have flown in fairly recently, have 36 of their genera and half the 238 species unique to Madagascar. Four bird families exist only here, and 20 more include only unique forms among their members. Not surprisingly, the running and perching birds differ most from their mainland counterparts, although some derive from Asia instead of Africa. Many waterbirds are widespread forms, but even among

Chameleon.

Chameleon (Berenty) looking two ways at once. Malagasy proverb: Don't be like the chameleon which keeps one eye on the future and one on the past.

Small chameleon (*Brookesia minima*).

Genet (*Fossa fossa*) (Tzimbazaza Zoo).

Fanaloka (*Eupleres goudotii*)
(Tzimbazaza Zoo).

waterbirds there are oddities, such as the Madagascar giant heron, or *Anas bernieri*, which is one of the world's rarest ducks.[25]

Bats, like birds, share some of their species with the mainland, but of the 26 species, 13 are unique to Madagascar. Again, these species are worth noting. The sucker-footed bat, *Myzopoda aurita*, forms a mammalian family of its own. The Malagasy bats have been little studied; several are known from half-a-dozen specimens or fewer.[26]

Finally, all the land mammals are unique: 34 endemic genera, with about 66 species.

Many land mammals never reached Madagascar at all—no hoofed animals except the African bushpig brought by early settlers and a pygmy hippopotamus who presumably swam snorting and puffing across the Mozambique Channel.

The seven genera of rodents are so different from one another that there is real doubt whether they are descended from one ancestor or seven different ones. The Madagascar giant jumping rat leaps like a springhare in a tiny region of the western woodlands; there are gerbil, mouse, vole, and rat-like genera, and one tree-climbing rodent which looks like a lemur.[27] No rabbits or squirrels came though, no jerboas or porcupines, not even true rats or mice until people brought them.

Eleven genera of insectivores have, similarly, diverged to fill different niches. There is a pseudomole, a pseudo-water-shrew, and five different spiny pseudohedgehogs, one of which can make supersonic remarks by rubbing together the quills on its back. As with nearly all the fauna, these animals have a confusing mixture of evolved specializations and primitive characteristics. The closest relative of the Malagasy insectivores as a group, and of the fat-bodied, tail-less *Tenrec* in particular, is *Solenodon*, a bad-tempered living fossil found only on the islands of Cuba and Hispaniola. Solenodon, like the tenrecs, has apparently survived nearly unchanged since the Eocene.[28]

All of Madagascar's seven native carnivores are viverrids, related to mongeese, civets, and genets in the large family which lumps many "primitive" species. There are no lions, jackals, or hyenas, no bears or otters, not even dogs and cats until people brought them. Malagasy viverrids include the elegant russet *Galidia*, the long-snouted *Eupleres*, and *Cryptoprocta ferox*, the fossa. A fossa is the size of a lynx and the color of a red fox, with short bristly fur like a kinkajou. It has square cats' jaws, retractable cats' claws, and a whippy tail behind which would do credit to an ocelot, being almost as long as the animal itself. This patchwork carnivore is the largest of the Malagasy viverrids, a tree-climbing predator which even catches lemurs.[29]

Madagascar has, finally, about 20 species of lemurs. I say "about" because there are more than 40 recognizably different forms, many localized in just one region. They range from the mouselemurs, smallest of primates, to the piebald indri, black-and-white and large as a three-year-old child, whose song resounds from hill to hill. These, of course, are the survivors—eleven more species of giant lemurs are extinct within historic times, that is, since man reached Madagascar.[30]

When the Old World monkeys evolved on the larger continents, and the mouse-like rodents and the modern carnivores like cats and dogs, these newer animals drove more conservative ones into marginal ways of life. In Africa and Asia lemur-like animals abandoned daytime use of the trees, social troops, and fruit-and-leaf eating to the true monkeys, if indeed they had ever tried such adventures. All the lemur-like animals that remain in Africa and Asia are nocturnal insect-eaters, who usually feed in solitude.

Yet on Madagascar this anatomically primitive stock radiated unchecked by competing simians. Lemurs bounce in noisy gangs through the treetops, dropping squashy half-eaten fruits on your head. They spring in ballet-leaps twenty feet from branch to branch, sunlight gleaming on white or orange fur. They have castes and complexes like any other permanently social mammal, including monkeys and certainly our own primate ancestors. Just as Madagascar is an alternate world, so lemurs are alternate monkeys. They diverged from the other primates during the epoch when our own ancestors began to evolve monkey curiosity and monkey cleverness. They tell us what potentials lay in our Eocene ancestor, which on one continent evolved the wide-eyed lemurs, toothcombing one anothers' downy fur, and on another evolved a primate which constructs a Telstar to transmit his wise or foolish words to the entire globe.

CONVERGENT EVOLUTION

All these animals raise the question of why, in an alternate world, so many of the same ways of life should appear. Why do Madagascar and Australia each have their "cats" and "moles" and "hedgehogs" and "monkeys," although in Madagascar the "monkeys" are lemurs, while in Australia they are tree kangaroos?

Unfortunately, although this is an obvious question, it is one that biologists have not been able to answer. All we can say is that in a complete biological community there seems to be only a certain variety of available ways of life, or ecological niches, and that, given time, plants and animals evolve to fill them.

Sometimes animals converge in bodily form, like the various "cats" or "moles."[31] Sometimes, instead, widely different animals find ways to exploit the same niche. Take, for instance, the world's woodpeckers. On all the large continents, the Picidae, proper feathered woodpeckers, hammer away at tree trunks and extract woodboring larvae. The Picidae never reached Madagascar, though, or New Zealand, New Guinea, and small oceanic islands.

A Darwin's finch on the Galapagos has taken the woodpecker's role, holding a cactus spine to spear insects instead of evolving the woodpecker's barbed tongue. On New Zealand a huia, or wattlebird, now extinct, became a two-part woodpecker. The males bore a stout beak to excavate wood, the females a slender one for probing insects out of the excavated holes.

On New Guinea and Madagascar the "woodpeckers" are mammals. A New Guinea marsupial called the long-fingered possum and the Malagasy aye-aye independently evolved bat ears to listen for insect crepitations within wood, beaver teeth to rip off the bark, and an elongate, clawed finger to extract the juicy grubs. Small matter that the possum's fourth finger is its woodpecker tongue, and the aye-aye's third finger—or even that the possum keeps its baby in a pouch like any other marsupial, while the

OPPOSITE: Falcon (Hiaraka).

aye-aye builds a leaf nest for her young. There is no question, that, in feeding ecology, these two animals have converged on a single way of life.[32]

The sum of the convergences of particular species is a convergence of communities. The shape of a whole forest tells at once whether it is evergreen, deciduous, or arid woodland. A mixed batch of photographs would be easy to sort by ecological type even if one does not know enough to guess if the rainforest is Malagasy or Amazon, or whether the deciduous woodland loses its leaves because of seasonal snow or seasonal drought. (A hot dry season can still be winter to plants.) Ecological constraints determine the geometry of whole communities—a much more general rule than the body form of a mole or the presence of some kind of woodpecker. Furthermore, we are beginning to understand convergences in forest dynamics: the quantity of timber on a plot of land, the turnover of new growth, the rate of respiration.

The Malagasy habitats, then, are as interesting in their similarities to the rest of the world as in their differences. They help to tell us which of our generalizations spring from fundamental ecological constraints, and which from the accidents of inheritance, whether the rules are as far reaching as the continuous canopy of lowland rainforest or as specific as that nature goes to inordinate lengths in the evolution of substitute woodpeckers.

It is in the most general rules that we finally reach the practical implications for people. People react to natural ecosystems in very consistent ways: we slash-and-burn forest; we pasture herds on grassy savannas. The same parameters of rainfall, temperature, and soil which determine the nature of climax forests determine the nature and success of our agriculture. If we can one day learn why and how a rainforest, or even a cactus desert, maintains tens or hundreds of times as much living matter on the same ground as does human agriculture, we may even arrive at a more efficient relationship with our own environment.

Yellow-billed kite (*Milvus migrans*) (Berenty).

PART 2
WINDWARD DOMAIN: WILDERNESS AS HOME

THE EXECUTIONERS

JEAN'S FUTURE

Bare feet splashed past the ditches and dikes of rice fields up into the shade under the trees. Bare toes curled over roots each of which outlined a step in the hillside. With a coupe-coupe over his shoulder and a brindled dog behind him, Jean d'Armand strode up the mountain path as though he wore Paul Bunyan's boots instead of cracked calluses upon his heels.

Jean is the rainforest's executioner. He is the last frontiersman in a world that has no wilderness to spare. In defiance of Malagasy law and all principles of conservation he still tackles the virgin forest with his *coupe-coupe.* He brings down rosewood, towering white ramy trees, and hintsy, the cabinetmaker's prize with its crimson heart. These rainforest hardwoods are too dense even to float and must rot for one or two years before Jean can burn their trunks to enlarge his little homestead clearing.

It takes stamina, patience, courage—the father of a family, felling on the slope below Jean, was killed when a trunk turned and hit his head as it fell.

Climbing behind Jean, more and more aware of muscles in the upper thigh I had forgotten were there, an invisible swamp pulling down my shoes, and sweat adhesive on back and face, I wondered if he and I could really be climbing the same mountain. To be fair, Mount Hiaraka reaches 1 km high only 3 km inland from the Bay of Antongil. Humidity hung near saturation, for we were inside the living climate of rainforest—air trapped beneath the canopy of leaves.

Foliage closed over us, layer upon layer. In this windless, shadowed world, trees are thin stemmed, their pale trunks racing one another upward to the light. Leaves are glossy, almost waxy, with drip tips to shed rain. Those plants which can reach the light by seed or spore leapfrog upward on the others: epiphytic ferns, strangler figs, 900 species of Malagasy orchids.[1] Trees that must support great weight throw out buttresses while they grow: the white wings of the ramy tree or the flying arcades of the abado fig.

25

OPPOSITE: Rainforest along east coast. Note fan leaves and slim vertical trunks.

This is the pattern of any lowland rainforest. It is the shape of wet jungle in Africa, Asia, South America, but we were in eastern Madagascar. This forest seemed at first glance like many others in its shape, in its frog chorus, its moldering smells, and the sodden air in my gasping lungs. It was, instead, a treasure house of wild species, nine-tenths of them unique.

"There! There! Up there!" Jean and Georges Randrianasolo pointed upward together. Branches slapped and parted. Sixty feet above us a female white-fronted lemur peered down. Her eyes widened with amazement in her grayish face. Her brown tail pendulum-swung in alarm, while she click-grunted in time to the swing. Bounce, off the loop of liana, slap went the leaves close behind her, and bounce, onto the same liana followed her male. His white mane surrounded his head and continued down his throat to the white belly-fur. He too swung his brown-plumed tail like a pendulum before leaping away.

Jean turned aside from the main trail down a faint track. Georges Randrianasolo, the Director of the Zoological Park in Tananarive, murmured conspiratorially: "Jean says that he will take us to his own illegal clearing. I did not exactly tell him we are conservationists."

We slithered down a ravine side, crossed the bottom on a felled ramy trunk, and scrambled upward, treading on one of Madagascar's fifty native species of wild begonias. We halted, dazzled, in sudden sunlight.

Banana palms balanced translucent sails against the sky. Jean touched the leaves of coffee bushes that glinted in the well of sunlight he has created among the gloom of the forest. He pointed to the table of lashed sticks sheltering his little clove nursery. In ten years' time those seedlings will begin to bear scarlet flower buds which dry to commercial cloves. Jean may then have a cash crop to sell the spice freighters that sail, once every four to six months, from our side of the world to the Bay of Antongil.

"These cloves will be for my children," he said, "when I am rich enough to marry one day."

Jean's story is a familiar tale. Millions of young men in the Third World leave home to seek employment. Millions are squeezed dry and thrown aside by economies that have no place for their energy, even for their existence. Jean is different only because he has found a way out, a path through the forest to independence.

He was born at Navana, 11 km away along the seacoast of the Bay of Antongil. One day his father said to him, "You must not call this *our* farm here at Navana, but *mine*, your father's."

Jean understood. He was the eldest son. His father had too many children to divide his land among them all. He left home to look for paid employment. He looked for three years. He worked as a cook, as domestic servant to Indian shopkeepers, as the unskilled assistant who packs people inside country bush-taxis and piles their baskets on the top. One day in harvest season he went to a farmer who owned land and clove trees.

"Give me a third of what I pick to sell for myself, and I will harvest for you."

"Come back at seven tomorrow morning," said the farmer. Jean was there, but the farmer told him, "Go away. I have enough labor."

Jean D'Armand, with transistor radio and sugar cane, in front of traveler's-palm hut (Hiaraka).

Red-ruffed form of *Lemur variegatus*.
Photo by John Buettner-Janusch.

There was an argument, with evil words between the two men, but again Jean understood. The man with land and trees will always be master. There is no future for a landless laborer. He came away to live beside the forest and to be his own master.

THE RED-RUFFED LEMUR

"What disappears here?" I asked Georges. "If Jean and others like him succeed in deforesting this peninsula, what species vanish?" Jean had given us permission to camp in his clearing, so Georges, photographer Russ Kinne, and I were luxuriating in the bird songs of forest dawn.

A barking roar drowned the answer. "Vary mena!" cried Georges. "The red-ruffed lemur! That's your first menaced species. Russ, grab that bazooka telephoto—and come!"

Georges led us uphill from a corner of the clearing to circle and catch the red lemurs above us. "They should be basking on a high tree by now, to catch the first sun. They sprawl back with their arms out like naked tourists on a beach. Our tribesmen call it sun-worship."

Again we plunged into the baffling interlace of rainforest: naturalist's paradise, photographer's nightmare. We had not seen the sky for some time, or rather only a postage-stamp collage of sky and leaf-layers, when Georges motioned us to stop. He pointed up a 30-m ramy that towered into the sunlight. On the crook of a white branch a lemur stared down at us. His russet ruff fur gleamed; his yellow eyes shone against the black face. He made suspicious, fruity grunts in his black throat. The red-ruffed lemur, and a second one, bounded away through the treetops.

"Come on, follow them!" Georges flitted through the trees ahead. "They are too lazy to really beat it. You won't see the red kind outside this peninsula. Even Nosy Mangabé (the island reserve in the bay) has only the common black-and-white form."

The ruffed lemurs, however, had evaporated. Georges guessed from their timidity, and the people of the region confirm, that "civilized" men sometimes come out from town with guns, lemur-hunting. The local people usually find lemurs too much trouble to catch and mainly set snares for wild boars which molest their crops.

"All right." Georges announced at last. "I am fed up with those clowns. We'll climb a bit and pick up another group on the way."

We climbed. A bird purred on a branch. "Blue coua, *Coua caerulea*." Georges had no need to look up at the call, for the blue coua is one of the "ordinary" members of the Couidae, a Malagasy subfamily of cuckoos which has radiated into ten endemic species. (Georges, after all, is a coauthor of the *Birds of Madagascar*.[2]) The coua, deep metallic blue with a bare patch of cerulean skin around its eye, flapped to a low branch where it could return our interest. A female, slightly smaller, followed behind. The male eyed her. He picked a morsel of glossy yellow-green leaf, held it in his beak, and flicked his tail. I assume the leaf was for her benefit since blue couas eat fruit and lizards. They themselves apparently are not eaten by anything much. Even Georges' bird book admits that they smell too nasty.

"That coua moves like an African touraco," Russ Kinne remarked.

"Exactly. Couas replace the touracos here, and have the same ecological niches," confirmed Georges.

"Dreo, dreo, dreo," shrilled something flying across the valley. "That is the vorondreo, the Madagascar cuckoo-roller," Georges told us. "Some authors allow a whole bird-family for this one species. Cuckoo-rollers always cry like that, all heart-broken when they fly. Maybe that is why the Sakalava tribe make love philters of their eyes and skin."

A yellow tag glinted on a tree trunk. "See that mark? Dr. Albignac of the university laid out transects here four months ago, in January. He planned to radio-track our Malagasy carnivores. He worked all month on his transects, measuring and tagging mapped squares, and cutting the undergrowth just enough so he could move in straight lines in this mess at night. Here is his camp—he actually found a flat place big enough for a tent and two stick tables.... Russ, the bird that flicked across that sky-patch was the Madagascar palm swift, *Cypsiurus parvus*.... Now, let me show you the other end of the transects."

The forest fell away from us. Tree trunks lay criss-crossed, newly cut. Microscopic orchids still bloomed on them, and the climbing ferns had not yet withered. The whole shoulder of forest, down to the next ravine, was freshly cleared for someone else's "future."

The insects loved it, not the insects of decay, for that had hardly started, but the forest ones which were used to making the most of sunny patches. A bright yellow weevil crawled up a trunk; two gray ones together looked much like boll weevils; a black and white weevil was outlined with white stripes like a diver with white tapes around his rubber suit. Three or four day-flying urania moths glinted over the clearing. All their iridescence is done by mirrors, from layers of prismatic scales that shimmer turquoise and orange without pigment of their own.[3] At one season the urania migrate like our monarchs, tens of thousands together, glittering in the sun.[4]

Even the urania moth paled beside a buprestid beetle which camouflaged its gray, lichen-colored back against a tree trunk, then flew, buzzing and bumbling, while the sunlight twanged off the chartreuse and fuschia of its ventrum.

"You hear?" Georges flung out an arm toward the valley on the forested side of our crest trail. "Toc, toc, toc. You hear them cutting over that way too? Soon there'll be nothing here. Zero. No study area for Albignac, that's tough, but no forest, that's catastrophe."

"Georges, come back to my first question. What happens if this peninsula is all cut over? What disappears? Red-ruffed lemurs and that bird people keep telling me about—the one with the enormous bill?"

"*Euryceros*, the helmet bird? That exists right through the northeast. It's never easy to see though. It's ultra-rare and it hides low down in the shadows, in the densest forest. No, the importance here is that the forest has been almost virgin, undergraded. There are few places where you can still say that. The Antongil region has its share of highly local species of course, but so does every part of Madagascar. The point is that this area used to be the least disturbed of all the lowland rainforest. This was the place to see the rarest species; those which cannot live with man."

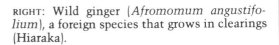
ABOVE: Farm clearing (Hiaraka). Virgin forest cut for fertile soil. Crops grow here for 2 years. Forest might regrow in 80 years.

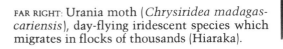
RIGHT: Wild ginger (*Afromomum angustifolium*), a foreign species that grows in clearings (Hiaraka).

FAR RIGHT: Urania moth (*Chrysiridea madagascariensis*), day-flying iridescent species which migrates in flocks of thousands (Hiaraka).

Later, as the evening light spotlit hanging lianas and white trunks, bare at the edge of Jean's clearing, Georges and I struck up through the tangle of wild ginger that sprouts among felled trees.

At the forest's edge we stumbled at once into a bird party. Here, as in most of the tropics, different species travel together in a flock, each helping to warn or guard the others against predators, and each taking a slightly different assortment of the insects they all stir up together.[5] Only this party was all Vangas, another family of insect-eating birds evolved in Madagascar. There was the tylas-vanga, green and gold. A tiny blue coral-billed nuthatch scuttled up a trunk, bracing itself with its tail and picking with its beak. It is a vanga, like the others, but offers one of the cases of convergent evolution between unrelated animals. It does everything a real nuthatch does except go head-downward. A white-headed vanga with its gleaming head and breast reminded me of the white-fronted lemur, swinging high on its liana.

But Georges was pointing low, not high, croaking "There! There! There he is! It's him! Do you see him, Alison? There!"

I peered into the shadow. A fourteen-inch black bird with russet wings plumped itself down from a perch 1 m off the ground onto an even lower and darker branch. Of course he flew awkwardly. His blueish beak was four or five inches long, shaped like a knight's helmet, or even a baby's shoe, stuck onto a bird's face.

"It's him," whispered Georges. "*Euryceros prevostii*, the helmet bird. It is the first time I have ever seen him in the wild. And you, you've the devil's own good luck, for you have seen him too."

It was only later that I realized another first: the first time I had ever seen a zoo director literally dancing on a log with excitement over an animal.

THE DISAPPEARING FOREST

The toulou-bird, the Madagascar coucal, was bubbling in the forest behind us. The Madagascar magpie robin trilled his night song in the forest to the right. Tree frogs began ratcheting to the left, while little evening bats hawked out of the dark trees before. As the sun set orange beyond the Bay of Antongil, the southern cross wheeled over Jean's clearing. We could imagine ourselves in intact wilderness, with jungle stretching in limitless circles from the central point of our campfire and the three mosquito-netted beds.

The wilderness is inhabited. Already the forest has been cleared from 80% of Madagascar's land; the rest may soon follow.[6]

About A.D. 500 the Vazimba, the proto-Malagasy, first settled in Madagascar. They sailed from Indonesia in outrigger canoes like those which still ply today among the islands of the Java Sea. Some may have crossed the Indian Ocean directly; some stopped in southern India and sprinkled their own polysyllabic tongue with tags of Sanskrit. Others settled for a time on the African coast, intermarried, and crossed the Mozambique Channel bringing African features, customs, and trade links. Indonesians were, in fact, long-distance sea-voyagers and traders for centuries before the Arabs ruled the Indian Ocean.[7]

The first settlers brought with them a tradition of shifting cultivation. They felled and burned clearings in the forest much as Jean does today. They did not plant tree-crops like Jean's coffee and cloves; they planted beans, root staples, and dry-land rice for their own subsistence. After two years or so of cultivation they abandoned their clearings to forest fallow to let nature herself restore the soil.

This system had worked well with low human populations in the evergreen Asian jungle from which the Vazimba came. It is still used throughout the world wherever rainforest survives. When the Vazimba reached the drier woodlands of interior Madagascar, however, their clearing fires became a holocaust.

The Great Fire is still retold in Malagasy legend just as westerners repeat the tale of the Great Flood. It burned over hills and valleys; it burned without ceasing until the center of Madagascar had burned bare. The Great Fire may have been one fire; it may have been a century of devastation summed together in tribal memory. It is, however, a fact. Fossil sites only 1,000 years old hold carbonized trees, the bones of extinct giant tree-lemurs and the pots where those lemurs were probably cooked. Only 1,000 years ago Madagascar was mainly forest; today, some 300,000 km² are prairie.[8]

Destruction on this scale probably resulted from a combination of causes, human and natural. The woodlands of Madagascar may well have evolved in earlier wet eras: the southern pluvials which correspond to the ice ages of the north. The forest survived into drier periods by maintaining its own microclimate of dampness trapped between canopy and leaf-littered forest floor. During the warm, dry, interglacial which includes all historic time, the forest gradually dessicated, becoming more and more vulnerable. Then, when the Vazimba came and set the sparks of the Great Fire, they "provoked the collapse of an already fragile edifice."[9]

Twenty years ago, only 21% of Madagascar was covered by trees.[10] For comparison, the United States with its Great Plains, its farmlands, and its urban sprawl is still 32% forested. The stretch from Maine to Virginia, with a population seven and a half times that of the Malagasy Republic in a similar area, has nearly twice as much woodland as Madagascar, in that 20-year-old estimate.

		Area (km²)
Madagascar, total		587,000
Eastern rainforests		61,500
Western woodlands		25,500
Southern spiny desert		29,000
Transition types		9,000
	Total forest	125,000
Degraded savoka		4,300
Arable land		29,000
Prairie		340,000

Source: Guichon 1960.

OPPOSITE: Eroded lands northwest of Tananarive. All once forested; now the hardness and color of brick.

France, which a visitor sees as farms, cities, and cathedrals, bears 26% of forest land—still more than Madagascar.[11] In France, as in Madagascar, the climax vegetation would be forest, not prairie. In France, as in Madagascar, most of the open spaces are due to man's destruction of the trees and to his replacing the trees with a landscape, or bioscape, of his own creation. The difference is that in Europe man has been chipping at the natural vegetation with flint, bronze, and iron axes since we invented farming in the Neolithic age. In Madagascar, man has felled and burned during little more than a thousand years yet achieved a similar ratio of cleared land to forest.

There is a second difference: Europe is roughly stable. Although agricultural land disappears under cities and roads, European forests are largely maintained because we see their value.

In Madagascar the forest which remains is not fragile like that which burned in the Great Fire. It must be actively felled, burned, or overgrazed to disappear, but it is disappearing, and no satellite map has yet been prepared to tell how much remains.[12] Since 1972 the government has been increasingly responsive to the needs of the people—needs for farmland not trees—so the rate of clearing has increased. This is why I can write about Jean by face and name. Even if this book reaches the Antongil region where he lives, it is unlikely that the forestry service will repay his hospitality toward us by jailing him. He is after all only one among so very many.

MONSIEUR EMMANUEL'S ANALYSIS

We were marooned. The storm broke at 3:00 A.M., deluging the clearing, our camp, and all the northeast coast. A black-and-white frog under my pillow, inside the mosquito net, drove me from cover far too early. We slithered down the mountain and took refuge in a spare house on the beachside belonging to the Emmanuel family, where we waited seven days for the sea to calm down enough for a launch to fetch us back across the Bay of Antongil.

Our house was about 2½ by 3½ m, entirely constructed of traveler's palm. Palm fronds, folded at midrib, made the thatch, which was adequate to keep the rain off, except for one corner in need of repair. Stripped midribs laced with vines were the walls; palm-trunk planks, flattened under stone weights, made our floor. Only the corner posts came from other forest saplings: stilts to hold our house above mud, firewood, and chickens.

Although it was convenient to pour away the rice water through cracks between floorboards without going outside in the rain, it was also a relief to visit our host, Monsieur Emmanuel, in his furnished family home. The Emmanuel house measured at least 3½ m by 4 m, to shelter husband, wife, three children, and two young men, who, like us, had taken refuge off the mountain. By day the house was lined with woven mats like a sweet-straw bird's nest. The cooking fire burned on three stones in one corner; wooden shelves, covered with a cloth, filled another; the free wall was covered with Adventist mission posters of the Story of Joseph.

By night an unbleached muslin mosquito net occupied the central floor space: a rectangle only two feet high but wide enough to hold all the family members. If you disturbed them too early, the net flapped in strange humps like a recumbant cream-colored elephant, and dark heads poked out from all four sides at once.

The Emmanuel family are respected people in their beachside community. Madame E. is the "nivaquinizateur": the hander-out of quinine for neighborhood babies. Monsieur Emmanuel, sitting cross-legged with his Adventist Bible, could read.

It is difficult to convey what reading means as an index of a peasant's strength of character. Fifty percent of Malagasy children attend school, but the *average* pupil/teacher ratio is 65 to 1, and in the Antongil region may rise to 260 to 1. It is not uncommon for primary school teachers to teach in two shifts, with over 100 children in the morning, succeeded by 100 different children in the afternoon. The teacher shuttles between two rooms, setting a lesson for the first 50 or 70 pupils, then moving to the next room to set a lesson for the concurrent 70. It would be easier to set lessons in this fashion if there were more than two or three books per class. In the circumstances, even conscientious teachers admit they concentrate on the first row of children and hope that information somehow trickles down to the back of the room.[13]

Of course, not all Malagasy schools are so crowded, but it is clear that for a rural child to learn, he himself must decide that he will be one of those few in the front row. Monsieur Emmanuel, as he welcomed us to his home, was already marked as a thinking man.

He began the conversation by saying that he believes in God. However, as he analyzed (his verb) the situation, this meant that man should also respect God's creation, even the unending forest. The real problem is that there is no more unoccupied land suitable for rice growing in the Antongil region, so what are young people to do except cut forest clearings?

Emmanuel had put his finger on the central problem of the Third World: government economists can only quantify his dilemma. Madagascar has barely an acre (0.47 hectares) of arable land per person of the agricultural population. This is small for an African country but average for the irrigated rice-growing nations of Southeast Asia.[14] There are 8 million Malagasy with a population growth rate of 2.5%. More than half the population are under 20.[15] Where can each year's wave of 20-year-olds go to make their living? What, Emmanuel asked us, would you do?

I mentioned jobs in towns, but Emmanuel shook his head. He, like Jean, has tried that course and failed. Again, the economists' statistics support his conclusion. Only 19% of the Malagasy work force have jobs outside agriculture, and only 5% of the agriculturalists receive cash salaries.[16] All the rest are subsistence farmers and their family helpers, peasants like Jean and Emmanuel, who live from their land and sell surplus crops when the opportunity arises. Even under the most optimistic assumptions about the future of the Malagasy economy, there can be salaried jobs for only a fraction of the people who want them.

Georges suggested emigrating to new agricultural projects where the government drains swamps for paddy rice and builds cement houses for settlers. He lapsed from his role as interpreter to tell me scornfully that most Malagasy are too conservative to leave their own regions. Emmanuel confirmed that he did not want to go away and live on a settlement scheme. He suspected that the government would not support its tenants so well through real crises as the ancient system of extended family. The land which Emmanuel farms on the beachside is not his own but belongs to a richer uncle. The rich uncle may retire to this plot, but Emmanuel thinks he will not actually turn his relatives away to starve.

The one real hope, for Emmanuel's family or for the rural population of the Third World, is to improve yields and cash revenues from their own farms.

Cash revenue, in Emmanuel's case, is derisory. The average per capita income in rural Madagascar is under $100 per year, including the nominal value of subsistence crops.[17] In this Antongil region 91% of rural *households* have an income of less than $200 a year. Three-quarters of rural households touch less than $80 a year in cash.[18]

Georges was too delicate to question the family directly, but he speculated that the Emmanuels kept no money whatever in their little house. Their bank was the chickens, sheltering noisily beneath the floorboards, the blond-hackled rooster and his harem. The interest on investment was a clutch of eggs one hen incubated in a straw basket under the eaves. When Emmanuel needs money, he walks into town carrying a hen.

What on earth can such figures mean? Any western housewife knows that as they stand they are nonsense. Two hundred dollars a year, spent as American dollars at an American supermarket, would mean the Emmanuel family have starved to death long ago.

Few Malagasy starve, and only one-quarter could even be called undernourished, though very, very few can afford to be fat.

Could these incomes just be a trick of the dollar exchange rate, such that everything in Madagascar seems cheap to an American? On the contrary, prices in the modern sector are frightening: hotels, meals, cement houses with plumbing, air fares, electricity. In Tananarive, American Embassy staff draw a bonus to cover their "high cost of living."

Here is the nonsense. The labor and products of peasants are valued as trivial beside the products of industry. The skills they learn from their fathers are valueless, in cash terms, compared to skills learned from a schoolteacher. That $200 does not measure the value of food to Emmanuel, his wife, and his children. It is what they would receive for their year's coffee, manioc, and pepper greens if they tried to sell their produce instead of eating it.

Michael Lipton calls this difference between traditional and manufactured goods the "price twist"—one of the ways in which the urban and modern part of almost any Third World economy sucks in real wealth from the traditional, rural, poorer parts.[19] Small wonder that such peasants have little surplus means and virtually no incentive to improve their one capital good—the fertile soil.

The prices Emmanuel receives for his chickens and his few kilos of coffee-berries are beyond his own control. The chickens sell for what townspeople pay. The coffee price relates ultimately to a commodity agreement negotiated in Geneva between rich country buyers and poor country sellers. Emmanuel, on a forest beach 11 km from the nearest jeepable road, is part of the global economy.

Vanilla beans (near Hiaraka). Madagascar is one of the world's two leading producers of vanilla, which is the northeast coast's main export crop.

Cactus (*Rhipsalis cassytha*) and orchid on beachside near Emmanuel's house. It is the only true cactus in Madagascar.

It is strange, perhaps, that the International Monetary Fund, UNCTAD commodity agreements, a frost in Brazil, or a hardening of tariffs in the United States has a decisive influence on whether Emmanuel's coffee or Jean's cloves will put a few francs into their pockets. Even the price of rice, which is largely an internal decision for the Malagasy government, is a price calculated between the rival claims of rural growers who would like the prices raised and city people who would like it lowered. When the price is kept low to pacify urban constitutents, farmers find it not worthwhile to sell their rice, so the government must subsidize massive imports from other nations. Thus, the Malagasy staple food itself depends on world trade balances. Neither a Third World government nor peasants as poor and remote as Jean and Emmanuel can escape the international economic order.

Fortunately, the cash returns are only part of Emmanuel's income. He needs cash for school fees for his eldest son in Maroantsetra town, and for the occasional family funeral. Day to day, however, his family lives from the yield of their rice and manioc plots, at the mercy only of local disease and weather, not of international economics.

I asked what he himself can do to improve yields on his own land. Peasant agriculture is often far more intensive in its use of land than mechanized agriculture, but it is still the "world's most underused resource."[20] If peasants were not hampered by lack of capital and by the fact that they cannot afford to take any risks, in many regions they could vastly increase the productivity of the soil.

Emmanuel answered that he was watching two experiments closely. The local agricultural extension officer had ox-ploughed a field and planted manioc, while a Frenchman in town was growing new-breed grafted coffee. The agman's manioc had wilted; the Frenchman's coffee was green as fine young rice. Emmanuel pointed out that the difference was not the farmers' race but that the Frenchman was working for himself and the extension officer for a salary.

He asked, in turn, what I would do. Georges helped me: compost pits, and a vegetable garden fenced off from the chickens. Emmanuel had already planned a vegetable garden, but compost was a new idea.

In coastal Madagascar there has always been enough land for the soil to renew itself by regrowing the rough secondary scrub called savoka. Savoka would turn into forest eventually, though you can see that the forest has once been cut even 80 years afterward. In practice, there is never enough time for regrowth. Once cut, the forest is irrevocably lost.

Twice-cleared savoka rapidly becomes too degraded for more crops, so people have moved farther and farther into the forest. Only now, as population grows and the forest retreats, is the crisis approaching when all Malagasy must grow their crops in permanent fields.

The change to permanent agriculture will not be easy in spite of the fact that the change has been made over and over, in different parts of the earth, from Neolithic Europe onward. Wherever there has been a welcoming forest, people have practiced the system of forest fallow; wherever population growth has forced them to change, farmers adopt compost, manuring, weeding, ploughing, and all the technology that permits permanent cropping on the same land.[21]

The approach to permanent crops must differ in tropic and temperate zones. Often traditional methods are better for the soil than ill-suited attempts to modernize. Emmanuel does well to distrust the agman's ox-ploughed manioc. Emmanuel avoids erosion instead by hoeing in hummocks as he always has, then protecting the soil with mulch or even weeds. Trees like Emmanuel's coffee or Jean's cloves can do their part to hold the earth together, while the apparently casual mix of manioc and pepper-greens and bananas minimizes the risk of tropical pests building up enough concentration to demolish any one food crop. Emmanuel's conservatism is forced on him in part because he cannot afford to take any risks: any change that might lose one year's harvest would condemn his family to a year's starvation. However, his conservatism also stems from the fact that he really knows more about managing his own land than do many of the outsiders who give him advice.[22]

But traditional peasant culture is not in ecological balance in the long term. In Madagascar man has never been in balance with nature: at least 80% of the island is now grassland or savoka. In Madagascar, as in the rest of the world, degradation is accelerating. Wild and mountainous areas everywhere are being cleared; steeper and steeper slopes are being hacked into farmland, then abandoned in shorter and shorter times. All the world's highlands face similar devastation, Andes and Himalayas and Ethiopian Rift, and their fate is linked to that of the plains below, where rivers alternatively silt and flood as the mountains pour down their soil.[23]

Much of Madagascar has already faced the need for intensive agriculture. Wherever the hills are wholly cleared, people grow paddy rice in the valley bottoms and abandon the infertile slopes. There is now a straightforward choice for those regions which still have forest: whether to adopt intensive agriculture 10 or 20 years before they are forced to and try to preserve the forested slopes above, or whether to cling to the older system, changing only when they must, with the forest reserves gone forever.

"What about the forest?" Georges challenged Emmanuel. "Do you think the soil will still hang about and wait for you when the trees are gone?" Emmanuel, who lives where the streams flow from rainforest as yet only pocked with clearings, had not considered erosion. He had a much more immediate worry: firewood.

In Maroantsetra Town, where he used to live, the people once cut wild trees for firewood and culled all sorts of useful tools from the forest around. For instance, the broom to sweep our house was a palm flower. "Do you think that's right?" stormed Georges. "What right has anyone to chop down a twenty-five foot palm at the moment of flowering just to make a broom?" Emmanuel conceded it was wrong but said the question no longer matters, for there are no more of those palms near Maroantsetra. Firewood, he insisted, is much more serious. Now the townspeople are reduced to burning planted cashew trees; soon there will be nothing left but bamboo.

Emmanuel was again stating one man's view of a worldwide problem.[24] One-third of the world's population cooks over wood or charcoal. Firewood is still free for many of them, but what happens when it is gone? First the women walk for miles to gather brushwood and carry it home on their heads. Then they pay for charcoal brought from farther and farther away. Then they burn dung, robbing the fields of future fertility— and then?

Above all, it takes time to grow even brushwood. The time lags are the desperate aspect of the whole question of human conservation: the time from first noticing the danger to realizing the needs are not just in Maroantsetra Town or Madagascar but in the world; time to gather the political will to act—and time for a tree to grow again where a tree has been cut down. And what if the soil for that tree has meanwhile washed away to the sea?

Monsieur Emmanuel concluded by saying that he is but a peasant, a small small animal and cannot hope to analyze the situation to its full extent—with a great grin. It makes me think that some economists are all right because their analysis tallies with Emmanuel's. Economists solemnly tell one another over their instant coffee that "the peasant" is far from stupid. . . .

The other incident of that day was that Georges bought coffee. We were down to drinking "presque cafe"—plain hot water. Russ claimed it tasted almost the same if it is hot enough. At least, if it is too hot to taste.

Georges had red coffee-berries chosen for him from Emmanuel's bushes. Madame Emmanuel roasted them on a tripod brazier with twisted legs, over the house fire, beside her big iron cooking caldron. (The devil turns over the souls of sinners with a long-handled iron spoon, like coffee-beans on the fires of Hell.) One of the young men who took refuge off the mountain went outside and pounded our roasted coffee in a rice mortar, sheltered by the overhang of the streaming thatch, while Georges sewed a filter of gauze from his dissecting kit. After about one-and-a-half hours' preparation, we ceremoniously brewed and filtered the best cups of coffee ever tasted.

RICE FOR TOMORROW

Rainbow! Doubled, momentarily tripled, into the sea behind the island reserve of Nosy Mangabé. Georges and I cried together, "God's promise there shall be no more flood!"

Georges folded his soaking tent; Russ washed his trousers. The tern by the sea was *Sterna bergii,* the Mascarene swift tern. The loud-squawking bird over the stream where we washed was a nelicouvri weaver, a genus confined to the eastern forest. The female with her bright yellow head and green eyestreak was bolder than her black and yellow mate. Their nest, so far just a woven ring, hung down over the stream. When it was finished its entrance tunnel would be 1 m long, its mouth decorated with green leaves. A flock of mister-now-you-see-me-now-you-don't, the wattled sunbird, popped in and out of the bushes like spots in front of your eyes. The wattled sunbird is not related to true sunbirds of Africa or the ecologically similar hummingbirds of America but is classified with the velvet asity in the Philepittidae, yet another bird family endemic to Madagascar.

Georges was happy, for Russ caught him a *Discophus antongilii*—a spherical scarlet frog the size of Russ's fist. This species is found only by the Bay of Antongil; Georges will take it back to astonish the zoo-going public of Tananarive. "That's a female," Georges told Russ. "Males are the same color, but only as big as a matchbox. How did you catch her?"

Russ lowered his voice. "She attacked me."

Dugout canoe from hollowed ramy tree on beach at Hiaraka, near Maroantsetra. Zebus in background are rare in this wet region but valued
for bride price and funeral sacrifices.

Pirogues, gouged from ramy runks, ferried people down the coast. One family drove a zebu cow along the beach, bound to be a bride price or a funeral offering. We could begin to see these people as they have always been. It is no new thing that Jean and Emmanuel have links with the outside world: this coast has been traded over for centuries.

After the Indonesians came Arab dhows and Portuguese galleons, then the British and French, rivaling each other for control of the Indian Ocean spice and slave trades. We should, perhaps, have taken the advice of Captain James Lancaster, who anchored in the Bay of Antongil on Christmas Day 1601:

> There blew an exceeding great storme, and those or our shippes that road nearest the small Island [of Nosy Mangabé] sped best: for two of our ships drove with three anchors ahead. At our going a land in the Little Iland, we perceived by writing upon the rockes, of five Holland ships which had been there, and had had some sickness upon their men, and had lost between one hundred and fiftie and two hundred men while they roade in that place. . . .
>
> We went a land to the Mayne Iland, where the people presently entered into barter with us, for Rice and Hennes, Oranges and Limons, and another fruit called plantans, and held all at high rates . . . for all these people of the East parts are very subtill and craftie in their bartering, buying and selling.[25]

This eastern coast, up to the Bay of Antongil, was the special preserve of pirates. There were Benjamin Bridgeman and Thomas Tew, Henry Every and John Avery, Captain England and of course there was Captain Kidd. Avery's pirate kingdom (which may be all Defoe's imagination) was supposed to be out in the bay before us, on the island of Nosy Mangab.[26]

No imaginary pirate kingdom can rival the real King of the East Coast, Tom Similo, an 18th century pirate's son. His buccaneering father sent him to London at age 17 to be educated as a gentleman. After three months he returned home in disgust and resumed his Malagasy name of Ratsimilao, "He who never asks pardon." He fastened the warrior's mother-of-pearl crescent to his forehead. Fighting with rifle and spear Ratsimilao unified the East Coast Betsimisaraka tribe, controlled the slave trade from the interior, made speeches still recorded for their eloquence, and magnanimously spared Englishmen shipwrecked on his shores. In 1746 Mahé de la Bourdonnais, the great governor of Mauritius, arrived storm-battered and dismasted in the Bay of Antongil. Ratsimilao's men helped the Frenchmen cut 24-m trees from the forest to repair their craft. Ratsimilao's kingdom lived on trade, a part of global politics like the pirates themselves, like Jean and Emmanuel today.[27]

In one sense, little has changed, but we are at the end of a historical era. To look about this village and imagine that we see traditional village life would be as much an illusion as to imagine the forest as untouched wilderness.

It was a Tuesday before we walked out along the beach to "civilization"—the day when Madame Emmanuel gives weekly quinine to the settlement children.

In these wet regions nearly everyone has seen a child die in the convulsions of cerebral malaria. Nearly every adult has intermittent fevers. They need no urging to bring their children on Tuesday to Madame Emmanuel—this is one government program widely accepted. I suppose that there must exist some conservationists who can look at these babies and see only the overpopulation of the future.

We have had an agricultural revolution in the Neolithic, an industrial revolution in the past 200 years. These changed men's lives merely by changing our means of production. The current revolution, the biochemical one, changes our means of reproduction. When a village woman gives out quinine, or help on birth control, or penicillin, she is altering the shape of family structure, of life and death.

Just as Jean with his coupe-coupe is the forest's executioner, who may end the traditional background of Malagasy rural resources, so Madame Emmanuel is ending the kind of families where half the children will die by the age of five. Between them they will change the structure of the tropical world before the century's end. It remains to be seen whether Emmanuel, the thoughtful farmer, can also play his role and find the means to feed that world.

After the quinine roll, Madame Emmanuel pounded the family rice in her wooden mortar, hollowed like a pirogue out of a tree-bole. THUMP-bump, bump, THUMP-bump-bump, Madame, her daughter Josiane, and a neighbor's teenager pounded together, the 1½-m pestles bouncing up again into their hands, the thuds in decreasing loudness according to each girl's strength. When Josiane grew tired of breaking rhythm, Madame and the teenager settled to efficiency, BANG, whang, BANG, whang. Madam Emmanuel stopped pounding and began to winnow, tossing the grains in the air from a flat straw basket. Two-year-old Ramiandrasoa "He who awaits a good future," seeing his mother busy, pretended to lift the rice pestle in his small brown fists, still dimpled over the knuckles.

Rice for today or rice for tomorrow? Will Madagascar have both? Will there be fields, and rice, and confidence in Ramiandrasoa's good future?

Bug in flower during rain (Hiaraka).

4

RAINFOREST

STARFISH IN THE RAINFOREST

We escaped to uninhabited land: the island reserve of Nosy Mangabé. This 5 km² hilltop in the bay has been bought by the International Union for the Conservation of Nature as a reserve for aye-ayes. It is not virgin forest—there were recent farms here and pirate anchorages or even "kingdoms." Sailors over the years have cut tall trees for masts. However, no one lives here now but a Forestry Service guardian. A one-roomed laboratory house offers visiting scientists the sort of cement roof and flooring they are presumed to need. The guardian even cuts trails—sometimes. Here if anywhere we could watch the forest alive, without considering the conflicting needs of humanity.

We set off toward the ship's beacon on the island's southern summit. Crimson-clawed crabs plopped into the streams. Only bulbuls flew about the trees, their black skull caps erect in a row of wet black points. They are interesting as one of the relatively few Malagasy species which have started from India, instead of Africa, but they are probably late arrivals, island hopping.

The path, after crossing a couple of streams on lashed-stick bridges, gave up entirely and slid downhill to the beach itself, so we splashed along the sand. Then the trail pulled itself together and started uphill to the summit in earnest.

The day before we had tried climbing in the forest without trails. We scrabbled and hauled ourselves up and down, occasionally making the mistake of grabbing the thorn-studded stem of a tree fern, often making the mistake of reaching for an apparently solid stick which collapsed into rotted fragments and a wettish cloud of fungus spores. We braided ourselves in lianas and clambered over buttress roots and slid downhill on the very thin layer of undecayed leaves which overlies almost sterile red clay.

The world of rainforest, here as elsewhere, is much like a coral reef. It is a three-dimensional world, layer upon layer, where birds insinuate themselves in the grottoes of foliage. The difference, as far as we are concerned, is that skin diving on a reef we are

44

Pirogue near tip of Nosy Mangabé, an aye-aye refuge.

among the flying creatures, soaring in the third dimension. Here in the forest we are crawlers, with the perspective of a bottom-living starfish. The forest towers over us, complex, impenetrable, mainly beyond the wit of our eyes or our minds to organize.

It is sheer size, first of all, which engulfs you. Malagasy lowland forest is not particularly high as rainforests go: canopy 15 to 25 m above ground, while emergent trees rise to 40 m or more. However Egbert Leigh, who has measured rainforests in many parts of the world, found that Malagasy forest is consistently denser—more trees set closer together. (I'm glad Egbert measured it—I thought it just felt that way when I tried to push through.) This relatively short, dense rainforest is common to lowland Madagascar and the northeast corner of Puerto Rico, which also alternates cool rain, cloud, and cyclones.

This rainforest, although not so high as Malayan or Central American stands, has all the true rainforest grandeur of massive trunks and continuous canopy—the solid occupancy of space. Rainforest may contain more than 200 metric tons of wood and bark per hectare.[1] Some northern woodlands exceed this amount but this is due to the longer life span of temperate trees. About 1% of lowland tropical trees fall down each year, with average life spans of perhaps 70–80 years.[2] The decaying stems we grasp are an index of the rapid turnover of wood: the production and decay. Lemurs, who are relatively less interested in inedible objects than most other monkeys, do not break off branches to drop on predators and primatologist, but one of the standard ploys of Panamanian Cebus monkeys is to leap to dead trees or tree branches, break them, and let them fall on the forest floor. So much decayed wood waits in the rainforest canopy that a 2 kg monkey can usually find a 100 kg branch ready to detach and drop, which at least makes a pursuer think twice.

The tropical lowland forest produces more leaf as well as more wood than temperate woodlands. Northern deciduous forests drop 3 tons (dry weight) of leaves per hectare per year, compared to 5 in Puerto Rico and 6 or 7 in rainforests of warmer, sunnier climates. Curiously, both the northern forest and Puerto Rico drop 6 hectares of leaves per hectare per year: the difference is that the tropical leaves weigh twice as much per unit area.[3]

Moreover, tropical forest is metabolically even more active than one would guess from its production of wood and leaf. Puerto Rico's rainforest takes up carbon dioxide four times as fast as its temperate zone counterparts, and less than one-quarter of its photosynthesis goes into new growth of leaf wood and root, compared to nearly half in a northern forest. Presumably the remaining metabolic energy pays the extra costs of extracting nutrient from poor soil and for defense against insects and fungi.[4] The respiration rate of a rainforest may also be double that of temperate controls, for the same quantity of wood and leaf produced. One Ivory Coast semievergreen forest breathed out 100 metric tons of carbon dioxide per hectare each year, that is, about twice the carbon dioxide content of the whole column of atmosphere above a hectare.[5]

Strangely, the size and the rapid turnover of the jungle are no guide to what man can grow on its barren soil. The forest (again like a reef) is an organic structure that perpetuates itself, not an outgrowth of some underlying resource. When a leaf drops to

OPPOSITE: Beach at Nosy Mangabé.

the forest floor, soil insects, bacteria, and fungi attack it. In six weeks the leaf has broken down to nutrient form, ready for recycling back into other plants. The six-week turnover of rainforest leaf litter compares to a year's turnover time in temperate deciduous woodland, three years in temperate grassland, and seven years in northern pine woods.[6] Each sort of forest is part of a cycle, in which minerals and organic matter go round and round from plant to soil, but in the north the cycle is slow, or even incomplete, so the humus may grow deeper and deeper with passing years. Not so in rainforest, where nearly all the resources blossom at once as living matter.

You can see the forest's reactions by looking down. Most of these huge trees have shallow roots, groping just under the surface for the minerals which have no time to sink deeper. The buttresses barring your way are a structural alternative to tap-rooted foundations. The ground's surface is knobbly with root-knees which trip your boots or conveniently outline steps in the hillside for climbing. Most rainforests grow on nutrient-poor, fragile soils, although the Malagasy ones do not have the extreme shortages of the Amazon basin. Decayed trees in the Amazon sometimes mysteriously stand upright—the live trees are so hungry that their roots have grown upward inside the dead ones! Even in the kinder soils of Panama, Montgomery and Sunquist watched three-toed sloths come down to the ground to defecate, drill little holes in the earth with their tails, and plant their fertilizer by the roots of their favored food trees—apparently a case of cooperative evolution between animal and tree.[7]

When the rainforest is felled for field crops, heavily logged, or wantonly defoliated, the tropic rains beat down on the bare soil and leach away even the small amount of nutrients which are left. In traditional slash-and-burn agriculture throughout the humid tropics, cleared fields grow a good crop the first year, a poor crop the second year, and no crop, no crop worth a peasant's time and effort, the third year. Where the soils are not quite so barren, as in eastern Madagascar and the outer islands of Indonesia, weeds choke the second-year fields, out-competing the planted crops for scarce resources, so the peasant is caught in two ways at once.[8] Then the field must be left to regrow. Given enough time, and if the clearing is not too large or the hill slope too steep, it will regrow. Given enough time, shifting agriculture is an efficient way to use the forest.

In the modern world, there is never enough time.

Madagascar is now cleared, most of it turned to man-made prairie. The red, forest-laid, lateritic soils leach away their minerals under the rain and set to concrete hardness under the sun. The common description of Madagascar is "an island with the form, color, consistency, and sterility of a brick."[9]

It seems strange that we cannot perpetuate the forest when it obviously renews itself. Trees grow, die, fall. When one of the giants succumbs to old age it crashes down, breaking those below. It leaves a gap—a sudden well of sunlight in the gloom. Light, heat, dryness. Wild ginger and light-demanding trees, whose seedlings may have waited years for their opportunity, grow up together in an impenetrable thicket. Young lianas entwine the growing saplings. Some of these light-demanders win their race toward the sun. The slower growing trees and the thicket bushes die off as the victors shade them. Lianas which are lucky in their choice of host live, too, stretching out, python-thick, as

OPPOSITE: Tangled jungle in aye-aye refuge along coast of Nosy Mangabé.
We braided ourselves in lianas. . . .

their host tree bears them higher. (Lianas are not lassos that fling out to grasp mature trees; they are lifelong parasites, and each has the same age as its principal host tree.)[10] After some decades, the gap has changed to forest in the building stage: a mass of trees all of whose foliage is roughly at the same height.

Beneath these building stage trees, the original thicket is gone, but a new crop of seedlings has started. These are the trees which can begin their lives in deep shade. These seedlings grow slowly, steadily. They could not compete with the riotous growth of the light-demanders. Many, in fact, would be killed by the heat and dryness of sunlight in a forest gap—and exterminated totally by the heat of man's clearing fires. This is one clue to our inability to perpetuate rainforest: many of its species can grow only inside the forest itself. In Madagascar there is an extra weakness in this step. Many rapidly growing trees and bushes are vigorous foreign plants, which the native Malagasy species find hard to dislodge.[11]

As the shade-tolerant trees are pushing up under the canopy, the building phase trees begin to space out in height. While they are all growing together they crowd one another into a vertical shape, their branches pointing upward, more or less parallel to a central trunk. As they reach their final height, some remain within the canopy, leaves interlaced with leaves of neighbors. But some grow taller, as the vast "emergents," where lemurs sun and bird flocks cry their morning chorus. The emergents relax, spread, their single trunks giving way to a fan of huge main branches, a candelabra of foliage 24 m above ground. Meanwhile, beneath the canopy, shade-tolerant species are forming an understory, sometimes as a visibly separate layer, sometimes blurring with the canopy itself.

The existence, or not, of separate layers of foliage is one of the great sources of argument among foresters. Whitmore seems to have largely settled the question by showing that the layers become clearer the longer the forest has been growing—but even in fully mature lowland forest there are older patches where the layers are sharp as well as younger, single-layer building patches and newly made gaps.[12]

This raises the question, What is a mature community? Ecologists speak of "climax": the form of life that will prevail in any given region if it is left strictly alone for a long enough time. A mown field in upstate New York grows up to goldenrod, then to brambles, then to second growth, finally to birch, oak, maple, beech. The climax, for that field, is beech–maple woodland, whose stable mix of species continues indefinitely. To recognize the climax, though, you must look at a reasonably large area, for any given tree will be growing or dying. In mature New Hampshire woodland, birch seedlings colonize gaps, sugar maple seedlings grow under the birch, and beech under the sugar maples; in each tiny patch of forest, species replace one another in turn.[13] How much more complex are the tropical forests! In the northern climax, birch, maple, and beech may account for 90% of the trees. In Malagasy rainforest, Perrier de la Bathie counted 239 individual plants in only 100 m^2, which represented 102 different species,[14] and in 1 acre you may find 60 different species of trees.[15]

Fortunately, we do not have to define a climax by the amount of time it has been

Rainforest at Nosy Mangabé: layers of foliage with emergents.

Strangler fig vine (Nosy Mangabé).

left alone or even by the species we see but instead by Odum's more abstract, and more satisfying, concept of energy flow in a steady state system.[16] When a natural community reaches climax, there is no net increase of plant and animal material. All the energy inputs are used up; the processes of growth, metabolism, and decay simply cancel one another out and are in perfect balance.

This may sound abstract, but for people it is the most practically important concept of all. What we usually want out of nature is that it produce things for us to consume. Whether that produce is grain or timber, we want to harvest a crop. The last thing we want is for nature to reach its own balance, with growth only equal to decay. Thus, the practice of rational forestry, whether temperate or tropic, involves keeping forests in the building stage, growing up timber for our own purposes.

When even the most idealistic of conservationists talk of a steady state, no-growth world, they mean a steady state with people considered as part of nature. In such a world a large part of the results of other animals' and plants' growth would still be channeled through people—their growth balanced by our decay. The "steady" aspect of the situation would merely be that people might agree to limit their demands to a constant share of the proceeds. The advocates of human growth, on the other hand, believe that we shall be able to claim an ever-increasing share of the proceeds of the system for ourselves by technology and management. After all, agriculture itself is a way of keeping natural communities in a building stage, building for our benefit. Why should we not go on exploiting the world with ever more efficiency? Why should we leave any natural community at its unproductive climax? Why not move at once to rational forestry—which means felling the biggest trees, poison-girdling the irrelevant ones, and keeping the rest in a fast-growing building phase for maximum sustained yield?

There are many reasons: logical ones, and emotional, aesthetic ones which overwhelm you when you are actually here, face-to-face with a rainforest.

In this organic world every species interacts with every other to provide fabulous richness. For people who come here from northern woodlands, it is like entering an Italian baroque church, after Scandinavian modern. Every scroll is embellished with further curlicues; every alcove is crusted with gilded cupids and mother-of-pearl. Literal alcoves, the circles of *Asplenium nidus*, an epiphytic fern, catch falling leaf litter, make their own soil, and provide brackets to support yet further epiphytes. The axils of palms and pandanus and cycads collect rainwater, like a great marsh split up into little ponds, at different heights above the soil. Thirty-eight species of insects may live in the leaf axil ponds of just one species of palm tree.[17] In a tropical rainforest there are a hundred ways to copy a dead leaf, from the first brown flecks on green to transparent latticework. Even when you see the dead leaf move, you do not know if it will metamorphose into a frog or a butterfly.

The trees even seem to mimic one another. Their slim, unbranched trunks lead the eye upward to similar branching crowns. The dark green ovoid leaves often grow horizontally along each side of a horizontal twig—a good pattern to catch the dim light without overlapping. A complementary pattern is the radial fan. Cyathea tree-fern crowns are fans; epiphytic ferns fan around their host trunk; the flat circular crowns of forest palms and the Colea tree copy the pattern. To a stranger, rainforest trees at first sight can seem very similar. Perhaps their similarity helps to baffle the ubiquitous insect pests, who must travel far to search out a second tree of the same species. Perhaps also, each tree fills its leaves, and seeds, with its own kind of poison, which only a few species of insect can cope with. It is harder for the appropriate pests to find a rare tree, so the forest is filled with many kinds of trees, none of them common.

Besides the defense against insects, rainforest trees probably conduct chemical warfare against one another, poisoning one anothers' root-ends as they grow. And any plant in this perpetual sog which did not provide its own fungicides would have athlete's foot.

The forest's complexity shows not just in species' defenses but in their interrelations. In this windless world, plants rely on animals for pollination. Flowers with open bowls, heavy fragrance, and abundant edible pollen are feeding dishes for beetles. Hanging nocturnal flowers wait for bats to sip their nectar while the shaving-brush stamens will dust pollen onto the bats' head and chest fur. (Bat-flowers often smell sour, reminiscent of the bats themselves.) The figs, strangest of all, keep captive gall wasps within their flowers, which hatch, metamorphose, and mate within the gall itself. The male wasps mate and then die in their gall-flower cradle; females emerge, gathering pollen from a male flower on the way. The female wasps fly off and pollinate either a female flower, which produces more fig trees, or a gall flower, which lets them lay eggs to produce more wasps. Nearly each one of the hundreds of species of fig trees has its own kind of wasp. One way to work out the figs' relationships is to see which species have similar fig wasps.

The complexity is there, even in the visual first impression. Furthermore, the longer you study and the more you measure, the more complex the forest grows. To give just one example, Tom Lovejoy spent two years at Belem, in the lower Amazon, mist-netting, marking, and releasing rainforest birds. He recorded not only species but individuals as well.[18]

He caught more than 200 of the 300 species reported for the region: about 15,000 separate captures, a total of 5,798 individuals. The unnerving part is that 35–45% of the species which he caught in each area were represented by only one or two individuals. That is, a very high proportion of the bird species were rare species.

The same sort of statistic could be repeated for rainforest trees, epiphytes, insects—perhaps even bacteria. Whatever you study here, you find that most species are rare species. This phenomenon has immediate implications for conservation. In disturbed habitats, and in stressed habitats, it is the rare species which disappear first. If the very nature of rainforest is the complexity of its fabric, whenever we allow a compromise which stresses the forest, we threaten that complexity. A little clearing, a little logging, a road which divides a forest block—all these might matter less in simpler environments. Here, where the web of life is almost infinitely ramified, the losses may be irreparable.

Despite this luxuriance of life, as we looked with our dim starfish perspective out through the dripping understory, through the canopy leaves of the trees on the hillside below us, out over the gray sea, no animals moved except peeping invisible tree frogs, one of which, when seen, turned out to be a peeping pale green miniature cricket.

At last we emerged to the hilltop beacon for a wide view of the tapestried hills of Nosy Mangabé. Then, as we watched the interwoven light green and dark green and new orange leaf-sprays, Russ said, "Alison, what is a black-and-white football doing on top of a tree in the rain?"

A quarter of a mile away, the ruffed lemur had curled up for a treetop siesta, black rope of tail thrown over white shoulder. Discovery: these rainforest lemurs, unlike my thin-fluffed ringtails of the south, are waterproof. We watched through binoculars, the mind, knowing the form and gesture of other lemurs, shaping the black-and-white spots into an animal at the limit of vision.

Very deliberately he pulled out his black face from his belly-fur—the round white half-moon of ruff, sideburns, ear-tufts all continuous—and then two more ruffed lemurs crystallized out of the light and shadow of adjacent trees.

Suddenly, a group far over on the hill to the right began to bark. Or perhaps, bellow: a harsh, in-and-out sawing noise, which filled the valley even cushioned as it was with layers of foliage. Our group became agitated, stood up on all fours, and swung their tails from side to side. A few seconds later they too began to call, their bellow alternating with high-pitched whinnying squeals. They are not much bigger than healthy house cats (although much furrier), and we could see that they were two-fifths of a kilometre away. Yet the din rolled like Rip van Winkle's thunder.

When the football group stopped calling, after a few more seconds a third group, farther toward the island's center, started in their turn. Meanwhile the football group moved to a soft green bamboo clump and settled to groom. Lemurs, like other primates, are contact animals, who enjoy snuggling against one anothers' fur and grooming with the toothcomb formed of all their lower canines and incisors.

As we traipsed back down, I kept staring at the trees in frustration that I could not understand what they meant to the lemurs. With my "own" ringtail groups, I soon learned to see tall tamarinds as sleeping and sunning places, long horizontal branches as highways, and tangled liana banks, shaded from noonday sun, as a lovely spot for a siesta. This is what Jakob von Uexküll called an animal's "umwelt": the world around seen from its own point of view.

This is the inside view of the same patterns I have tried to describe from the outside when talking about the complexity of rainforest. Each of these myriad species has its own niche, its own way of life. The way each perceives and reacts to its environment defines that way of life. An umwelt is an ecological niche seen from the inside.

Thus, for our pale green peeping cricket a tree is only, perhaps, a color of green that its eyes are tuned to appreciate, a scent of food, perhaps a texture on its tarsal claws. For the lemurs, each separate branch has a known potential in terms of food or travel. Above all, for these ruffed lemurs which were so quick to react to the calls of other groups, each tree may well have an emotional value of "ours" or "theirs" or "shared" or "disputed." Only by spending months on Nosy Mangabé could we find out if the ruffed lemurs actively defend territory, that is, particular pieces of geography, or if they simply space out a reasonable distance from the next bellowing troop.

Hilltop view of rainforest at Nosy Mangabé (black and white ruffed lemur area).

Land snail (Nosy Mangabé). Snails are very common in rainforests, which have much decaying vegetable matter.

Tree frog in rainforest (Hiaraka).

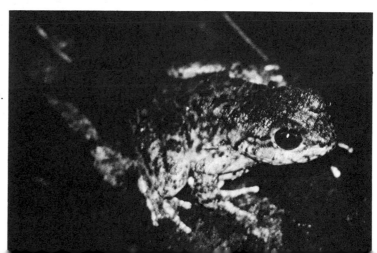

Leaf-tailed lizard (*Uroplatus fimbriatus*).

Hunting kingfisher (*Ispidina madagascariensis*).

And knowing that the lemurs' viewpoint was all there to find out, all I could see in my own umwelt was the soft tapestry of treetops viewed from above and the maddening tangle of stems viewed from underneath.

THE MOUSELEMUR AND THE EARLIEST PRIMATES

As night fell, Russ and I put on our headlamps, not miners' lights, but the weaker lights which alpinists use when they must start a climb at three in the morning. A forehead torch beam moves just where you are looking, so an animal's eyes which look toward the light reflect directly back to your own. The dimness is an advantage. Strong light makes night creatures blink and turn away.

First, ruby-red eyeshine, then a bark-colored shape plastered to a vertical tree trunk, only a yard above ground. Its splayed suction-toes and the frills along its sides merged with the bark. As we approached, a leaf-shaped tail lifted away from the tree, perhaps a distraction to make us think the head was at the top and not the bottom, although I don't know what predator could miss seeing the crocodilian eyes and skull-angle. Even camouflaged, the concentric vertical arcs of its pupil seemed like a night-dragon's eye. Leaf-tailed lizards are common on Nosy Mangabé, apparently because there are no cerulean couas here to gobble them up. They are common here but nowhere else: they are one of the six Malagasy species in an endemic gecko genus.

I grabbed the little dragon—and it grabbed me.

It won the first round and sprang straight up with all four legs outstretched at once, as though worked by a spring in its stomach. But we won in the end. It stayed with us long enough to pose in sunlight.

After we caught the little lizard, we amused ourselves picking up the reflections of spiders' and moths' eyes, while a bat flew figure-eights between us down the trail. The next high point was *Ispidina madagascariensis,* the hunting kingfisher, sleeping on a low twig over a stream.

He was a tiny bird, russet above and white below, with a tail so short it seemed some naughty child had taken scissors to it. Since this kingfisher catches insects, not fish, I should think he would need more steering apparatus.

To make up for lack of tail, its head was top-heavy, with beady black eye and long, strong, coral-pink bill. When we first saw him, he was pulled out thin with alarm, quite hammer-shaped, although too sleepy to get up off his haunches even when Russ and I stood with our headlamps 2 feet below him.

On our way back, the little kingfisher had gone to sleep, fluffed out into a perfect sphere, like one of those German woolly-ball toys which appear in the shops at Christmas. Even his color you would choose for a woolly-ball, orange top and white bottom. And, from what must have been under one wing emerged the very tip of a coral-pink bill.

We had been seeing pairs of tiny orange eyes, in bushes and lianas and small trees, every hundred metres along the trail. No, not tiny eyes but tiny blazing searchlights, set less than an inch apart.

It was *Microcebus murinus,* the mouselemur, smallest of all primates. They do

Mouselemur (*Microcebus murinus*).

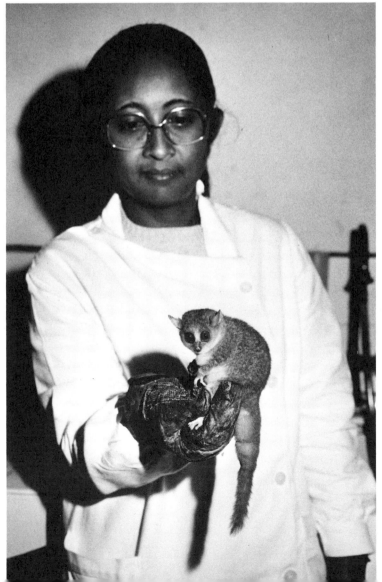

Rabodo Andrianatsiferana with mouselemur.

not seem to realize that you can see them in the lamplight almost as well as they can see you. One mouselemur in a low bush, its mouth full of a grape-like berry, sat with its tail curled in a spiral beneath it, staring at Russ through the drizzle as hard as he stared back.

Mouselemurs have attracted a great many lemur-watchers: Jean-Jacques and Arlette Petter of France, Bob Martin of England, Jay Russell and Lee McGeorge of America, Rabodo Andrianatsiferana of Tananarive.[19] It would be uncharitable to suggest that all the scientists like mouselemurs because they are easy to feed in laboratories, live in convenient trailside bushes, and obligingly shine their eyes at you to show where they are.

The real fascination is that mouselemurs are the nearest modern animals to the ancestor we all started from: the first little primate scrabbling about in a bush not too long after the last dinosaur relinquished mastery of the earth.

That ancient primate had eyes which could focus on objects: to move quickly on branches you need pattern vision which will register detail in three dimensions. It had the beginnings of hands: divergent fingers that gripped around small twigs, not just claws that dug into bark. Matthew Cartmill thinks that, very early on, the ancient primates were insectivorous.[20] Forward-facing eyes, which later evolved to true binocular vision, are characteristic of the hunters, not the hunted. Grasping hands allow primates (and chameleons) to sneak up on their prey without shaking the branch. Besides, all the nocturnal primates use their hands, not their mouths, to catch insects.

That ancient tree-climbing hunter may have looked a bit like a mouselemur and probably lived very much as mouselemurs do. They hunt alone because there is not enough of most insects to share, even with your best friend.

Like most generalizations, this one is not absolute. Squirrel monkeys in South America hunt in large troops. Insects fly up as the monkey gang disturb the leaves, and one of the monkeys is generally ready to pounce.[21] Insect-eating birdflocks, like the vangids we saw on Hiaraka, can work with the same methods. However, there is a complex of behavior that often goes together: small size, nocturnal habit, insectivory, solitary stalking of insect prey. Because mouselemurs show the same sorts of behavior as their relatives the African bushbabies, and their further cousins the lorises and pottos, we can conclude that this is a widespread way of life. On the other hand, when mouselemurs eat in a fruiting tree or bush, they may join in twos or threes—but not two or three at random, for they all know who is who.[22]

A male's range overlaps the range of several females—his harem by location. Some of the females may also overlap with other males, but the males rarely associate. You (or Bob Martin) fairly often find a mouselemur nest with several females sleeping together in a furry ball, sometimes a male with a few females, rarely several males.

Of course there is a great advantage for such small mammals to sleep together just to keep warm. Arlette Petter went so far as to take rectal temperatures of mouselemurs and found they are much less accurately adjusted than the rest of the mammals.[23] Rabodo Andriantsiferanana has found that their body temperature can vary as much as 10°C from their outside environment while they are asleep, although they pump up to normal while they are awake. She has even showed that mouselemurs can go into hibernation if kept in a cold room at 15°C. They sharply reduce their breathing and heart rate to a kind of steady torpor but wake up quite naturally once a day to forage.[24]

Quite aside from keeping them warm, the mouselemurs' social structure would be a reasonable starting point for the evolution of permanent social life. Primates, more commonly than other mammals, tend to live in troops where males associate with females throughout the year and throughout their lives. The mouselemur pattern of overlapping home ranges may be the way our own ancestors started to evolve toward our own society.[25]

For almost as long as it has taken to write these paragraphs, the little mouselemur held still, goggling at Russ's headlamp, its berry unchewed between its teeth. Finally Russ could not stand it any longer, reached out very gently—and tweaked the little lemur's curled-up tail. It came to with a jerk and scuttled away down its branch into the darkness.

AYE-AYE

There was one real disappointment in our trip to Nosy Mangabé. We never saw a wild aye-aye.

Aye-ayes are a story of people not zoology. The zoology is bizarre enough: a mammal with bat ears, beaver teeth, two skeleton's fingers, and a black and silver tail like an overgrown ostrich feather. It took scientists a hundred years to conclude that the aye-aye is a lemur not an order of mammals all by itself.

One must admit that the aye-aye, however eccentric, is not unique. A New Guinea marsupial, *Dactylonax*, the long-fingered possum, has converged with it, which brings us back to the "woodpeckers" of chapter 2. No matter how odd the way of life, animals of different continents may discover each niche. Both the aye-aye and *Dactylonax* use their bat ears to locate burrowing insects inside trees, their great incisors to strip away the bark and wood, and their delicate, elongated finger to probe in the insect's hole and impale a plump larva. The aye-aye as well raids coconut palms, chiseling holes in the green fruit much like a man with a coupe-coupe, then flickering its skeleton finger in and out to bring up drops of coconut milk.

But the aye-aye is only an animal. What makes it dramatic are the fears (and the hopes) that go with it. Malagasy fear it. It brings bad luck or death to any village where it appears. The only escape is to kill it and if possible to burn down and relocate the village. Even dead, it is powerful magic. The sorcerer who dares to keep its finger has occult strength and, I have been told, even more if he has the courage to twist, or bite, the finger from the still living animal.

Russ and I, looking at the only living aye-aye in captivity, in the Tananarive zoo, could not believe that anyone would want to persecute this soft mammal with the rich black-and-silver fur and the great appealing eyes.

Now, though, Georges has let me walk in the zoo by moonlight and watch the aye-aye as it climbs and leaps about its cage. Now, under the moon, I can see those eyes as baleful beacons. I can see the face as somehow wrong: a primate's eyes with the jaws that could tear. Even its movement is uncanny: it leaps between branches balancing with the plumed tail, not like a lemur but more like a fox-sized squirrel. Above all, the bony finger would explain the superstition. It is too long, and too delicate for ordinary locomotion. Whenever the aye-aye's hand closes on a branch, that one finger still angles away, ready, with its claw, to point out death.

The terror of the villagers has roused almost equally strong emotions among conservationists. Jean-Jacques Petter estimated that the world population of aye-ayes may be only 50 animals. Even if this estimate is too low and there are others secreting themselves in the Malagasy woods, they are certainly one of the world's most threatened mammals.[26]

Jean-Jacques Petter and André Peyriéras raised money from the IUCN, scoured the east coast, climbed trees, and hauled protesting aye-ayes out of their nests—at the cost of scratches that took a month to heal. Sometimes they reached a village too late, to find one of the rarest mammals reduced to a drying skeleton and a few wisps of black-and-silver fur.

In 1966 they released nine aye-ayes on the beach at Nosy Mangabé. One female and her half-grown offspring made themselves immediately at home. They climbed up and began nest building in front of the goggling movie cameras. The others disappeared into the trees. . . . Where are they now?

For ten years no one has known.

Guy Ramanantsoa, professor of forestry at the University of Madagascar, thinks they may all be dead. The high salt content of the leaves, under perpetual sea wind, may disagree with them. Guy camped two nights at the topmost ridge of Nosy Mangabé without so much as hearing the characteristic cry of "ha-hay," a soft sound like someone hammering on a piece of tin. (The aye-aye in the zoo said "ha-hay" at me without opening his mouth, just squeezing the noise out of his dilated nostrils.)

André Peyriéras, the only person who has hand raised a baby aye-aye, and one of the founders of the reserve, thinks some must still be alive. He has seen one of their leaf nests in a tree this year. For my part, I can only say you could hide a dozen aye-ayes in my field of vision on Nosy Mangabé, and in that density of forest I might not see them. This, of course, is their protection. When fishermen come to the beach, or root diggers evade the Eaux et Forêt's guard and penetrate the woods, the aye-ayes can simply hide.

I suspect, in any case, that the stormy career of Nosy Mangabé is far from finished, and the story is far from over.

All the fundamental questions of conservation can be raised about this little island. Is it worth saving climax forest at all? If the answer is yes, is it worth saving small islands? MacArthur and Wilson have convincingly shown that the number of species which survive in small areas decreases as the area decreases: the rarest species become so rare that they arc extinct.[27] Perhaps this fate overtook the aye-ayes. The rarest species are often the largest animals, especially carnivores at the top of the food chain—the very ones which impress us to see as well as piquing our curiosity by their scarcity. Nosy Mangabé is only 5 km² in area. This is a beautiful size for a laboratory or a study site. It is small but not vastly smaller than the Smithsonian Institution's island of Barro Colorado in the Panama Canal. The 15.5 km² of Barro Colorado has inspired much

Aye-aye (Tananarive Zoo).

André Peyriéras with baby aye-aye (photo J.-J. Petter).

of our understanding of tropical forest ecology: interrelations of trees, howler monkeys, and three-toed sloths. But considered as a reservoir of species, 5 km², or even 15.5, is nearly nothing.

Yet, practically, Nosy Mangabé is defensible. The conservation lobby could encamp there as did the pirates, distrustfully glaring over the bay toward people and their human needs on the mainland. The aye-ayes, or their ghosts, ironically are guarding the forest because their emotional appeal pulls in foreign money.

A second problem, however, divides the conservationists. How far are we justified in introducing species to our reserves and in managing the reserves in the interests of the weird or beautiful creatures that appeal to us? Where, on the gradient from captive breeding in zoos to semiwild breeding on managed islands to fighting to save extensive tracts against all the human pressures, should conservationists concentrate their efforts? The answer, of course, is everywhere. In the short term species and races will survive only if saved by any means at hand. However, in the long term breeding programs, or even island zoos, are mere stopgaps. The real question is whether people of any nation will wish, or will be able, to save their wilderness, the "unproductive" climax.

The story is not finished, for all the arguments can circle back to the tiny forest island of Nosy Mangabé, and to the aye-aye whose skeleton finger may now be pointing to its own doom.

Foresters have discovered five leaf nests together in the extreme southeast corner of Nosy Mangabé, perhaps made by one aye-aye, perhaps by two. Liz Bomford of the "Survival" television program, walked the six hours across the island to camp near the nests. She saw the orange gleam of aye-aye-sized eyes "so big that when they blink you actually see the shutters coming down." Hooray that the tale has a happy ending—for now.

Aye-aye (Tananarive Museum).

5

THE ZEBU LICKS BARE STONE

KING AMADA AND HIS FATHER'S GHOST

I *never* spent so much of a day learning etiquette. When you shake hands with a King, use both hands. When you meet a lady possessed by spirits, don't greet her in the road, say "Bonjour" when seated inside her house. *Whatever* you do, don't kill a sacred lemur, for that means certain death.

We were in Nosy Bé, on the northwest coast, preparing to leave for Lavalohalika. island of the sacred lemurs. No Europeans before us had visited the village of the royal tombs on Lavalohalika. Much more important, no government officials or other outsiders have lived there to disturb the coherence of the peoples' own traditions, except Guy Ramanantsoa, assistant professor of forestry at the University of Tananarive, and his wife Lily. Fortunately, Guy was coming with us, for the islanders would never accept us without his presence. To make doubly sure, we had to bear a letter from King Amada of Nosy Bé. Finally, because on Guy's first visit the villagers argued that if Guy could write he could also forge letters, we should ask the King if he could ask a minor princeling, farther down the coast, to send an emissary with us. I'll call that one the Duke.

Just for contrast, Nosy Bé itself is the most cosmopolitan part of Madagascar, and always has been. To start with the present, Nosy Bé (or Great Island) is the one region of Madagascar arranged for tourists. Package tours will bring you here for two weeks of guaranteed bliss, in a luxurious beach hotel, with trips to undersea gardens and uninhabited atolls.

The French were here long ago: a Sakalava queen ceded Nosy Bé to France in 1839, fifty-eight years before France colonized the mainland. They built Hellville in the verandaed, spacious style that mid-19th century Europe thought right for the tropics, much like Balboa in Panama. They named it proudly after Admiral de Hell, with no afterthoughts about an English interpretation.

64

OPPOSITE: King Amada of Nosy Bé.

Fishermen on botrys (boats of Arab design) at Nosy Mangabé with smoke from cooking fire on fore deck.

Woman and child at Nosy Bé collect shells at low tide for sale in market.

Long before the French, Indians and Arabs traded at Nosy Bé, sailing their dhows and botrys and goelettes on the thousand-year-old trade routes across the Indian Ocean. Africans came here through the centuries. many as slaves. And first of all the Vazimba landed on this northwest coast, having sailed their outriggers from Indonesia via India and East Africa.

Not since the Vazimbas' landfall has Madagascar been truly isolated. Settlers and traders have influenced each other over the centuries, and even so apparently isolated a spot as Lavalohalika surely is touched by, or reacts against, the outside world. As for Nosy Bé. . . .

We met a boatbuilder called Ali, who still makes and repairs boats to the ancient Arab designs: one-masted botrys whose cumbersome sails have to swing around the front of the mast to change tack, and two-masted goelettes. However, as you might suspect from Nosy Bé's sophistication, Ali's latest goelette was built as a charter yacht for cruising tourists. Also, as you might guess from Nosy Bé's fusion of tradition and sophistication, the masts for the charter yacht were cut, by royal permission, from King Amada's personal forest.

Before visiting the King, we called in at the Hotel Palm Beach to hire a boat for the voyage to Lavalohalika. We saw a vast thatched verandaed restaurant, one side open to the coconut palms and the Indian Ocean, and a few beautiful tourists parading around in swimsuit and suntan. Only here can you find the kind of international traveler who does not care where he is so long as it feels the same.

All right, that was sour grapes. Part of me was heartily jealous of that girl in the yellow bikini, in a thatched hotel cottage, eating Nosy Bé lobsters with French mayonnaise and salad flown in from Tananarive. I was also jealous of her suntan and her shape.

We slept in an Eaux de Forêts resthouse, a couple of cement closets the French thought good enough for Malagasy foresters, whose doors opened onto a drain full of giant snails. Madame Rodin, the forest guard's wife, kindly offered to put a bed into my closet and to sweep the floor for Russ and Guy. On the other hand, it was free—Guy's entire professorial per diem would not buy one meal at the beach hotel.

Now to the important part of the day: a postluncheon meeting with King Amada of Nosy Bé. It had to be lunchtime because during office hours he is switchboard operator at the police station; so he is only King when at home in the palace.

King Amada greeted us on his palace veranda, in his switchboard operator's outfit of white shirt, dark trousers, and packet of Gauloises. He welcomed us upstairs to the sitting room: four armchairs in as many corners, cowries and coral on the coffee table.

Guy explained, in flowery French so that I could understand, the purpose of our visit.

I, Madame Le Docteur Jolly, had read in America the article which Guy wrote for the Defenders of Wildlife about sacred lemurs in Lavalohalika.[1] I had been so much touched by the islanders' devotion to their lemurs that I had traveled to Madagascar to bring a present for the upkeep of the Lavalohalika tombs and temple. For Dr. Jolly was also much devoted to lemurs.

King Amada did not comment on the likelihood of the story. He and Guy were operating on an allegorical plane, where style outweighed content.

Instead, he countered by telling us the origin of the sacred lemurs.

There was a little princess, Tsimisarakarivo. Her father was dead; her mother Rasilimo was sent away as a prize of war to marry Radama I, the Napoleon of the far-off Merina tribe of Tananarive. The orphaned princess went to live with an aunt, the queen of the island of Lavalohalika.

The first pair of lemurs came to the island as pets for the lonely princess. The male was black, sporting chin and ear tufts of long jet whiskers. With him stalked his golden female, her mane a sunburst of white whiskers around her face.

In time, the princess grew up, as even princesses will. But the day her aunt the queen died, Tsimisarakarivo died two hours afterward, hence her name "she who is not separated."

The two women were buried in the same royal tomb. If it was like a Sakalava funeral nowadays, there would have been weeks of drumming and dancing and many zebu killed.

All this happened early in the nineteenth century. Then, as Ramada's Merina tribe came conquering farther and farther north out of the central highlands, the inhabitants of Lavalohalika took fright. They all fled away to the north, which is why the royal family still lives at Nosy Bé. After some years, though, an ancestress of King Amada (the same queen who ceded Nosy Bé to the French in the hope of protection from the Merina) sent back settlers to Lavalohalika. "For," she said, "it is not fitting that the tombs of our ancesters should be unguarded."

When the new guardians arrived, they found the island and its village of royal tombs deserted and rank with second-growth forest. Yet the tombs themselves were safe, for Tsimisarakarivo's lemurs had come out of the forest to guard them. The people of Lavalohalika concluded that lemurs served the spirits of royal ancestors, and have worshipped lemurs ever since.

Guy then told the King how the turning point in his own acceptance by the islanders came when he pointed out that Princess Tsimisarakarivo's mother had indeed married Ramada, who, being a Merina, was of Guy's own tribe, so there were links of friendship as well as fear. The islanders were delighted to meet someone who knew so much royal genealogy. They asked Guy if he would like to meet Tsimisarakarivo's mother? She was currently reincarnated in a local woman, so it would be a simple matter for the lady to go into a trance, if Guy would like to converse with the long-dead queen.

Guy duly went; the lady duly entered her trance; the queen duly spoke through the lady. To Guy's amazement, although the tranced lady normally talked only in the Sakalava dialect, the dead queen had lived so long with Radama in Tananarive that her spirit spoke pure highland Merina!

Eventually King Amada promised to write us letters of introduction both to the Duke and to the islanders. Russ and Guy, deferentially, asked permission to take the King's picture. As they were unpacking cameras the King disappeared into another room. He emerged in traditional cloth skirt, carrying his spear-scepter. He posed, first in his armchair of honor, then on the veranda. I suggested, then unsuggested, that Russ take his picture with the framed telephone operator's diploma—it seemed too easy to

Old Indian tombs at Nosy Bé.

poke fun. But then, King Amada actually winked and said, "Oh well, it was the Swedes photographing me last month. I've had Americans here and Germans—no English yet, but they'll get round to it!"

I thought that was all. I thought we would leave on that note of cheerful complicity, all playacting together. But just as we were leaving, Guy turned back, and abruptly asked the King, "Is it true that the woman Soajama knew facts about your father that no living person could know?"

"Yes," said King Amada. "I judged the woman myself. Perhaps you know that when a person claims possession by a reincarnated spirit, that person must be judged to see if the claim is false or true. When the King my father, who died in 1968, possessed Soajama, they brought her here from Lavalohalika. I sat in the chair, there, where you photographed me, with my family and my councilors as witnesses. Soajama, speaking in trance with my father's voice, said many things which were public knowledge, or which close friends might have told her. But in the end, she spoke of a disc of gold that was given my father by a person who owed him money. Only my mother and myself knew what my father had done with it—not even my brothers and sisters knew."

"Soajama turned to my mother and spoke in my father's voice: "My wife, where have you put the golden disc which I gave you? Do you still have it?"

"Then, we were forced to believe."

We bade farewell to the King. We bought provisions for the voyage and tried to memorize Guy's rules for the sacred island: never extend your feet to the East, always tie your hair back, men and women must wear wrapped skirts. This meant Russ and me buying skirt lengths. Mine bore a motto: omby milela-bato, matin'ny tany maha-zotra. Guy translated: the zebu will lick bare stone, and die in the earth of the place he loves.

To the Malagasy this is a beautiful symbol of lifelong fidelity but to me a grim prophecy of what may happen if some of their customs do not change.

ON THE EDGE OF THE INDIAN OCEAN

I sat on the bow of the diesel launch, eleven hours out. The sun was still high at 4:30 P.M., but the burn had gone out of it, as it accelerated toward the horizon—the reverse of the sunrise behind the volcanic peaks and craters of Nosy Bé. Adabé, our boatman, caught three fish during the day, each a yard long—no, truthfully, two two-and-a-half feet long and one mackerel for supper that measured fully a yard.

Our boatman bore a glorious name. "Adabé" was the title of one of the Sakalava officers, described in 1844 as "simultaneously herald, hussar, and aide-de-camp of the King, a personage with a long bonnet, bedizened with silver and armed with an ebony staff."[2]

The line spun out again. Adabé left the tiller to Russ and sprang to the reel, hauling in fishline hand over hand, not waiting to wind it. . . .

Nope. Something very large bit the wire trace in two, presumably swallowing the six inch spoon.

Again the foreigner saw a picture opposite from the one seen by the man who belonged here. Our figure was Guy's space, like a reversing illusion. Russ and I looked along the miles of empty, coconut-fringed coastline. We asked to stop, somewhere alone and idyllic, where we would all swim. Guy replied: Well, this village or that village, perhaps we could ask them to quickly cook us some rice, perhaps we could go on for a longer visit with the Duke. To Guy, this "empty" beach was a road, lined with paths leading to the houses of people he knows.

So on to Duke Magnitry's village. He too was addressed as Mpanjaka, King, and he effectively ruled this coastal area, including Lavalohalika. He was a gray-haired man with black felt hat for coronet. His two littlest sons or grandsons crowded in around his knees while he talked, frightened of us and taking refuge. He cuddled the boys throughout the interview in his coconut palm house, wallpapered inside with old magazines. His senior wife braided raffia basket handles on the veranda; a younger woman fed a new baby; an old woman, drunk, claimed she knew me of old; a very old man with one pigtail over his right ear wanted his picture taken. One son of six or seven was very ill with whooping cough. They had taken him to the dispensary but found no medicine. There is a Malagasy herbal cure for whooping cough, but the Duke said it was dangerous, curing one child but killing another.

At last the Duke designated a guide to come with us. We sailed on to a village on Lavalohalika island where the people fish for sea turtles. In a village beyond they specialized in dugong and whales. Of course, dugong are on Madagascar's protected mammal list, but I had realized at least since the Bay of Antongil that conservation laws are relative—relative to the distance from a forest station. People harpoon the whales (sometimes dolphins but occasionally southern right whale), wait until it is exhausted from loss of blood, and then tow it in behind a fleet of pirogues to shore. (There is a picture of Malagasy dismembering a whale caught this way, in 1601.)

I asked if we could see shells or skulls of any of these animals.

"Sorry," said Guy. "The whale skulls are taboo for women to see, so they must be thrown back into the sea. Dugongs are protected animals, illegal, so their skulls are hidden. Turtle shells are sold for jewelery and eyeglass frames. Sea-turtle meat is taboo to sell. Turtles are cooked immediately, after which the whole village comes and helps themselves.

"Fisherman catch four species of turtle off this coast. The loggerhead, or fano mamy's flesh is tender. The green turtle, fano zato, and olive ridley or mindroy are middling. The fano hara, or hawksbill, is both tough and complicated. When you catch a hawksbill, you must pray. When landing it, you must pray. When dismembering it, you must pray. Certain parts must not be eaten, but you tie them in a bag, cook them with the rest, then throw them away. The oddest part of all, to me, is that this turtle is boiled in seawater.

"All these species of turtle are threatened because of hunting on the nesting grounds. The hawksbill may disappear first of all, which is the source of true tortoise shell for export and for our traditional jewelery, as well as the center of so many nostalgic rituals."[3]

The launch sat acant on the mangrove-sprouting mud flat, tide out. Men from the village of the turtle fishers launched an outrigger pirogue at the flat's edge, with

Duke Magnitry (Anorotsangana).

Duke's wife, braiding raffia (Anorotsangana).

Outrigger pirogue and motor launch at low tide on mangrove flats near
Lavalohalika. Root-noses are in foreground.

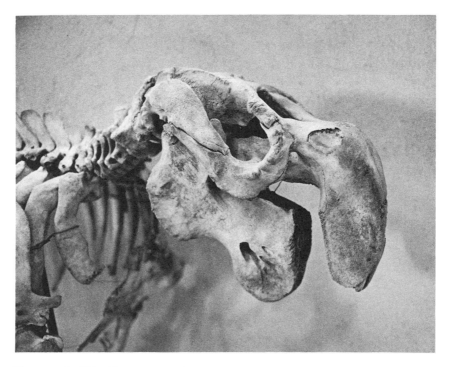

Dugong skull in Tananarive Museum.

Fiddler crab on mangrove flats (Nosy Bé).

Adabé with breadfruit (Anorotsangana).

Mudskippers on mangrove flats.

Villagers hiking through swamps carrying scientists' gear (Lavalohalika, on northwest coast).

V-shaped struts for the square sail instead of a central mast. This design is Indonesian, apparently unchanged since the Vazimba first came.

The villagers housed us in a clean coconut palm rest house lined with sweet-straw matting, in luxury undreamed of at the tourists' Beach Hotel. Adabé cooked a glorious stew of his glorious mackerel in a borrowed pot. Our second fish went to the village to split and sun dry with their own catch. The pirogue just leaving carried the third, an inedible species, already cut up for bait.

The mangroves around the channel grew like mangroves anywhere in the tropics—except that Madagascar, even on the beach, manages to have an indigenous species, *Ceriops boviniana.* Some mangrove species stand on tiptoe on straddled roots. They drop seeds which float away on the sea tides. The roots, although they look like the support braces of forest fig trees, have a totally different function: if you cover them permanently, the tree suffocates. Another ploy of mangroves is to send their roots down into the mud, then turn them around to grow upward again, so the flats sprout thousands of little points which are mangrove root-noses panting for air. *Ceriops boviniana* is related to this latter sort of mangrove. Its seeds grow on the tree into ready-formed little plants, which drop like darts into the mud beside the parent tree. This may be one reason for the fact that this species stays confined to Malagasy sea shores.[4]

Between the pointy roots darted myriads of fiddler crabs. Mudskippers, the fish that stump over the mud on their forefins, goggled at me from their burrows. Both fiddlers and mudskippers keep enough water closed in their gills to breathe. The mudflat is an upside-down interface, where water-breathing animals promenade about the land, while air-breathing trees stand buried in water.

Guy told me more and more about local beliefs, while I wondered more and more about Guy. He is the kind of intellectual who combines scientific rigor toward his lemurs and chameleons with the courage to be sympathetic, or even sentimental, about the feelings of people. He spent two and a half months in Lavalohalika this year, bringing Lily, his bride of a week. What a honeymoon for a girl who had been studying business management at the university!

They watched the lemurs but above all talked to people. Guy's own mystic brand of Catholicism, far from interfering with his respect for other traditions, makes him all the more sensitive to their beauty. He was half playing the game, like all of us, but perhaps, just a little, convinced. . . .

Adabé summoned us to a luncheon of mangrove crabs. Monsieur Le Reste, a zoologist from Nosy Bé, had been studying the mangrove crab. They lay their eggs in the sea and then, when still a weird and uncrablike larva, the offspring swim into brackish estuaries to grow. People start catching them from that moment on in woven fish weirs or even just on strings with a bit of fish tied on. The crab lacks the sense to let go of the fish, and the fisherman simply hauls it in. But most of the free-swimming crabs are too small to be worth the bother. If left, they can grow up to 18 cm wide and 1½ kg in weight. Then each male moves to a traditional crab tunnel among the mangrove roots, housecleans it, and for three days walks around piggyback clasping his chosen female.

She finally molts. While she is still soft shelled, they mate at the bottom of their 1½ m deep tunnel in the mangrove mud. Mating can last up to 24 hours.

But very likely, during low tide, while the female is soft and vulnerable and the male, in M. Le Reste's phrase, is "very, very occupied," Adabé or one of his friends comes checking the neighborhood crab holes with a long, hooked stick. If he finds a crab or two at the bottom, he plunges his arm in mud to the shoulder and hooks out the defenseless animals.

Somehow, when the caldron appeared with crabs boiled from sea-blue-green to lobster-red, I forgot all about M. le Reste's account. Russ immediately produced crab-cracking pliers from his sack. When I accused him of traveling prepared to eat lobster on any beach of the world, he had the nerve to claim he brought the pliers for camera repairs. Guy told us the local endearment, "I love you as much as the little crabs. I could gobble you toes and all."

What paradise!

Hitches in paradise. Not beriberi from overpolished rice, or the aftermath of un-treated syphilis, or children dead of whooping cough, which is the dark side of paradise for the local people. Just minor hitches. The first guide the Duke sent with us to show us the mazy channels through the mangrove swamp did not really want to come. He arranged a second guide who agreed publicly to take us. Mr. Turtle the turtle fisher said he would join us too, so Guy brought out a Sakalava proverb that we would then be in knowing hands, like a man's penis in the hands of his senior wife. They all roared with happiness at Guy's wit and knowledge.

Whereupon the first guide went home, and the second guide decamped.

"That," said Guy philosophically, "is the inconvenience of Malagasy politeness. You must say yes when asked a favor, so the two guides simply said yes. The same thing has happened about the tide. The villagers said last night that high tide is two o'clock in the afternoon. I misheard and said, 'Ten o'clock?' They said, 'Yes, ten o''clock. . . .,' then added in a whisper, 'Two o'clock.' "

The upshot was a postmidday start, then disembarking at quite the wrong landing because Mr. Turtle knew the channels there, then somewhat irate disinclination of Russ and me to start an unnecessary 10 km walk. A villager appeared. Mr. Turtle recounted all our journey from Nosy Bé on in a storytelling singsong. The villager countered with a singsong of his own, equally long, which Guy explained afterward was the entire story over to show he had understood. He then reached the heart of the question in one sentence: "Since these visitors have disembarked at my home, I'll help carry their baggage."

We started off, through the secondary woods and erosion gullies that remain from the slash-and-burn cultivation of mountain rice. The soil grew redder and redder and sadder and sadder in the sunset—but the walk was barely 2 km, not 10, until we arrived at the ring of real forest which is left by taboo around the sacred village of Mahabo. Suddenly we were breathing the cool, damp air that is chambered between a roof of leaves and a floor of humus, instead of dessicating wind over barren ground. There is of course a science of climate and microclimate, which deals with the large- and small-scale effects of vegetation on the atmosphere. No one could doubt that there is an effect, blatant to the sensitive thermometers of human nose and skin. This northwestern woodland is wet, with leaves all year, though not so tall as true rainforest. Even in this little relict, the presence of trees was enough to preserve a microclimate of moisture.

The trees, the microclimate, the shelter were enough for a few animals, for there coiled a dô, the Malagasy eastern boa constrictor. Russ and Guy, both serpent collectors, picked it up correctly, supporting its stomach by lodging it around their necks. Such a snake, used to the constant support of the ground, can break its back if picked up carelessly by either end. Russ showed me how to recognize the typical broad head and hefty build of the boa, although previously he had seen only the distant cousins of the dô from the South American fragment of Gondwanaland.

Our guides stared at us in horror. They said that, although they were forbidden to kill the denizens of the sacred forest, we could oblige them by releasing the dô very far off the path.

The one European who attempted to reach the village of royal tombs before us was a policeman, who shot a sacred lemur as he disembarked from his boat. The villagers prevented his coming farther. They recount his punishment: at that moment his daughter died, and later he himself went mad.

We reached that flat stone, where all must stop, take off their shoes, and don a wraparound skirt in respect for the traditions. I reflected again how privileged we were to quit Tananarive by jet Friday morning and to stand barefoot at the sacred village's stone doorstep on Sunday as darkness fell.

WHERE THE LAND BLEEDS INTO THE SEA

It was noon in a house that grunted. The sacred lemurs staged a raid in the morning and made off with half our bananas. They still hung around the ridgepole hoping for more.

Crash! went the coconut frond that led to the roof. Rustle, rustle, rustle went the thatch. Grunt-grunt-GRUNT-grunt—and a face with black nose, yellow eyes, and an aureole of back-lit white ear tufts appeared in the doorway, halfway up the doorpost. It was mostly the bolder females who came so far, while the black males held back. "Scram! Shoo!" I shouted at the overtame lemur. "You'll have to wait for the ceremony, just like the rest of us!"

In contrast to their lemurs, how dignified the people were! They greeted us as hosts and welcomed us with formal courtesy to their home. Saha Malandy, who is said to be 100 years old, agreed to summon the spirit of Princess Tsimisarakarivo by a trance. (Saha is a title of respect meaning the possessed one). Thus we, who have traveled all the way from America because of the sacred lemurs, would be able to thank the princess in person. People of Mahabo may not know where America is, but they appreciated the effort it took to come from Nosy Bé.

Furthermore, two other possessed ladies, the princess's aunt and the princess's mother, might call up their spirits as well. The old lady who reincarnated the princess's mother is called Saha Bé, the great possessed one, because her spirit is the eldest of the spirits, although that old lady is younger than the other two old ladies.

Before the trance we would have a ceremony of thanks to the lemurs, which mostly meant giving out bananas, and of thanks to the village, which meant giving out rum. Locally distilled rum is the island's chief export because it is too far for the police to come and tax the stills.

The spirits themselves receive a cash present for upkeep of their tombs.

Mercenary? Less than we are.

No, just like us, a mix of many emotions, but the islanders believe, while we distantly respected their beliefs. We did not even have the thrill that Guy draws from bending the knee to the Sahas and returning to a tradition elsewhere dead.

While waiting for people to assemble for the ceremony (the lemurs had already assembled) Guy took us to see his "grandfather."

When Lily first came here, she was horrified by an old man named Tefindrazana, quite so openly depraved that he addressed her warmly as his "wife." She was also heartbroken by Guy's putting up with it, for she had been Guy's own wife for only a week. Guy explained that the old man was simply showing appreciation of Lily's beauty and admiration for Guy as Lily's husband. Lily conquered her scruples. She settled to addressing the old man as "husband" too. Guy then regularized the situation by adopting Tefindrazana as his "grandfather" and the "grandfather's" nubile granddaughter as his, Guy's, "second wife." By this time, Lily fell in with the game, addressing the girl as "co-wife"—as long as there was no doubt Lily remained the senior one.

If it seems complicated so far, the Sakalava change sex as well as kinship in their terms of address. A woman possessed by a male spirit is called "he," a man possessed by a woman "she." Tefindrazana's own real wife is usually called "Njarini Ravo," or "Father of Ravo," to show how much people respect her for being the mother of Ravo.

Guy explained all this over his shoulder, as we traipsed behind him up the path to his "grandfather's" rice clearing. After we left Mahabo's circle of sacred forest, the path was cut and gullied where the rain had found it an easy channel in the bare earth. Hillsides, first cleared for mountain rice, formed dunes of lunar barrenness. The lateritic soils of Madagascar are so fragile that they die when once cleared.

The slash-and-burn farming of mountain rice is the staple way of life for the people of Lavalohalika, like much of the rest of coastal Madagascar. Guy thought they plant perhaps only 1 hectare of rice for a family which needs 2. From the land's point of view this is all to the good, but the people finish their supplies within six months. This year had been too dry. They expect to eat their crop in three to four months, then buy their staple food from the mainland. At least Lavalohalika has its rum to sell the mainland in exchange.

It is men's work to clear the forest, women's to sow and reap. A field's fertility does not last more than two years. There are no primary forests left, except the sacred one (and that one is full of calcereous rocks with cutting edges called tsingy), so the men now clear the sparse scrublands or occasionally stands of wild guava trees disseminated by the lemurs in their droppings. This, people point out, is yet another kindness by the lemurs.

Guy and Lily Ramanantsoa of Tananarive University outside their house.

Ravo with basket of mountain rice (Lavalohalika).

Erosion in gullies near Lavalohalika.

Guy's grandfather, Tefindrazana, (Lavalohalika).

Tefindrazana's rice field had just been harvested, with the burned stumps of saplings sticking up through the straw. We met Ravo, his son, on the path, with heavy baskets of golden rice heads. Now was the time of plenty.

Tefindrazana himself greeted Guy warmly, but his wife, "Father of Ravo," was ill and badly frightened by Europeans calling at her house. I had never seen a house like it, with palm leaf walls as well as thatch, and an extra door placed like a picture window to command a view of the valley. The traditional three-stone hearth burned in full sun from the valley, instead of being tucked in the darkest corner. When I asked if Russ could take photographs, the old couple hesitated, but Guy explained that he himself would like pictures as souvenirs to remember his grandmother and grandfather. They at once smiled and agreed.

Then we went down to see a magnificent rice field, paddy rice on flat land, guarded from zebu by a fence, guarded from crows by three little boys to throw stones, and guarding, in turn, two bushy raffia plums. Raffia, like rice, is essential to Malagasy life, the basis of all woven articles. It is a swamp-living tree, whose roots turn up for air like mangroves'. (*Raffia* is the only English word which derives from Malagasy.)

I asked how many such permanent fields there are—very, very few. I asked, too, if people make any use of fertilizer, have any knowledge of recycling apart from scrub regrowth of old fields. A few have seen that manure makes a mango tree bear more fruit, but no one puts manure on fields or makes compost. Agriculturally, the island is just at the moment when traditions must change and farmers learn new ways. Now, on the ravaged hillsides, the zebu licks bare stone.

Lavalohalika is an endpoint. Climax forest like the relict around the sacred village was cut by the first executioners. Centuries, or even decades, have now reduced it to scrub and wasteland. Shifting cultivation has served these people well. They have built their families and their culture on it since King Amadas' forebear sent them back here in the 1840s. Now the first permanent irrigated fields coexist with the dry-land ones, and soon there will be nothing left of the old ways.

Masalina, Lily's co-wife, was drawing water at the well by the rice field. She told Guy she was engaged to a local man. Guy teased her that he would tax his rival 30,000 francs for her release. She giggled and laughed and talked of plans for the wedding, which will take place as soon as her fiancé raises the bride price of two zebus. She and her fiancé had been sleeping together for six months now and looked forward to being married so she can move from her parents' home and live with him.

By local custom, even after marriage, either partner has the right to dissolve the union. If the wife leaves within the first year, her family has to return the bride price; so she is under strong pressure to give it a year's fair trial. After a year, or if the man sends his wife away, he forfeits his zebu, so the husband is under a certain pressure as well.

I asked about children of a divorced couple, thinking back to situations in Africa where even highly westernized town women may remain in miserable marriages because the husband has absolute rights to their children. Guy looked astonished. "Why, the children just go where they want to."

These cheerful customs are interesting not just as local gossip but as interplay with the economic basis of life. In this and in other Malagasy tribes, kinship and marriage

OPPOSITE: Masalina, Guy's second wife, on the edge of a paddy rice field.

customs are tied to the pattern of land use. Shifting cultivation of mountain rice needs labor to clear the forest but supposes that the forest itself is without limits. People like Masalina and her family, then, can marry unrelated people from neighboring villages. By contrast in the tribes which grow paddy rice on permanent fields, land is obviously limited to fertile valley bottoms. When the people of Lavalohalika finally change to permanent cultivation, the family might put pressure on Masalina to marry close kin in order to keep their lands within a strictly defined group of relations. Probably they would also increase the sanctions against divorce. Giving up a husband or wife may matter much less, in society, than divorcing the spouse's rice field.[5]

Thus, the change to permanent crops as the last hillside soil leaches away will mean not just harder work, not just new techniques, but change in the relations between man and woman, parent and child.

Watching Masalina's coquettishly tressed hair and the back of her neck in the sun the color of a well-polished horse chestnut, it seemed a good thing Masalina did have a fiancé, or Lily might stand some real competition.

VILLAGE OF SACRED LEMURS

At last the village notables and the possessed themselves assembled for our ceremonies. First, we must give thanks to the lemurs, then to the people. An official reception by people for us would follow and, finally, our combined thanks to the spirits.

Guy and I mounted the temple precinct. The temple itself was taboo for this month to anyone except lemurs, but thank-offerings took place on the raised log step which marks the edge of temple ground near a little storehouse on stilts for the sacred drums.

Guy spoke for me, accouncing my gratitude to all concerned. The Sahas shrilled, "Guidou, Guidou, Guidou!" The lemurs had been waiting their cue but, having already learned where the bananas were kept, began by trying to break into our house again. Soon, though, they came tumbling over the roofs, down the great sacred tamarind tree, and on to the zebu-crotted precinct ground. One female was so eager she bounced three times on her hind legs, arms and nose out beseechingly.

The ground was covered with milling lemurs, black backs and golden ones jostling and jumping. I handed out bananas by halves; Saha Malandy came to help me, and so did the village chief, putting them down by handfuls. Too slow a source of supply might have started the animals fighting. A few spats began even so, but I tossed half-bananas out to the lemurs who had none.

In the furry maelstrom I counted (I think) 14 jet-black males and 8 golden females. Black lemur troops have a majority of males—extraordinary among primates. No one knows how or why they manage it.[6]

This large troop may itself be a conglomerate of two or three smaller troops, which forage independently by day and then congregate to sleep at night. Of course it may also be that this gang knows that where the spirits protect them, they get fed, and so they stay together all day to scrounge.

As the last lemur licked the last squashed banana off my fingers a villager handed me a cup of white alcohol from a 1-litre bottle, then was much concerned that I sipped

OPPOSITE: Black lemur (*Lemur macaco*) at Lavalohalika.

Female black lemur (*Lemur macaco*).

Male *Lemur macaco*.

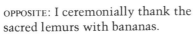

OPPOSITE: I ceremonially thank the sacred lemurs with bananas.

Formal welcome at Lavalohalika.

Prayer session at Lavalohalika. All are facing
east. It is forbidden to extend feet to the east—
where spirits of ancestors are. Left to right: Mr.
Turtle, three women I don't know, woman who
incarnates Rasalinio, Saha Malandy, who incarnates Princess Tsimisarakarivo, and Guy.

instead of knocking it back. The rum made the rounds to a more appreciative audience, as Guy herded us toward our house for the reception.

You must understand that we had been greeted, and welcomed, and talked to steadily since the night before. The most extraordinary greeting was the lemurs', who congregated staring at Guy, not at us, from the moment of our arrival in the village. It is certain that they recognized him as their special friend and provider of four months earlier.

People, as well, had flocked to talk. One man came in such a hurry that he started right in speaking as he entered the house, without waiting for Guy to say the householder's "Kabary mba," or "What news?" and giving the formal answer, "Tsy kabary," "No news, nothing urgent." His scandalized friends shushed him up to let Guy speak first. He excused himself with the Sakalava proverb: "Those who love each other too much kiss even with snotty noses."

At the *formal* reception, no such mistakes were permitted. We were sat down on our mats (being careful no one's feet extended to the east) and made speeches to and about, with a fine variety of singsong oratory so the words should not wound our ears. Guy sangsong back, and I did my best.

At last they came to the embarrassing part. They had all forgotten in the flurry of our arrival that it was dark of the moon! Trances are flatly not permitted at dark of the moon. Could we not stay till Saturday, when the moon returned, the temple would be opened, and we could perform the full ceremony, annointing my forehead with chalky earth as a symbol of purity?

There flickered through my mind Guy's eldest daughter's first communion next Sunday, my own family flying from England, Russ's airplane ticket to America—and the daily hire of the diesel launch. No, I said with the utmost regret, perhaps some year we may return, but we cannot stay till Saturday.

In that case, they said, they were deeply disappointed. Would we be content with a prayer to the spirits, offered in a house? Russ would be welcome to take pictures.

Guy, by what circumlocution I am not sure, pointed out that in that case I would make only a small gift to the community, not the large sum I had planned for each spirit.

They replied with dignity, with a proverb to the effect that the impossible cannot be bought.

Our respect increased.

Then they offered us a formal gift of hospitality for ourselves: a hen and a vast bowl of rice. Knowing that chickens are taboo anywhere near the Mahabo, for the owner of a chicken that strays inside the tomb fence must "wash" the tomb with zebu's blood, we knew that someone walked miles to fetch us that black hen. As for the rice, all of us were aware that they would run out of rice for themselves in three or four months.

So we moved to a house near the temple, where they dedicated my paltry francs to the spirits, as we sat with cupped hands, facing toward the tombs. One-hundred-year-old Saha Malandy, who had already decided that I was an innocent, to be taught the words to say on entering houses like a two-year-old, set me around in the right direction. I had a momentary memory of my daughter Margaretta remarking in second grade, "Mummy, you should really come to school and watch us all pretending to pray."

The chief led the prayer, holding up my money. He was simple and direct and made sure to mention everyone's name: both those of this generation and of those present only as reincarnations from the past. Guy had to prompt him with the town version of his name. Then all of us shook hands, except one man who had been away to school, and who embraced me French-fashion to squeaks and "Eeeeh's" of approval from all.

So, amid congratulations we trundled to our house, collected the baggage, and forded streams and climbed stiles and flushed whirring guinea fowl out of the scrub until we reached the boat. I thought that dear Mr. Turtle never would catch up (he had bought a litre of local rum all for himself) but he brought up the rear unfazed. He pointed out that he had fathered twelve children and had two married grandchildren, so he was entitled to drink. Any great-grandfather who makes a habit of harpooning 100-kg sea turtles and towing them home behind his pirogue must take some stopping.

So home, through silky sea, with jellyfish the size of dinner plates phosphorescing in our wake.

Now what? Tourism? Guy would love to put Lavalohalika on the tourist circuit—an obvious benefit the lemurs could bring their people.

"Oh, no!" I protested. That girl in the yellow bikini at the Palm Beach to come and point and snigger? It would destroy your paradise quicker than anything else. You'd have to arrange the village for the bikini-girl's benefit. A little shop down near the landing, selling ceremonial skirts to wrap around her. The bikini-girl would like that part, and you'd charge her triple the town price. Next, a little stand in the forest by the flat stone, where she'd check her platform shoes. The village would have to be cleaned at ground level, removing that pink-flowered creeper that kept jabbing you and me in the instep, and picking up the zebu crotts, although they could profitably be put on a rice field.

And never again would your proud people refuse a foreigner's money.

Besides, what would the tourists come for? They can go to Nosy Komba, half an hour from Nosy Bé, and *there* the black lemurs will jump on their shoulders for bananas. No, you would have to play these up as sacred lemurs. You could let tourists in to see the relics in the royal tombs, where only descendants of royal slaves are now allowed. You could schedule ceremonies every full moon, but they might need jazzing up a bit. How about old Saha Malandy taking a course of fire-walking? Best of all, you could have a tourist shoot a sacred lemur and die within the week—though it might just tempt others to try it too.

Guy countered, "Tell me an alternative. A government agricultural officer would say lemurs are inefficient, why not eat them. A missionary medical dispenser would say lemurs are idolatrous, turn away from them. Tourists would at least say lemurs are beautiful and pay the village money to prove it.

"You cannot just hide from the world, and hope that Lavalohalika will hide from the world and that the princess's spirit will make the rice harvest last all year."

OPPOSITE: Mr. Turtle. Any great-grandfather who hunts 100-kg turtles takes some stopping, even with ceremonial rum.

Town west of Moramanga: rice fields, cleared hillside, and first step of escarpment.

6

THE MOST HATED MAN

THE ROAD TO INDEPENDENCE

Our Land Rover tipped down the first of the faulted steps of Madagascar's eastern escarpment. The road wriggled beneath us like an insecurely caught serpent, coiling itself around vertical flanks of viridian rainforest, slashed by crimson landslips. The world itself seemed to turn vertical while the road clung desperately with its belly-scales to the faulting land, but the earthquake which raised that thousand-kilometre escarpment took place long ago in the timescale of drifting continents.

Half a mile below us, clear of forest, lay the rift valley of the Mangoro River, squared off into rice fields around the railway depot of Moramanga.

Roger Ramanantoanison twisted around in the front seat of the Land Rover. He said mildly over its clatter, "My mother's brother died down there, in Moramanga."

"What was he doing there?"

"The French brought him, in May of 1947, in a railroad car, with a hundred and sixty-five other men. He was a dentist from Fianarantsoa, on the plateau. The French arrested any Malagasy in that town prominent enough to be noticed. They executed some of them on the fifth of May. The rest they kept until the eighth without food or drink, then decided to kill them too. Soldiers machine-gunned them, machine-gunned them where they were, huddled inside the railroad car.

They are buried, of course, in a mass grave. We cannot even find my uncle's bones, to let him lie in our family's tomb."

Europe has been the overriding political fact of Malagasy life since Radama I invited the first British missionaries to come in 1820, as well as Sargeant Hastie, his military adviser. With Ramada as general, and with British muskets, the Merina kingdom conquered most of Madagascar and unified its diverse tribes. Succeeding Merina kings and queens westernized on their own terms, inviting technical aid but at intervals barring both foreign commerce and foreign missionaries. By 1895, on the eve of coloni-

Road at Moramanga.

Moramanga station, where Roger's uncle died.

zation, 160,000 children attended Protestant primary schools. The Malagasy kingdom, in fact, passed a legal statute in favor of universal schooling in 1881, one year before France voted universal schooling for itself.[1]

Twenty-five years later, after the French conquest, the numbers in school had dropped to 25,000. Colonial administration brought the usual combination of benefits and abuses, self-sacrificing colonists and self-enriching ones, and many who did both in perfectly good faith.

Political resistance movements simmered among Malagasy intellectuals while the mass of people tried unsuccessfully to ignore their alien rulers. Then, in 1947 a full-scale revolt broke out along the eastern escarpment and down the trading towns of the eastern coast. Five major towns fell to the revolutionaries in the one night of March 29, 1947. Colonists and the Malagasy who helped them were slaughtered.[2]

The French flew in troops from Senegal and gave them license to kill. Not only Roger's uncle but an unknown number of other Malagasy died. Estimates vary between 10,000 and 80,000 dead in that year of repression, amid chaos inside Madagascar but in almost total secrecy from the outside world. Malagasy who were young in 1947 still wake with nightmares that the great black Senegalese have come.

France apparently won—but only on the Malagasy front. Indochina and then Algeria took up their own battles. At last, in 1958, after some 10 million Algerians died in their own war of independence, General de Gaulle delcared the French Empire at an end, to be replaced by the French Community.

Madagascar, again a nation, gained full independence in 1960. Independence within the community, however, remained paradoxical. The new Malagasy Republic still traded almost exclusively with France. French officials remained in most government offices. French aid balanced the government's budget.

In 1972 General Ramanantsoa took power. He began a further step toward self-determination. His successor President Ratsiraka has continued the route toward valid independence, with socialist central planning and Soviet as well as Western aid. At last the government is genuinely Malagasy, but it is caught like most other countries of the Third World bargaining from a position of weakness and relative poverty against trading partners who are rich and powerful.

To people who have seen both rich countries and poor ones, the economic fact of richness or poverty touches every argument, every aspect of life. When thinking of forests and forest reserves, one might, momentarily, imagine that certain climax forests, certain regions of beauty, should be preserved for humanity wherever they are. The threats and the benefits of commercial forestry may indeed be similar in rich and poor countries. Aside from commercial forestry, however, it matters enormously whether the human threat to a wild landscape comes from hamburger stands, parking lots, snowcats, and speedboats, or whether it comes from a million farmers with their coupe-coupes.

It also matters whether the forest guard is a local fellow who might equally well run the hamburg stand or whether he is sent out by the central government from a different tribe and region and was recently servant of an occupying, foreign power.

"You should realize, Alison, that the forester is the most hated man in the Malagasy Republic," said Roger. "Let me tell you how he looks to the peasants."

I must have raised an eyebrow at Roger to think of him as a peasant's spokesman. He visits rural areas with sports shirt still impeccably ironed after a day in a Land Rover, and the gray silk scarf at his throat still neatly tucked in.

He laughed. "I haven't always been an economist in the central planning office. My first job was *animation rurale*—what the English call community development. I was based down below us on the eastern coast (that narrow strip beyond the Canal des Pangalanes) five hundred kilometres of sandbank with warm, fishy lagoon behind and only the shark-infested surf before.

"My job was to interpret government programs to the villagers, and the peasants' views back to civil servants. I used to go to a village, introduce myself, talk things over. Some local notable would ask me to stay. I would sleep on sweet-straw matting in his house, sometimes for as long as a month while we discussed the needs of the region.

"Then I was chosen for graduate study in France. I flew from the coconut-frond coastal houses to Paris in the space of a week. Do you know the Champs-Elysées in November, the Parisians scurrying head-down into the winter wind, all wrapped in coats and gloves and mufflers? They do not glance at a stranger in the street; they do not even show bare skin where you might shake their hands. . . .

"When an east-coast peasant goes to clear the forest, Alison, you see only the destruction of the wilderness you love. He thinks, however, of the field he has left behind, for nature to restore and heal, fertile as before. Here in the east, nature is kind. Banana trees spring up untended in the woods, among wild guavas. Dry-land rice is an easy crop—you simply clear a field and sow, then you wait until harvest. Rice itself seems a gift of the forest, in this bounteous country.

"Now consider the forester's role. He is like a gamekeeper in feudal Europe, who used to hang yeomen that poached the nobles' deer. He decides which parts of the forest may be cut, and forbids people to clear the richer stands. When peasants make their fields as they always have, according to the traditions of their ancestors, the forester arrests them. He is not only policeman, but judge. He recommends the sentence: prison, fines, or forced labor for the Forest Service itself, which is supposedly "educational."

"Of course, since we gained true independence, since 1972, we have relaxed the foresters' power, so that they can no longer cripple our people's wishes. When you think how peasants felt about foresters under colonialism, however, you will see it as a mark of our tolerance and understanding that the forest service still exists."

THE FORESTER

"Come and meet the ogre! We have an interview with the forester this morning."

Roger's silk foulard blew back in the wind from the sea; his plimsolls crunched slightly on the sand beneath us. All around, dune-grass clung to the sand, springy as rolled English lawn, although it was instead untended vegetation of the beachside.

On our right hand, to the east, the beach shelved down to rolling surf, an endless swell under the southeast trades, a beach of 800 km in a straight line north and south, parallel to the escarpment faults we had driven down. It ended to the north in the Bay of Antongil, itself a rifted trench whose floor is invaded by the sea.[3]

We did not swim in that surf. There was a French lady in Manakara who thought wading might be safe, so she tucked up her skirts and stepped in, only to have a shark sever her foot at the ankle. Eleven species including the real maneater, the great white shark, patrol just offshore. The same species hobnob with swimmers on the west coast, which is shallow and fishy. Here, instead, the beach shelves rapidly to deep, poorly inhabited waters. The sharks hang off the lagoon mouths, waiting for Malagasy endemic mullet, or perhaps an unguarded toddler, to stray out into the waves. . . .

To our left, beyond a belt of coastal trees, lay the Canal des Pangalanes, a 800-km lagoon where all the east coast rivers drop their silt. The lagoon is fringed with reeds, small houses, and dugout pirogues drawn up on the shore. It is crisscrossed with the stick fences of fish-weirs, some of their fresh-cut posts sprouting from the lagoon floor into new trees.

Between sea and lagoon grows the forest of the Malagasy littoral. This coastal woodland is not quite so peculiar as the inland Malagasy forests. A mere 20% of its plant species are endemic.[4] Many plants are far-flung sea travelers, familiar on most Indo-Pacific beaches, like the filao or horesetail tree. Others are Malagasy species but closely related to those of the eastern tropics. The bishop's-bonnet tree is a local species of a widespread genus. It grows along all the eastern seashores, its glossy, paddle-shaped leaves shading the forest stand behind. The pendant bishop's-bonnet fruits hang near the tips of its branches, while the multistamened flowers fall rose and white on the sand below like the souls of hedgehogs in paradise.

Many of the coastal trees resemble the bishop's-bonnet, with round glossy leaves. Among them grow thin-fronded trees: palms and pandanus—some forty endemic species of pandanus. There is also the palm-like *Cycas thouarsi,* one of the cycad group which links ferns to flowering plants, a kind of coelocanth of the vegetable kingdom.[5]

The coastal forest is not, perhaps, so precious in endemic species as others, but it is the most threatened of all Malagasy forest types. The east coast is densely populated, and except on wholly sterile sand, men attempt to clear the land.

We walked into a denser stand, a wide part of the sandbank, where species of lowland rainforest could grow sheltered by the hedge of thick-leaved bishop's-bonnet from the steady beat of the southeast trades. Louis Ratisbourne Randrianasolo, chief forester of Ambila, joined us.

Louis Randrianasolo is a civil servant like any rural doctor, agricultural officer, or inspector of schools. He seemed an unlikely candidate for one of the Malagasy Republic's most hated men.

He is responsible for all the forest estates and water management of the subprefecture of Brickaville. His terrain includes Brickaville, a town of some 10,000 people, as well as orange orchards and sugar plantations, the forested foothills of the eastern escarpment, and the sandbank. There are three forestry stations and one fish hatchery, but only six technically trained staff, counting himself, and five unskilled laborers.

Beach at Mahambo on east coast.

Canal des Pangalanes and east coastal
forest, near Mananjary.

Fishing dugout and shark (Lokaro peninsula).

Fish-catching weir on Canal des Pangalanes. The sticks are sprouting.

Sea-grape trees and bishop's bonnet along beach at Mahambo.

The worst problem is that he has no transport, not even a motorbike. He spends 22 days each month "on tournée," surveying the work of his district, but much of this time he wastes just walking, or waiting for a vehicle, official or unofficial, to take him where he needs to go.

His work includes classifying the forest into stands which the peasants may or may not cut for their rice, planting small plots of pine and eucalyptus, and some 1,600 hectares of grevilea, the Australian silky oak. Grevilea is important because it enriches the soil rather than impoverishing it like eucalyptus, or poisoning it like pine.

"But it is always foreign species that you plant!" the naturalist in me burst out. "I *know* how important they are—eucalyptus and South American mimosa are all the firewood of the central plateau, and pine is all the building timber. I *know* that reforesting has to be done with fast-growing softwood. But not one of your Malagasy forest species will grow beside eucalyptus; not one of your animals can eat it!"

"Look here, then." The forester stepped off the forest road near a blazed tree. He led us a few yards from the path. "Look, do you see this sapling? It is hintsy, one of the eighty species of Malagasy hardwood which we use for fine cabinetwork. We have planted a dozen hintsy here in the forest station, and ramy, and Malagasy rosewood, to see if we can enrich native forest with our most precious endemic trees. There is no question of planting these, though, in thousand-hectare blocks. They are slow-growing species of the deep shadows. We are simply experimenting with these transplants to see if we can make them grow at all. No forester has yet succeeded in regenerating Malagasy rainforest."

I looked at the gray smooth-barked hintsy sapling, so small my finger and thumb would meet at breast height around its trunk. I saw, instead, Jean in the virgin forest of Hiaraka, beside the 1½-m crimson bole of a fallen hintsy, whose centuries of growth will profit no one.

"How do the peasants view your work?" Roger interrupted my thoughts.

"They vary. Many hate us. Some ignore us. But recently, a few have asked us to plant them trees."

"What determines their attitudes?"

The forester laughed. "The extreme case was two villages of people living right inside the forest, good, primary forest in the foot hills above the coastal plain. We tried to move them out to permanent paddy fields we had irrigated for them. They simply threatened to bash our men until we gave up. We never did get them moved.

"The most discouraging part of our job," he continued, "is that we build dams and irrigation projects, and find that no one will use them. There is a combination of reasons: the extra work in growing paddy rice and the traditional attachment to home. Besides, in the end, mountain rice tastes better than paddy. In their place, I probably wouldn't move either."

Again, the story repeats itself. People who have forest, and the fertile soil beneath, have every reason to continue with shifting cultivation or else with tree crops like bananas and cloves. This was the kind of agriculture we saw among the executioners of Hiaraka. People whose soil is cleared, exhausted, are forced to change. They reach the

OPPOSITE: Burner of charcoal on road between Tananarive and Perinet. Planted eucalyptus like this can forestall burning Malagasy forest.

turning point we saw on the island of sacred lemurs. Most of the east coast plain is at or past this stage. It is farmed on large-scale plantations with modern methods or farmed by cultivators who must go farther and farther to find scrub worth cutting for a new field.

There is one hopeful development, however. Some villagers have begun to come to the forester to ask for trees. This is a direct result of the new Malagasy government and its system of delegating power to local village councils. The village councils have no intention of punishing shifting agriculture, but they also can foresee their own needs for firewood. A few, a very few, of the village councils send requests for a village stand of eucalyptus.

It is always eucalyptus, of course. It seems insane that the Malagasy Republic must destroy its own forest heritage only to replace it with alien woods. Why not skip the interval of denuded, degraded soil and preserve woodlots of real forest instead of eternal eucalyptus? Why must Madagascar of all places be covered with the one tree that is only fit to burn?

The forester looked at me: "When we are richer, we can afford to guard our native forest. When we are richer, with more modern agriculture, and villages which trade with each other, our people will understand the need to preserve what is left of our forest. Until then, we can only salvage, with eucalyptus for firewood, pines for building, and grevilea for the soil. . . . In the meantime, I could use a motorbike."

He did not need to add, When we are richer, people can afford to be sentimental about their own natural heritage instead of seeing conservation as the foreign whim of a foreign power.

About 80 km north of where we walked at the forest station lies another beachside forest, by the coastal village of Mahambo. The people of Mahambo have a taboo against killing aye-ayes. Rationally or not, through their own traditions they have preserved these strange denizens of the coastal woods.

In 1960 the World Wildlife Fund bought a portion of forest beside Mahambo to help the aye-aye. Zebu graze now in that little forest; the blackened stumps of trees decay among sprouting rice. Why should any Malagasy inhabitants of the region take note of the rusty sign which proclaims The World Wildlife Fund Preserves This Land for the Children of Our Grandchildren?

Whose land, preserved for what nation's grandchildren?

The sign is written, on both sides, in French.

ORCHIDS AND INDRI

We turned the Land Rover inland over barren dunes and foothills, where once the massive trunks of lowland forest marched down toward the sea. One tree remains: the traveler's palm, *Ravenala madagascariensis*, symbol of the Malagasy Republic. The palm grows here because it is an opportunist among forest trees, sprouting in forest clearings in the sunlight, its prussian blue seed so hard that it resists fire. The spread fingers of its crown faced the westering sun, stamped against the sunset as it is stamped with the Malagasy seal on every official document. The traveler's palm is the symbol of

Decrepit sign marking aye-aye reserve between Mahambo and Tamatave. Because it is in French, most Malagasy cannot read it.

Zebu feeding in same aye-aye reserve.

a land unique—and symbol of a land transformed by man. It is also, in its own way, a symbol of nature as man's shelter and succor. Its leaf axils hold pure water for the traveler; its fronds and trunk provide housebuilding material for nearly all the eastern peasants.

The Land Rover climbed the lowest scarp as night fell, slithering into ruts, hooting monotonously like a ship in fog on one-lane passages where recent earthslides had blocked the road, always on hairpin turns. This red clay track is the only road down from Tananarive to Madagascar's main port, but it has been deliberately left in a state to offer no competition to the east coast railway line. The dizzy engineering of the railway was a colonial triumph of 1905: now it seems that the coastal road may be paved by Chinese aid.

At midnight we reached Perinet, 925 m above sea level, but only some 50 km due inland. Clammy mist closed around us—the chill of night in hill forest. Winter monthly minimum temperature at Perinet is 10°C (50°F). After the balmy coast, the foresters' rest house loomed out of the darkness like a cement mausoleum.

Roger and my husband Richard were in no mood for half-measures. They swung back the rest-house double door and drove the Land Rover straight inside. Our family rolled out into a room on the right; Roger opted for the kitchen space on the left, saying, "I shall build a fire and be warm."

Richard offered, instead, "Lets take the headlamps and find some sleeping indri."

"This is ridiculous." Such is my suggestibility, at least to my husband's suggestions, that I did my complaining while walking down the path with him, with a headlight that barely reached the tops of the planted pine trees. "Russ Kinne and I have already tried night-walking here, with Arthur Rakotondravelo the forester. Total catch was one little lepilemur, which left Russ so frustrated he flashed away at it like the fourth of July."

Of course, we might have seen all sorts of animals and plants. This forest is still rainforest, although higher and colder than the ones we visited before. There are, for instance, nine species of lemur. Mouselemurs like Nosy Mangabé's here make their nests in hollow bamboos. Fat-tailed dwarf lemurs sleep through the coldest season. Lepilemurs bounce vertically between the tree trunks like Ping-Pong balls. Avahi, the woolly lemur, browses nightlong on leaves and peers at intruders with enormous nocturnal eyes, as placid as a koala bear. Those four are all night creatures. The five diurnal are, first, common brown lemurs (a black-faced race of Hiaraka's white-fronted lemur), and the black-and-white-ruffed lemur we saw at Nosy Mangabé—although these have apparently disappeared in the last 20 years. Then there is hapalemur, which sits on its haunches and eats bamboo. Hapalemur, like giant pandas, are one of nature's specialists: they live only among bamboo groves or lakeside reeds. Arthur the forester, however, knows two troops which have learned to take revenge on the peasants and raid new clearings of mountain rice.

The fourth diurnal lemur is most beautiful of all: the diademed sifaka. I remember once that at Perinet in 1962 storm clouds were lowering over the forest and golden late

OPPOSITE: A pair of indri, one of which clings and reaches in typical fashion.
Photo by Jonathan Pollock.

sunlight shot through beneath the storm. The spindly white trunks of the rainforest stood tall and bare, like trunks stripped by fire. Suddenly, five diademed sifaka materialized on a tree 20 m above the trail. One after another they leaped across. Their orange-gold arms and legs gleamed in the sunlight. Their charcoal backs were still lighter than the black cloud backdrop of their leap. Each leap was perhaps 6 m, the great jumping hind legs propelling them out and down, then doubling in midair so the legs again broke the force of their landing.

Then they were gone. And now they are truly gone from that forest of Perinet. The pressures of clearing and of hunting have already been too great.

No zoologist has yet made a detailed study of diademed sifaka or of hapalemur, avahi, dwarf lemurs. They have studied a western race of the lepilemur, but out of the nine species at Perinet only mouselemur and indri are scientifically well known.

At least, I reassured Richard, if we can show Roger an indri it will be worth seeing. Black and white and 1 m tall; it can leap backward nearly 10 m. Its song carries for 2 km, to a human ear, or at least 3 to another indri's. It has, besides, an honored place in Malagasy folklore, whose many legends call it a man of the forest. One of its Malagasy names is babakoto, which may derive from Ibabanikoto, the ancient being who first separated the ancestors of lemurs and of men.

If ever there was a place, or an animal, to touch Roger's pride in the aesthetic value of his own heritage, not simply its long- and short-term economics, this should be it.

Richard, more practical, wanted to know what chance there was that we might drag Roger all over the hill next day and see no indri? Roger was dubious enough about wildlife already.

I admitted that given the solidly braided tangle of Perinet's forest, there was a very good chance we would find no animals in all our visit.

Even that prediction proved optimistic. Richard and I saw no animals on our night walk, but Roger, who had roasted us a feast of sweet mealy east-coast manioc on the rest-house hearth, spent the rest of the night hurling lumps of firewood at the rest-house rats.

We walked in the morning by a still river that circles the hill of forest reserve. A wailing rose from the hill, a rising tone like an air-raid siren, pitched soprano, ultrasoprano, and still rising. Several voices began together, with a barking roar, and then rose, false thirds apart so you yearned for a piano tuner. First one voice, then another broke off, leaving one alone to continue the downward half of the siren's note. Then, as this group died away into silence, they were answered by a second, and a third group, the wails echoing over the water, reflecting one another as the still river mirrored the hill. An indri female sings through the whole song, the male for only a part, juveniles for still less. Each animal sings in its own voice, so the echoes and reechoes told each group where every indri was upon the hill. Eerie and beautiful, yet the only human cry which can compare is a child in extreme hysteria. The kind of sound which we make with larynx squeezed rigid and emotion out of all control is, for the indri, a song.

We climbed through the now familiar pattern of wet forest; although the trees grow lower the canopy becomes less dense at Perinet halfway up the escarpment than in

Orchids (Hiaraka).

Diademed sifaka (*Propithecus diadema*)
in the Tananarive Zoo.

the lowland forests of Hiaraka and Nosy Mangabé. Cerulean couas and toulous and magpie robins fluttered and twittered and purred, but no lemurs crashed through the trees. "You will have to look for the indri, not just listen, or expect to see movement," I warned Roger. "Jonathan Pollock, who has finished a fifteen month study of Indri, says that they are sometimes awake no more than five or six hours a day, particularly now, in the colder season."[6]

Even then "awake" means merely that they have stretched, defecated, and moved out of their sleeping place for the morning and not yet settled down again for the night. Much of the intervening time they rest, or feed languidly in one spot, Their langor is not surprising, for they mainly eat leaves, spending only 25 to 30% of their feeding time on fruit or seeds. An indri's intestine is 15 times as long as its body, with an extra intestine, or cecum, folded up in their abdomens that is three times as long as their bodies. (The cecum is the equivalent of our own thumb-sized appendix.) This apparatus copes with the bulky and indigestible mass of leaves they must consume each day simply to provide enough energy to keep moving. Leaves contain more protein than fruit does, but a diet of leaves is very low in fats, sugars, and starches—any source of energy. Leaf-eaters tend, then, to low metabolism and travel about much less than their fruit-eating relatives. This is paradoxical, for many leaf-eaters travel in beauty. When you see a Malaysian siamang swing away from you into the jungle, arm over arm beneath a branch, its body and legs pumping up and down like a child pumping on a swing, or when you see an indri, crouched black against a vertical branch, then apparently doubling in size as its jumping hindlegs propel it backward into space, you think these must be the most controlled and acrobatic of creatures—Nureyevs of the animal world.

It is, to be frank, a bit of a cheat. In three or four glorious leaps they eclipse themselves in the foliage. Then they sit and watch you blunder half a mile beyond them underneath. Jon Pollock eventually outsmarted them by bluffing himself. He went past and then doubled back and waited, sometimes for hours, until they gave themselves away.

Jonathan Pollock's study, to show anything about the indri at all, needed to be a quantitative record of animals in relation to their environment. If he had simply noted down interesting incidents, he might easily have ended his fifteen months with lyrical descriptions of indri's beauty and a handful of obvious social interactions. By systematically recording the animals' positions and movement, he showed far more than one could have guessed.

This did not stop him naming and enjoying "his" groups. The hill where we walked with Roger really belongs to Bigears and Leftear, a well-established Indri pair. Their young, Yam, Yaf, and Whitethroat, were born at three-year intervals. Indri are monogamous. Apparently, like gibbon and siamang, they maintain their bond on a basis of sex for a week or so every three years. Since no scientist has yet watched an indri in estrus, we are not even sure whether the pair bond survives this crisis intact.

During ordinary, sexless years, the female takes precedence over the male. Bigears fed high up among tender shoots of the canopy, while her male Leftear contented himself with perches lower down, among structural branches. Perhaps he was not content. Sometimes Bigears supplanted him on a choice perch or actually cuffed him over the muzzle, driving him lower in the trees.

There is probably an evolutionary advantage for the female having more to eat, for she is usually pregnant or lactating. A monogamous male, or rather, the mate of a monogamous female, can also gain by self-sacrifice, for he is furthering the health of his own children. Female dominance, however, is far more widespread among lemurs than monogamy. I first saw it among ringtails; brown lemurs and sifaka behave likewise.[7] It is probably an inherited trait in the lemur strain. In contrast our own relatives, the Old World monkeys and great apes, all share some form of male precedence over females.

Leftear, the male, may not have had the best feeding spots, but he came into his own defending the feeding territory. Primates which eat mature leaves can find food throughout the year without moving far afield, while their limited energy supply constrains the distance they can travel. It is apparently more efficient for them to defend a small permanent "rice field" than to range widely to trees in sporadic flower or fruit. Bigears and Leftear probably knew their 9-hectare hilltop in great detail. They ranged methodically over it, stopping to browse even in the parts they visited rarely. In contrast a newly established couple on the next hill was much more uneven in their ranging. They apparently did not yet know their territory well enough to exploit its possibilities. The territory is a group's livelihood, and a really familiar territory is the most efficient livelihood.

Once, Bigear's family was feeding near their border when they heard another group about 150 m away. The two groups leaped toward each other, wailing a fugue of song and answering song. Bigears wailed loudly from within the territory, just as a gibbon or siamang female cheers on her champion with hoots and howls. Leftear, her male, leaped forward, cheek-marking branches and ricocheting through the trees. At one point, before both groups retired, he sang continuously for nine minutes flat. Indri's song close by is at the pain threshold for human ears, so Leftear tested not only the other group's courage but Jon's scientific detachment as well.

In short, an indri male's role is not simply to defend his female but to defend their joint property. Again we come back to economics: animal economics, which says that the shape of a kinship system links up with the regular or sporadic use of a piece of geography. The relation of an animal to its food resources molds social behavior, just as much as diet molds the crowns of its teeth and the coils of its gut.

Indri are reassuring animals because they confirm our picture of other leaf-eating primates. Many leaf-eating monkeys live in small, relatively immobile groups in a range which they defend for their exclusive use. Such knowledge, of course, constitutes a major part of lemurs' scientific importance; they are a separate evolutionary line which can help to confirm or disprove the theories we make about other primates, including our own ancestors.

"Excuse me," said Roger. "Indri are surely of interest, but we have walked at least five kilometres back and forth over this hill. I would really prefer to go down and look at the forester's orchid collection. Besides, the fisheries guard wants to talk about using pigsties to fertilize fish-culture ponds."

Sadly, we watched him go. Fair enough—among Madagascar's 900 orchids is one of the most famous in all the world. The tubular nectary of the comet orchid is 38 cm (15 in.) long. When Charles Darwin examined the flower he predicted that a hawkmoth with a 15 inch tongue must exist on Madagascar to fertilize it. The moth was found at last and named *praedicta*.[8] Orchids and their moths are also part of Roger's heritage—and fishponds and pigsties.

At last Richard and I slid down a hillside among tree ferns. We looked up to see a black-and-white figure sprawled on a branch. The long legs stretched luxuriously forward, the black belly toasted in the morning sun; teddy bear ears framed a black face with lemon yellow eyes.

I had seen indri here, once twelve years ago. That group converged on us, leaping low. They stayed long enough to stare, each clinging to a vertical stem, then put their heads back and bellowed alarm. This was not the indri-to-indri wail but an in-and-out sawing roar, with little round red mouths pushed forward from the black faces like flappers' makeup of the twenties. Then they leaped away, their huge thighs pushing them off into the air. They turned to cling again on landing. After a last look over their shoulders, a second leap carried them into invisibility.

The indri above Richard and me did not leap, bellow, and soar into invisibility. He peered down at us, then settled his belly even more comfortably toward the sun. He reached out a long black hand and hooked a spray of leaves toward his muzzle. "Why, that's Yaf, Bigear's son," exclaimed Jon Pollock, much later in England, looking at my ill-snapped photo. "He's a bit embarrassing. I named him Young Adult Female, then he matured into a male. I am so glad he's still there—and still tame." But when we returned with Roger and our children, only empty blue sky showed in the tree fork where Yaf had been sitting. Susan, the concerned child who had mothered the dying sifaka, asked for them all, "May we never see an indri any more?"

Our children, and our children's grandchildren, may never see an indri. In twenty years they will be rare as aye-aye, to be found only if one has time and money to seek out survivors on the remotest hills. Far worse, Roger and his children may never see an indri, unless they themselves decide that indri are part of their nation's pride. And what of the children of Bigears and Leftear and Yaf? Will the children and grandchildren of the indri, who sing so bravely to defend their home, have a home to defend?

PART 3

CENTRAL DOMAIN: WILDERNESS AS A LUXURY

Boy with slingshot. The schools can teach him that wild birds are precious—but he also needs enough to eat.

THE BARE PRAIRIE

Do people actually need the wilderness? We have seen some of the economic and social pressures to destroy the world's wild places. It is worth asking soberly how much the wilderness is worth to us.

A naturalist may grieve as virgin forest is felled, but farmers ask for firewood, soil, and flood control, not wilderness. Are human lives the poorer if tigers become extinct, or blue whales, indri, or aye-aye? Will anyone mourn a Malagasy scaritine beetle, cremated by the bushfire that sears its earthen burrow before its gargoyle form is figured in the annals of the Paris Museum?

Most people of the Malagasy central plateau would answer: No. No, they do not need wilderness. For 800 or 900 years they have not had wilderness. The forests which covered the plateau at the time of Charlemagne have long since burned to a few remnant copses. Plateau people have permanent agriculture, rich local cultures, a history of kingship, and a present of national political activity. They do not need wildlife as well.

Enthusiasm for the wild is relatively recent even in European culture. Petrarch was the first European to climb a mountain simply for the view (at least, the first to record his emotions).[1] Romantic forest gloom and windswept heights are largely a creation of the early 19th century Romantics. In the Middle Ages, when forests existed in Europe, they were nasty places full of wolves and outlaws, while the Alps seemed merely a hazard to transportation.

Let us turn then to the plateau people. In this chapter we will see what their cities and farms are like, how rich their culture is, how impoverished their natural environment, so that we may understand these people who have no mystique of the wildneress.

CITY OF A THOUSAND VILLAGES

Tananarive is gneiss and granite, the bones of Gondwanaland. Its ridges are crumpled

Queen's Palace at Tananarive.

Ranavalona II.

Andrianampoinimerina.

Radama I.

together like old newspaper, baffling to those who know glaciated hills that run north and south, or the tectonic east–west humps of English downs. The granite ridges float, apparently, on water. The floodplain of the Ikopa River encircles the capital. In its season the city's peak is mirrored from the still waters of fallow rice paddies or, as the new rice sprouts, rises like Mont St. Michel above an incoming tide of tender green.

The Queen's Palace crowns Tananarive. Ranavalona I, who ruled from 1828 to 1861, built the palace to proclaim her glory. It stands in traditional Malagasy fashion around a central tree trunk. Two thousand slaves are supposed to have died in bringing that 39-m-long trunk (125 ft) to Tananarive from the eastern forest.

The rise of the kingdom began at the end of the 18th century with Andrianampoinimerina. His somewhat daunting name is pronounced Amp'nimern, which means Lord of the Merina people. It was he who established his capital at Tananarive and rebuilt and enlarged the dikes of the Ikopa River. By a system of forced communal labor he drained the marshes, established local markets, and laid out canals to let people carry their rice for sale as much as 48 km away. Above all, systematic water control meant that two crops of rice could grow on the Tananarive plain, where only a wet season crop grew before. Later interpreters stress the despotic or communal aspects of his reign, according to their own bias, but none disputes his accomplishments.

Andrianampoinimerina wore only a white lamba, rather like a bedsheet, after his people's tradition, and the warrior's mother-of-pearl shell on his forehead. His home was a one-roomed hut where he slept on a wooden shelf with his fourteen wives. To westerners who are used to the idea that palaces make kings, it may seem strange that such a chieftain could create an agricultural infrastructure or leave such oratory as his deathbed speech to Radama I:

"Dama Oh! my eldest son, oh fragment of my life. May I go before you to the tomb! How beautiful you are! You do not resemble the commonality of men; you are like a god fallen to earth; you are not the issue of my flesh but come out of my mouth, for you are the fruit of the creator. I do not die, I who have such a son, for you are a beautiful bull."[2]

Radama I fulfilled his father's prophecies. He opened Tananarive to British missionaries. His army, drilled by Sargeant Hastie, conquered from east coast to west and drove the Sakalava kings from the island of sacred lemurs northward to Nosy Bé. He forbade the slave trade, which was largely an economic measure to undercut the coastal tribes, and among his own people abolished infanticide and trial by ordeal. When Radama died in 1828, at only 36, he had transformed the life of Tananarive. His people buried him in a coffin made from 12,000 Spanish silver dollars and with his wardrobe of eighty British uniforms, hats, feathers, and a golden helmet.[3]

Queen Ranavalona, his massive successor, reacted against the west. She wrote an open letter to Europeans to thank them for their wisdom and knowledge but warned that if they broke the kingdom's laws they could be put to death, just as in any other country. For, she claimed, "I have no shame and no fear for our traditions."[4]

She outlawed foreign possession of land and, for a time, foreign trade. She viewed local christians as imperialist spies. They were sewn alive in raffia mats and rolled off the granite cliff face before her palace.

At the same time, however, the queen welcomed a few foreign technical advisers. The most extraordinary was Jean Laborde, who began his career in Madagascar as a shipwrecked mariner and ended by directing factories that produced guns, gunpowder, brass, steel, swords, glass, silk, lime, paint, ink, soap, candy, potash, bricks, tiles and lightning conductors.[5]

The pulling toward and away from the west has continued to the present day. The visitor to Tananarive has an overwhelming impression of its Malagasy and Merina traditions, with an overlay of outside cultures. Redbrick balconied houses cling to the hillsides, like a rosy Italian hilltown, as in Italy, footpaths and staircases serve for streets, with mediaeval sewage and garbage disposal. Below in the valleys, modern office and government buildings rise four square, looking up at the occasionally occupied bedrooms of the Tananarive Hilton. Jacaranda trees from Brazil and flamboyants from the Malagasy west weep their scarlet or lavender petals on the sidewalks. The modern and traditional buildings join without suture, for Tananarive is a city which has grown organically, not merely a coagulated set of official decisions.

Descend from the spur of the university, cross a valley with sodden fields of canna lilies destined for the flower market, dive into a road tunnel under the ridge of the Queen's Palace. You emerge in Analakely, which means "the little woods." No trees grow there now—instead the crowding white umbrellas of the Friday market, or zoma. The zoma sells fruit, vegetables, furniture, trinkets. There are litchi sellers and green pepper sellers, tortoiseshell jewelery from the coast, gems from the plateau. Malagasy nature contributes the indigenous butterflies; local technology offers raffia mats, mohair carpets, aluminum cooking pots; craftsmen dig, smelt, and mold aluminum in family forges.

Dive beneath another tunnel from the market, under the spur which bears the modern president's offices. You emerge in a different valley, with a jacaranda-fringed lake, and then over another spur to the valley which holds Tananarive Zoo.

Classic buildings in blond cement look down on a botanic garden. This is the Directorate of Scientific Research, housing students of demography, geography, agricultural genetics, and medicinal herbs. The institution was once French, founded by Raymond Decary, whose patronym echoes in the Latin names of Malagasy creatures from the little cave-dwelling daddy longlegs (*Decarynella gracilipes*) to the three-cornered palm tree (*Neodypsiis decaryi*).[6]

Here, below the research laboratory, lies an oasis of green, where botanical specimens collected throughout Madagascar grow beside three small, stepped ponds. Cages hold chameleons, birds, lemurs—almost the only lemurs on the plateau.

The people of Tananarive stroll here: teenagers in blue jeans, ladies with white lambas around their shoulders and pastel parasols, soldiers out on a day pass. This park has the only woods in the city where young couples can be alone, the only wild animals for children to see.

"It is a great responsibility," confesses Georges Randrianasolo, the park director. "This park represents the one place where plateau people can learn about our own heritage of nature."

OPPOSITE: Zoma, or Friday market, in Tananarive.

OPPOSITE: Hardware at zoma.

Raffia lemurs (*catta*). Plateau people have never seen lemurs, so there is more art than accuracy in these versions.

Fruit at zoma.

Raffia bed and floor mats.

Butterflies for sale, including huge comet moth (*Argema mittrei*).

Tananarive Zoo. The zoo and museum are the only place where people of the capital can see their own fauna.

Crowned sifaka (*Propithecus verreauxi coronatus*).

Buff-backed heron.

The ladies in their lambas lean over the crocodiles' cage—creatures pictured over and over in local carvings as dismembering men or, strangely, locked in battle with giant sharks. In one lake in the far north, crocodiles are sacred. People call them to shore with a dish of blood, then throw in chunks of sacrificed zebu.

The largest crocodiles used to reach 6 or even 8 m long in the lakes of the interior. No wonder they slide evilly into so many tribal legends.

People stare as well at the wild boars, at the Madagascar horned owl drowsing its life away in a cage, at the five species of egret and heron that nest in a bickering colony on the little lake. They gasp as lemurs and sifaka leap from branch to branch of the bare trees on their private islands.

Almost no one knows, however, that the mother sifaka, staring with glazed eyes at the cage wire around her, is probably the natural inhabitant of "the little woods" (the copse that grew where the market umbrellas cluster). She is a crowned sifaka, with brown head and white-blazed nose. She comes from the relict of plateau forest near Tsiromandidy, 240 km away. As far as we can tell, her ancestors ranged in historic times to the woodlands of Tananarive.

She clutches the precious baby, cradled between her hairless black knees, but it will die. The zoo at Tananarive has not even enough money to feed its animals the diets they need, and far too little is known about keeping the rarer animals of Madagascar.

Tananarive, then, is a city like other cities, with its own history, economics, architecture, and even a zoo for the city dwellers' bow to nature.

There are differences, odd differences, in the immanence of nature. No city dwellers expect wild animals on Fifth Avenue, or Analakely. Still the New York child may realize that white-tailed deer once roamed Manhattan. The New York child at the zoo reaches out toward the well-known, well-loved Bambi. In Tananarive, no Malagasy child has a book of lemurs to love. The New Yorker need travel only as far as New Jersey to find farmers complaining of the rabbits and white-tailed deer; the Tananarive child must be prepared for a 240-km expedition over unpaved road and a two-day hike into forest, if he would reach the last home of the crowned sifaka.

The lambaed ladies and their children drift from the huddled sifaka to the museum. Suddenly, the scale enlarges. Here are lemur skeletons almost as tall as a man, bird skeletons that tower over a man. Here is a crocodile skull as large as a baby's cradle. Here is the carapace of a tortoise 4 feet in diameter. Here, at last, is the natural history of Tananarive.

It is as well that people do not miss wildlife unless it is incorporated in their own culture, for the truly spectacular wildlife of the Malagasy plateau is extinct.

INSEPARABLE AS RICE AND WATER

"What is your village commune—a bunch of men or of grasshoppers?" shouted Georges. "Do you call yourselves socialists? Then show these foreigners that socialists can lift *anything*!"

Forty people materialized from the apparently empty rice fields and set their shoulders to the Land Rover, which canted at a 45° angle in a pothole in the road verge, ready to roll into the paddy below. They heaved and cheered and set us straight again, on the road to Ampasambazimba, the graveyard of giant lemurs.

Scarcely a tree punctuated the highland landscape, except lines of planted eucalyptus. There was water aplenty, for the crystalline bedrock is impervious to water and each dimpled valley is a natural reservoir.[7] But water, and soil, are controlled by man, not nature, by terracing, not trees.

Every patch of flat land is irrigated and diked with earth. Every crinkle of hill is terraced, the little fields rising up its sides like contour lines on a map. It is all green and red—red earth, red houses, red people hoeing the mud—green rice, green hills—tending to gray in the dry season. Only the ducks flapping in the empty rice ponds are allowed to be frankly black and white, offset by the multicolored laundry which blooms on river banks to dry.

Decary, who founded the scientific institute, wrote with love that a rice growing landscape is in human scale.[8] Just as a prairie of wheat can stretch your eyes, open and billowing as the empty sea, so the cupped hills and contoured terraces, or the square fields of the plain, enclose the eyes and the spirit. Each outline of little mud dikes speaks out to say, "I am human livelihood. I belong to a man, a family, a village. I am a pattern in earth, pattern to the eye, a pattern of peoples' lives."

Paddy rice is no easy crop. First the field must be tilled, by using a hoe to break the soil into clods, which dry and aerate. Then the dikes of field and irrigation channels need repairing. At last the water is let in, to lie placid among the little dikes, a mosaic pavement mirroring the sky.

While the men are preparing the main fields, women have planted nursery fields where the first shoots push up through the shallow water, violent yellow-green. In some regions, where land is still abundant, rice can be sown directly in the growing fields, but in Imerina, and the even hillier Betsileo country to the south, virtually all irrigable land is already farmed. Sowing in nursery fields increases yields by a quarter. Plateau people accept the necessity of labor to wring more from their land.

When the nursery rice is ready for replanting, the main fields must be churned to liquid mud. This can be done by hoeing but is commonly done by trampling. On an appointed day the men of the region gather with a small team of zebu. Young men and boys clap and whistle and dance and whack the animals with sticks. The zebu, whites of their eyes showing, plunge and bellow and circle in the mud. The men plunge in after them, sinking kneedeep in ooze. In some regions, men even dress up as monsters "to frighten the cattle." We saw one stalwart in the south with square straw hat, bare hairy chest, and then a skirt of trailing banana fronds that flapped and rattled as he capered in the slime.

At the end of the day the fields are an emulsion of clay and water while men and zebu alike are coated and caked the color of their own fields. It is a party, not an ordeal. At evening the man whose fields were trampled that day offers a grand dinner for all with meat to eat. Besides the hilarity of trampling and the welcome feast, the working group has expressed their solidarity. A man asks his "kinsmen" to the trampling party. If they are merely neighbors, or comembers of the village commune, he still calls them

Plateau rice (Betsileo). Mud bricks for houses are at left center.

One stalwart near Fort Dauphin wore a skirt of trailing banana fronds as his zebu plowed and trampled the rice paddy.

fictional kinsmen. The old kinship bonds can, if all goes smoothly, blend into the modern community bonds, in part because paddy rice demands cooperation of labor.[9]

After the men it is the womens' turn to work together. They replant the rice, bending from the hips, with a bundle of seedlings in the left hand and right hand rhythmically plunging a young plant into the waiting ooze. Sometimes a woman works alone in her own fields. Often, instead, a file of "kinswomen" move together, each planting a share.

So through the seasons. The rice must be weeded, the dikes tended, Above all, the water level must be watched and raised as the rice grows higher to support but never cover the lengthening stalks. Decary quotes the Merina proverb, "Don't be ambitious if you don't work, for the rice of the first harvest is not for the lazy man" and that other proverb which sums up the peasants' love of the land: "inseparable as rice and water."

In the end comes the harvest, reaped by women and carried by men, and the Tananarive Festival of First Rice, when men march through the streets with ripened stalks in their hats and sheaves in their arms to present the first fruits—in pagan times to God, in Christian times to the King, and nowadays to the State.

Irrigated rice is an intensive culture, demanding care and labor, and well suited to accept improvements in technique. New rice varieties of the Green Revolution, for instance, are gaining ground in Imerina. The new varieties demand fertilizer and attention, but since there is already a tradition of careful husbandry and of fertilizing the fields, the changes are acceptable. Even without miracle plants, the apparently simple improvements in microhydraulics popularized by the government during the 1960s could raise yields from 2½ metric tons/hectare by traditional methods to 4½ tons/hectare.[10] However, it is equally revealing to compare the 2½ tons of traditional paddy rice to the 1 ton/hectare from mountain rice, in places like Lavalohalika, or the 5 ton yield in Mauritius or the United States and the 6-ton yield in Japan.[11]

Irrigated rice accepts an almost infinite increase in labor on the same land. In Java, one of the most intensively populated paddy rice regions of the world, the population increased from about 7 million in 1830 to about 42 million in 1930, while yields per capita remained nearly constant at 106 kg before 1900, and 96 kg after 1900. The increase in total yield was not due to increased acreage or modern fertilizers but to ever more intensive driving of the paddy terrace: weeding, draining, and finally harvesting the rice heads singly with a tool like a razor blade.[12]

In Java the result has been a rococo involution of the social structure, where tiers of sharecropping and work agreements divide the crop of lilliputian rice terraces.[13] In Imerina the social structure hardens, to exclude "strangers," that is, anyone outside the family group.

A Merina tribesman ideally marries within a close group of villages which comprise his extended family. Merina explicitly recognize the fundamental role of property: a proper marriage is called "inheritance not going away," or "closing the breach." Where land, and the capital investment of terracing and drainage, are the limiting factors, people acquiesce and develop a cultural rationale for their behavior.[14]

When a Merina speaks of people, he normally qualifies the term: "living people." Dead people, the ancestors, are his spiritual link with his land.

OPPOSITE: Rice fields east of Tananarive.

The family group traces itself back to a family tomb. The living are united with, and tied to their ancestral land by the present dead. Furthermore, the living hold celebrations for the dead. Every few years they return to the tomb en masse, open it, take out the bodies of their closest relatives and most recent dead, dance with the wrapped bodies, and sprinkle them with rum. Villagers enter such a ceremony in real terror, not just with the emotions of recent loss but also with horror and revulsion as the living approach the forbidden world of the dead. As the afternoon wears on, though, and the women dance more and more wildly, the terror turns to bacchanalian joy. After formal eulogies (and often a blessing by a Christian catechist), the bodies are rewrapped in as many as 12 new *lamba mena*—the red or black silk cloths which the dead wear, as distinguished from the white shawls of the living. Then dancing and drinking begin again. At last the corpses are carried at shoulder height three times clockwise around the tomb, while the brothers-in-law play tricks on their relatives as they did in life, trying to stop his or her return to the tomb. Some of the corpses are thrown up and down, and the bones can be heard to crush. Afterward, women fight and scramble for the mats used to carry the corpses, for sleeping on these mats brings fertility.[15]

I have never seen such an exhumation, but one friend has told me about the ceremonies in her own family. She is no villager but a chic, petite university English major, descended from one of the 12 kings of Tananarive who predated Andrianam-poinimerina. "My family tomb has over 500 corpses," she said. "Of course the older bodies shrink. Some are no bigger than four loaves of bread parceled up together. (She held her hands with their manicured fingernails at the imagined ends of a French loaf.) And the stench when the tomb is opened! Revolting! I couldn't bear to go inside a tomb. The whole thing makes my flesh crawl, not to mention the risks of disease. Fortunately we pay special people, who make a living at it, to go in and turn over the corpses on their shelves until they find the ones we want taken out. . . . We drink and dance and make speeches at the tomb itself, but the main corpse, the person in whose honor the ceremony is held, we carry to a house in the valley. We put the body on the dining room sideboard and celebrate for another day and a half, toasting the spirits of the dead and sprinkling rum. Of course, my family are declaring their status. Most people could not afford to entertain all their relations with beef and rum for an extra day-and-a-half before the tomb is resealed. People even take full bottles of Scotch whiskey to pour over the dead."

"But how do you *feel*, eating and drinking with grandmother on the sideboard?"

"Very gay. It is a family reunion, not just with the living people, but all the dead as well. Of course we are happy that our ancestors are joined with us, and the family is united. Tell me, how is it in the West, that when you bury your dead, you try never to think of them again? And that you even cast off your old people, who are near death? I have read about "old people's homes. . . ."

That conversation ended with my trying to explain the more horrifying habits of my own tribe.

The Land Rover jounced along the twisting roads of the plateau, past brick-verandaed houses, past the little cups of irrigated fields. The plateau peoples' lives are cupped in like their rice, linked to their fields, their kinsfolk, their family tomb. And yet, how much more tolerable life would be in the valleys if only there were still trees on the hills! No silting up of the rice fields, no scarcity of wood or charcoal for the fire to cook the rice.

Rain tears away the red laterite soil, slashing the slopes into deep gullies called lavaka. The hills erode in sheets, grain by grain, and in gullies that grow deeper with every storm. Lavaka are a good deal more than simple gullies. These ravines do not merely become deeper, but wider, ramified, as the hard upper layer of laterite clay slumps into the softer gully base—more on the scale of earth-moving than erosion. Le Bourdiec estimates that three-quarters of Madagascar's surface is severely degraded.[16]

Boiteau wrote in 1946: "About 20 million hectares annually undergo the regime of wild (grass) fires, uncontrolled blazes which destroy in passing forest relicts, reforestation efforts, even isolated homes and villages. If we estimate the dry matter so destroyed at 2,000 kilos per hectare, and the nitrogen content of that dry matter at two percent (very moderate assumptions) then every year 80,000 tonnes of nitrogen go up in smoke.... Counting in the forest destruction, we reach the painful conclusion that the value wasted every year by this stupid process exceeds the yearly total of Malagasy exports."[17]

Above us, a fortified village of the last century guttered downhill like melted candlewax. Before the Merina kingdom pacified the country, people built on hilltops, with a deep moat dug for protection, in the worldwide pattern of moated hillfort. A very similar Iron Age ditch encircles Mount Caburn near our home in England, stabilized over millennia in the chalk of the Sussex Downs. Here in Madagascar the ring of moat had merely channeled erosion. A lavaka began from its low point and reached upward, engulfing more and more of the moat and the hill crown, a flayed red hand clutching with bleeding fingers at the crumbled walls of the ancient village.

I, though, see only the land—I do not see the Malagasy love of their land. Let me quote Dox instead, most famous of Malagasy poets. I cannot render the many-voweled quality of Malagasy or the rhyme which is always on a diminishing cadence, for words are stressed on the third syllable from an end. The last two syllables of each rhyme are breathed, or anticipated in the mind, the final notes of a running chord. Here, at least, is the English substance of Dox's poem "Red Island."[18]

> I am moved at the sight of certain places in Imerina with their red soil.
> Is this not why, if one thinks of it, that people give Madagascar the simple
>   name of "Red Island" ... evocative name.
> Evoking the hills worn by the fire and ravined by the torrents of rain.... It is
>   there you will see, with their road-ravines, the ancient villages con-
>   structed by our ancestors.
> Villages whose face is the gable roof, the chicken hut and the cattle corral in
>   the courtyard. But the well is down there in the valley ...
> Their descendants shall think of them, and raise up ramparts which silently
>   shall replace these villages, villages of red walls that ask our compassion.

Volcano—extinct, the top of the cone fallen in like the lips of a toothless old man. The soil had changed from red to pale yellow, the rocks from gneiss and granite to friable black lava. Madagascar has no live volcanoes, but the Itasy region of the central plateau is pocked with craters and pimpled with ash cones. Many of its springs still bubble out hot soda water.

Years ago a lava flow dammed up the River Mazy, a little stream which now makes a lazy semicircle around a natural basin. Georges parked the Land Rover where the last field track ended. We hopped across terraces where cooking-pot greens grew in the outflow of a perennial spring, toward the rice fields of Ampasambazimba, "the Vazimba's tomb." We had reached Madagascar's most famous fossil site. When the lava dike dammed up the Mazy, this little basin was a lake. The giant lemurs of all-too-recent times came down to browse and to drink at the lake edge, died, and were fossilized in its limy ooze. Successive paleontologists have reverently dug them up, and successive farmers have hoed them out of the way, ever since.[19]

As we jumped from dike to dike or stumbled among the drying clods, the farmers gathered and immediately recognized we would be interested only in fossils. The oldest peasant pointed to Georges' ten-year-old son, Mamy. The ancient said that he was just Mamy's age when Lamberton last came to dig. He had hung about the excavations, helping to carry baskets. Look, he would show us the place Lamberton made his final trench. . . .

Unfortunately the site is not adapted to modern paleontology, because early diggers have confused the fossil layers. It would be difficult now to correlate pollen and soil strata with the fossils in order to gain a record of vegetation and climatic changes.[20] We have, at least, one date. A bit of *Megaladapis* tibia, from Standing's collection in the British Museum, radio carbon dates at 1,035 years old (give or take 50 years). We do not know if this was the bottom or top or middle of the fossil deposit, but it is nonetheless one anchor point.[21]

We do not need the date to know that extinct lemurs were contemporary with the earliest men. In the middle of the fossil layer lay an intact earthenware jar, and an ax-head made of the shank-bone of an extinct flightless bird, lying beside a cut stick which was probably the ax-haft. There is no question of the workmanship. The bone is beveled and polished to a sharp blade, the stick still has cutting marks, and they fit comfortably together. The whole sequence is there: the extinct animals, the ax that dismembered them, the pots they were cooked in.

What was this valley like when the first Vazimba came over the hills, and what were the animals they found watering at the lake?

First there was forest: lush at the lake edge, sparse on the crests, instead of the present golden panorama of grass, and a lavaka in the hill just beyond funneling its soil down to the Mazy River. Through the forest roamed imposing animals, for almost all the creatures now extinct were larger than those which remain.

Pygmy hippopotamus wallowed in the lake, surfacing to blow with their piggy nostrils. Giant crocodiles, monsters of 7 and 8 m, basked at the bank, pretending to be

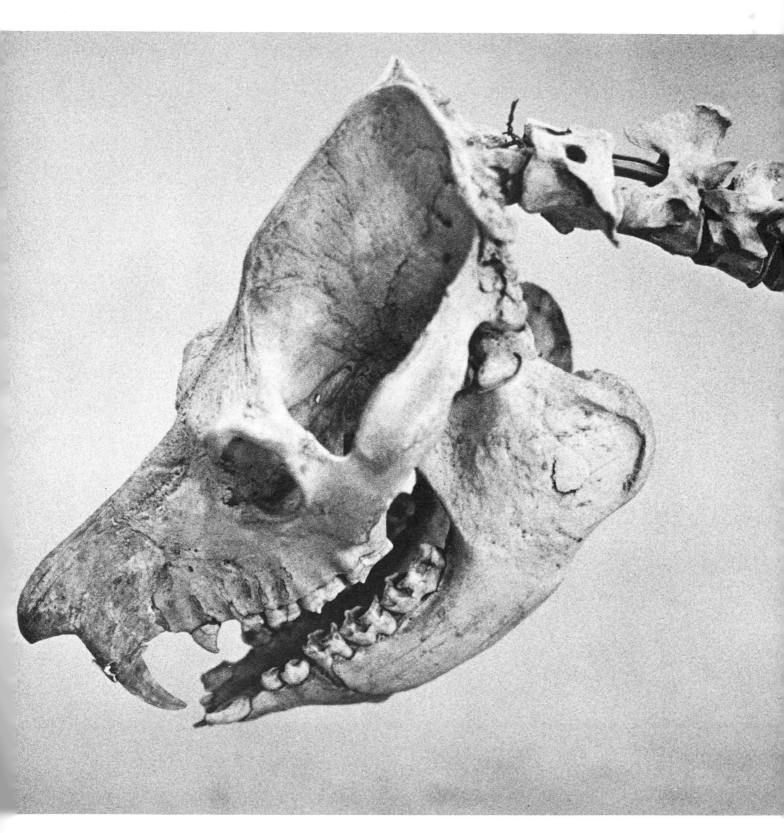

Megaladapis skull (Tananarive Zoo Museum).

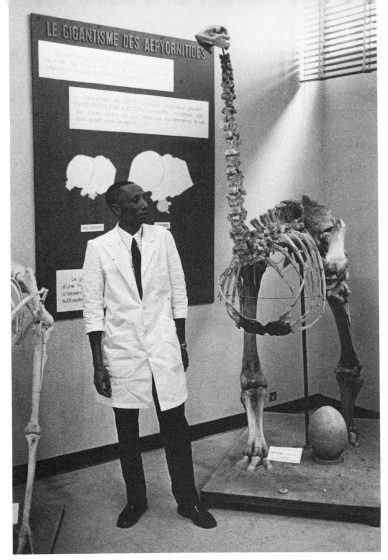

Georges Randrianasolo, director of Tzimbazaza Zoo in Tananarive, with aepyornis skeleton and egg.

Megaladapis (Tananarive Zoo).

improbably large tree trunks. Giant tortoises tiptoed under the trees, one carrying a shell 1½ m long, which makes it bigger even than the present-day tortoises from the Seychelles and Aldabara.[22]

Occasionally aepyornis or mullerornis minced past the turtles, flightless birds related to ostriches. At least mullerornis may have minced—that was the one whose shank turned into a hatchet-head. Mullerornis was the graceful version, only tall enough to look a 1½-m Vazimba hunter in the eye. Aepyornis clumped, instead. It was 3 m tall, the heaviest bird that ever lived, with legs and thighs like an aging weight lifter. The kick of an ostrich is said to be enough to kill a leopard. One images the little Vazimba people taking no chance with the kick of an Aepyornis.

They did take chances, though. They gathered the 10-litre eggs, if not for a 2½ gallon omelet, at least for water jars or grain jars. Aepyornis lived throughout Madagascar, from southern beach dunes to Diego Suarez in the north (eggshells from the north and south have also been radiocarbon dated at about 1,000 to 800 years old).[23] Climatic change may have contributed to the great birds' disappearance, but it is difficult to suppose a change that struck the whole island-continent in the past 1,000 years. More likely they dwindled from hunting, and egg collecting, although it takes two hands to collect one egg.[24]

We have missed these elephant birds by very little. The Sieur de Flacourt wrote as late as 1661: "Vouron patra is a great bird which haunts the Ampatra region, and lays eggs like an ostrich, it is a kind of ostrich. The people of the said region cannot catch it; it seeks the most deserted places."[25] Arab traders told Marco Polo of a colossal bird on an island called Madeigascar which entered European legends as Sinbad's roc.[26]

As well as giant birds and reptiles, there were giant lemurs, the only candidates to fill the herbivore niches left vacant by the absence of hoofed mammals. Perhaps a troop of baboon-sized creatures sauntered down to the lake shore, plucking grass-stems with their hands to eat, keeping their distance, but only just, from the elephant birds as African baboons do from an ostrich. This was archaeolemur, whose equal-length limbs and grit-worn teeth show that it was a partially terrestrial lemur.[27] The "troop" is just a guess, based on analogy with ground-living baboons. A baboon troop protects its own members from attack as they forage away from the safety of trees. The large argumentative troop also provides a complex of social relations. They have lifelong kinship patterns that require an individual to relate to brothers and aunts as well as to mother. Their dominance relations require judging the temper of others and who will support whom in their daily bickering.

It is maddening that archaeolemur is just lying there, in fossil swamps or in museums, instead of trotting around from trees to ground to provide a distinct line of terrestrial primates which we could compare with baboons and their ilk. The extinct lemurs might have given us another version of a primate's adaptation to ground-life—like, after all, our own ancestors. It is maddening that hadropithecus is lying there beside archaeolemur, a long-legged, fleet-limbed form which ran where archaeolemur trotted. Hadropithecus may have fed on small hard objects such as grass-bulbs or grass-seeds, which also probably nourished the Miocene ancestors of man.[28]

Maddening—but such animals would have come immediately into conflict with the Vazimba by raiding crops as well as by being meat on the hoof (or rather on the hand). One archaeolemur skull from the site of Andrahomana was pierced by an ax-like instrument with rectangular cross section—no naturally round stick or stone or canine. The wound was made while the flesh was on, for the pieces of bone are still attached where they folded in to crush the brain, not loose as they would be if someone had casually smashed an old, dry skull. Archaeolemur leg bones from the same site have been cut and burned.[29]

All these animals spent some time on the ground. A different group of species used the trees that clustered around the lakeshore. At Perinet, in the rich forest of the eastern escarpment, nine species of arboreal lemur coexisted. Here in the trees of Ampasambazimba there were at least twelve arboreal species. Six of them are from genera still living in the western forests today. The full complement of modern forms appears among the fossils, which is hardly surprising. You would not expect new genera to evolve in the last thousand years. Modern lemurs' presence at Ampasambazimba simply proves that it was an ordinary Malagasy woodland.

The seventh was an indri. That indri bothers me. Indri are now confined to the wet forest of the eastern escarpment. A thousand years ago Ampasambazimba may have had lush vegetation like that of the east. Yet all the surviving plateau vegetation indicates that the plateau region shades toward drier and drier woodlands and that there has been no change of climate. Possibly indri was far more robustly distributed in the past, popping up all over the plateau wherever a lake or stream supported year-round rich vegetation. Alternatively, perhaps indri, like many other lemurs, had a western species which could tolerate plateau conditions.

Two of the extinct lemurs were tree-living quadrupeds running about on branches like modern *Lemur*, only bigger. Two were vertical-bodied forms, like modern sifaka or indri, only bigger. But they did not leap like a sifaka or an indri; they clambered. Paleopropithecus, the size of a modern chimpanzee, apparently hung or even swung from its arms as much as jumping with its hind legs, and archaeoindris, with rounder skull and flatter face, probably did the same.

My own candidate for the funniest of the tree-living lemurs is the last, megaladapis, which had three species, large and small. The largest may have weighed 200 kg, as much as a male orang. It was stout like a plump bear, with enormous hands and feet that would have wrapped right around a tree trunk.[30] Its skull and snout were long and heavy and cowlike, bent upward to be almost a continuation of the neck.[31] Probably, while the quadrupeds scuttled or sauntered past and the vertical-bodied lemurs swung by their arms, megaladapis just clung onto trunks like an overblown koala. It reached out the fingers of one of those elongated hands, hooked in a branch, extended its neck and muzzle, and browsed from the twigs and leaves without moving from its tree. When it came to the ground, it may have simply shuffled from one food tree to another, or perhaps it stayed upright and made short, frog-like hops, like its short leaps in the trees.[32] This Malagasy koala-cow hung fat and furry, peering amiably downward, when the Vazimba came.

Of all these extinct lemurs, only one quadruped was smaller than indri, the largest survivor. As forest shrinks and hunting pressure increases, it is the biggest animals who disappear.

How long did it take to dispose of the extinct giants? As the Great Fire burned off the hilltops, the megafauna took refuge in wetter, more resistant forests in valley bottoms like Ampasambazimba. The Vazimba felled trees from these more fertile lands. Their hunters haunted the waterholes. The net squeezed tighter and tighter. The lake bed turned from sanctuary into trap, from forest to grave.

And yet there are still forests in Madagascar. There are still Malagasy legends of ape-like giants and hippo-like water-beasts.[33] There is still the tale told by Monsieur Andrault, a retired forester.

In 1932 or 1933, said Monsieur Andrault, he was hunting deep in the eastern forest, in the area near Perinet. Suddenly he came on an animal only 7 to 10 m distant, clinging to a small bushy tree. It stood about 1¼ meters tall on its hind legs. This huge lemur resembled an indri in being tailless, with black and white fur, but had a far heavier build, especially about the shoulders and arms. Andrault described it as "trapu, costaud, lourdose" (squat, robust, heavy-set). Further, its face was flat and black, not muzzled like the sifaka or indri. Later, Andrault saw a picture of a gorilla and recognized that the gorilla resembled his animal of the forest, but at the time he thought "This has face of one of my ancestors."

He stared at the animal for about five minutes, while it watched him. He considered shooting it, then thought it would be a pity to kill so fine a creature. Besides, he was no scientist and had no means of making an autopsy, although his Malagasy laborers would have been glad to have the meat. At last he stepped nearer.

The beast leaped away, on its hind legs. Its trunk remained vertical, its arms up and out from his shoulders, hands a little above shoulder height: it used its hands for support at each landing. Andrault was amazed that so heavy a creature could move with such lightness. Then, in four or five leaps, it disappeared.

Is the tale true? At least the six friends who listened that evening were convinced. Perhaps we were largely impressed by the succeeding story, a hilarious account of a 4-m crocodile stuck in a turbine pump, under the opaque red water of the Betsiboka River. We reasoned that if M. Andrault could give such a good rendition of the crocodile, he would have made up a far more elaborate version of his giant lemur, once embarked on fiction—even if it were a fiction he believed himself. The very baldness of his account made it convincing: the lemur was there, it looked *so*, it moved *so*, and then it was gone.

The last European before Andrault to claim a sight of a giant lemur was Flacourt in the 17th century. He glimpsed across a pond, the "Tratratratra, large as a two year old calf, with a round head, and a man's face, front and hind feet like a monkey, frizzy fur and short tail."[34] Perhaps it is just wishful thinking on our part or M. Andrault's, but perhaps we have missed seeing such a beast by only 40 years instead of 300 or 1,000 years. Or just perhaps, in the depths of the eastern jungle or the crags of the West, we might find their traces still.

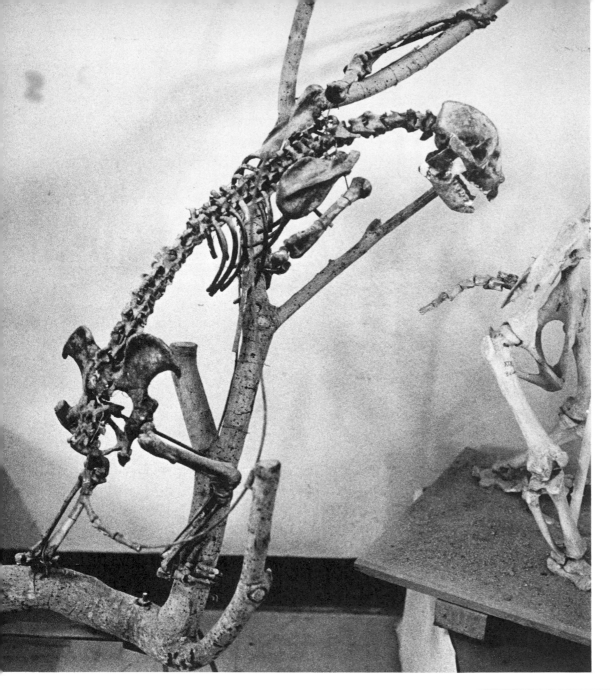

Subfossil lemur (Tananarive Zoo).

Monsieur Andrault, who may have seen *Paleopropithecus* in the early 1930s.

In any case there are no giant lemurs or elephant birds or crocodiles at Ampasam-bazimba. The grass shimmered in the heat waves rising from bare hills; clods of hoed earth lay drying in the sun. The old man who had helped Lamberton excavate called out to one of the farmers, "Where's the fossil you found yesterday?"

"I chucked it on that stone pile."

Georges took the piece. "Look, there is a jaw embedded in the matrix, with teeth sticking through."

The farmers offered another, and another, fragments of limestone bone from the graveyard of the lake bed, and at last a nearly complete skull smoother than a lemur skull, its nasal bones pulled out flat and long.

Many months after, Ian Tattersall suggested that the skull was most likely a fossil aardvark. Aardvarks are as aberrant as their name suggests, a zoological as well as philological joke. They have been unrelated to other mammals since the Paleocene and then most closely to the ancestors of hoofed mammals. Our Malagasy aardvark was the most aberant of all. It not only ate ants and termites, lapping them into a tubular toothless snout, it not only burrowed into termite hills with sharp, hooked claws, but it jumped. African aardvarks, if beset by dogs, turn somersaults to gain time for digging; possibly the Malagasy aardvark surprised predators by springing straight up in the air. Very likely it jumped right up into trees, like the leaping lemurs, to scale and raid the nests of tree-termites as well as the ground-termite hills.[35]

Georges asked in the end, "If we can find no more fossils, can you show us the Vazimba's tomb for which this valley is named? Do you have a tradition which says just where it was?"

"Of course we know where it is," the farmers replied. "We may not bother over fossils, but we wouldn't lose track of a tomb."

A little aside from the lower part of the basin, above the old lake bed, one of the rice dikes gave way to a pile of heavy stones, untended, sprouting long grass. "It doesn't look like much," the farmers admitted, "but then, he lived too long ago for any relatives to remember, so no one tends the grave. It has been here since the beginning. . . ."

I looked at the few stones, and the gleaming grass-straw, and wondered. If the tomb was really a Vazimba's, perhaps he lived in a time when the fauna of Madagascar were complete. The herbivores' niches that, on other continents, are filled by cows or kangaroos or koalas, baboons or patas monkeys or chimpanzees, were all free here for the lemurs to fill if they could. The niches of all the large carnivores were free, too, with only one extinct fossa, half again as big as the modern one, to fill them, perhaps with its cat-like teeth and claws tearing at the jugular of animals heavier than itself.

As I looked at the tomb, I thought: Vazimba, if you destroyed all those animals, you are in good company. Evolving man in Pleistocene Africa killed off the mastodons and giant pigs, baboons and giraffids, and probably ten other genera of outsized mammals by hunting and by changing their habitat. The first Americans eradicated elephants and ground sloths from the Great Plains, wild camels and horses and four-horned antelopes. Europeans urged on the extinction of cave bear and mammoth, while the ice sheets retreated. Later the spread of European agriculture removed wild horse, auroch, bison, and wolf from one country after another, the survivors surviving only by human permission. Maoris wiped out the moas, which was all the big game New Zealand had to offer them, as recently as you destroyed your elephant birds.[36]

If Madagascar is an island of empty niches, so are all the other continents—wherever man has gone, a wave of extinctions went with him.

But, Vazimba, you and your like in other continents took only the largest, most vulnerable of wild animals—you did not finish the job.

You have left that to us.

THE FROG-LADY'S PICNIC

"Don't underestimate the plateau," said Marguerite Razarhelisoa. "At last we have reached a prairie which has nothing to do with man. We are now at 2,000 metres above sea level. From here on up to the highest peak of the Ankaratra massif, at 2,600 metres, the montane heath is above the tree-line."

"When can we start frog-hunting, Mam'selle?" asked six-year-old Morris, bounding with eagerness to reach the object of our expedition.

"Lunch first," replied Marguerite firmly. "I have brought my university students here on field trips year after year, and I know that no excursion succeeds if you neglect lunch. Look over that way, Morris, see if you can make out the palaces of Tananarive. On a clear day you can see the city, 150 kilometres to the north."

Marguerite unpacked a rose-patterned rice salad, its tomatoes and olives in concentric whorls, with lettuce leaves as outer petals. As we ate, we stared up the mountainside to the curls of mist at the peaks and out over the valleys, the unpolluted air so transparent that we imagined falling sideways into space, falling in the line of vision forever.

"Don't underestimate the plateau." Marguerite returned to her theme. "In relict patches, like the little woodland on the Forest Station just below us, there are Malagasy reptiles and amphibians and insects enough to keep biologists studying for years, not to mention the plants which remain. You may mourn the giant lemurs; but adjust your minds instead to look at other forms of life."

"What started your own interest in amphibians?" my husband Richard asked.

"Necessity. My students will mostly become teachers in ill-equipped provincial high schools, where they must catch their own study animals. For their sake, I developed local teaching materials and found myself with a research theme. We have something up to a hundred and fifty species of frog, of which only two are found elsewhere—no newts or toads, though, at all."

"Is it true that frogs for dissection were imported here from France? That actually happened in some West African countries."

"Never!" Marguerite was horrified. "The only French frogs in Madagascar were two I brought in myself for comparative study. My whole aim is to prevent such a thing ever happening. As in Europe, every school biology student dissects his frog if he does nothing else. Our available books were all written in terms of *Rana esculens*, the European frog whose natural habitat is garlic butter. My first work, then, was a dissection manual for the sarobakaka, *Rhacophorus goudoti*, a frog the size of a man's hand which lives in our irrigation ditches. Now I am writing a similar fish dissection manual, which is more of a challenge because it is in Malagasy, not French. You have no idea of the ingenuity it takes to create Malagasy equivalents for anatomical terms!"

"What animals have you studied yourself?"

"Oh, various groups. Perhaps the most amusing is the burrowing frog, *Pletodontohyla tuberata*. It lives on the plateau, in the region we have just driven through. It thrives near man because it likes the soft earth of cultivated fields. The burrowing frog is almost spherical, with a grass-green hieroglyph on its back and a brown background that matches the light volcanic soil of this region. As soon as you put it down on loose earth or sand, it starts to swim backwards into the ground, kicking up concentric waves of sand around its hinder end. It turns as it goes, corkscrewing downwards. In seconds the frog completely buries itself with only a little depression of trembling sand above the animal's nose to show where it is still digging. At last even the depression disappears.[37] Unfortunately I won't bother hunting one for you today, because they hibernate 30 to 60 cm underground, during our winter, and we aren't organized for a day of random digging ourselves.

"Morris, if you'll consent to wipe the chocolate mousse off your chin we can now go frog-fishing. No, not up, down among the trees. Don't slip."

We skidded down almost vertically through the protecting ring of forestry plantation pines. At once moisture engulfed us, as though the air were filled with fine spray from an icy waterfall.

Tree ferns and ground ferns bent downward in the windless air and gave way to sloping carpets of smooth moss where sheets of water flow downhill whenever it rains. Mountain orchids perched on the tree trunks. More different orchids grow at these heights even than in lowland rainforest, as well as 178 species of fern.[38] A bouquet of pink orchids bloomed from a headless tree-fern trunk as though they had chosen a 6-m tall flowerpot. Even the light twinkled like sun breaking through a spring shower, catching up and dancing with the last drops too slow to run away.

The montane mist (or moss) forest is lush in a very different fashion from lowland rainforest. The whole scale is smaller, not just total height but the details as well. Lowland forest is an interlace where lianas and trunks and aerial roots and tree-layers twine and arcade about one another. The montane lushness, instead, was furry; layers of green plush were around everything, almost as though the plants were keeping themselves warm.

The stunted forest of mountains may be so because they are too wet, not just too cold. In the moisture chamber of moss, leaves cannot transpire excess water to draw up nutrients from the soil. They are starved of nutrients like Japanese bonzai. Hordes of epiphytes—ferns and orchids—perch on the soil itself as though it offers no more sustenance than a tree branch. The highest, most extreme mist forests are called elfin woodlands, for their tiny growth in enveloping cloud.[39]

"Mademoiselle Frog-Lady!" called Morris in the all too clear tones of childhood. "Mam'selle Frog-Lady, I see just what you mean. A frog would *love* it here."

Marguerite beamed. "Quite right, Morris. Some species of frog spend all their lives in the moss, never moving to a stream. The perpetually wet ground is a perfectly congenial habitat for tadpoles."

The ravine engulfed Marguerite, who set a fast pace, children and assistants slithering down the gorge side after her. When we caught up she was in the streambed, fishing at the foot of a tiny tumbling cascade with an ordinary kitchen sieve. At each sweep she pulled up one or two wriggling tadpoles. "These are *Mantidacytlus leavis.* They are such strong swimmers they can live even at the foot of waterfalls. Morris, try fishing over here, where the water has swirled and scooped out a sandy basin under the rock like a micro-swimming pool—you'll find tadpoles clustering on the sand.

"Ignace," she called to an assistant, "What is the water temperature?"

"Twelve to thirteen degrees."

"That's 55° Farenheit. Don't fall in."

Morris and Georges Randrianasolo's sons Solo and Mamy took turns sieve-fishing while the university technicians collected stream water for analysis of oxygen, organic content, and minerals. Marguerite amiably watched the boys' efforts to make sure they were not too successful, for she will return in a month's time to compare the tadpoles left in the stream with those she is cultivating in the laboratory.

"Probably these tadpoles will not develop at all for the next two months," she explained. "They overwinter as larvae in the cold streams, and only metamorphose when spring comes. Those that hatch from spring eggs, however, change into adults before the next winter season."

At last we turned uphill, one technician photographing orchids, another lugging water and tadpoles. Then Solo found the swing—a moss-fringed liana big enough for all the children at once to swing on, soaring far out over the soft slanting hillside, while the liquid gold sun flowed endlessly down through the rows of the tree ferns.

So, down from the mountain. Down past the open-field foot of the same stream where Marguerite promised, "Only ten minutes," but Solo and Mamy fished for an hour, catching four species of frogs and tadpoles. "They'll be zoologists like Georges their father," she approved. Even tadpoles in a fast stream have their separate niches: *Mantidactylus cowani* clung to the bottom with a sucker mouth; *Mantidactylus brevipalmatus* floated near the surface from a distended lower lip, which is both its plankton funnel and its water-wings.[40] Down we went past the "Cold Lake," flocking with 300 of the widespread red-billed duck of southern Africa. There Morris promised he wouldn't fall in, but did, in thigh-deep mire. Solo played hero by excavating him and returned with the claim to have caught the biggest burrowing frog of all. Down past somber pine plantations and gleaming high altitude rice fields, with the two boys, mudded to an identical hue, ostracized to the far back of our Land Rover.

"You see," concluded Marguerite, "You may mourn the giant lemurs; but you may also rejoice in the variety of life which remains, and the fascination still to be found. What remains are gentle, little animals—the sort which appeal to the minds of children and biologists. Should we not simply be grateful for those?"

OPPOSITE: Plateau forest near Fianarantsoa.

$$8$$

SAVING THE UNKNOWN

LEUKEMIA FLOWER

What use, then, is wilderness? People who live in towns and cities and on permanent farms scarcely seem to need it. Even those who do find pleasure from the wild can go to the zoo or study the frogs of tiny relict forests. Do we still need nature wild, uncontrolled, unknown?

The answer is a paradox: we can never know how much we need to unknown. Only when we capture a new species or a new idea in the net of our economic interest, do we suddenly find how much we needed it.

Twenty years ago one Malagasy species turned from the obscurity of the unknown into a vedette of modern medicine. The Madagascar periwinkle, *Catharanthus roseus*, emerged from the rubbish tips of tropical villages to be hailed as a cure for childhood leukemia.

The Madagascar or rosy periwinkle began as a highly local weed. Its pink flowers and glossy leaves evolved in southeastern Madagascar, near Fort Dauphin, one of seven related species that bloom in their own corners of the Malagasy landscape. The periwinkle escaped the island as botanical specimens sent to Paris in 1655 by that same Sieur de Flacourt who wrote about surviving elephant birds.[1] By the 18th century it grew in London's Chelsea Physic Garden, was elegantly figured at Kew, and named by Linnaeus.[2] It did not long stay cooped up with the botanists. It grows in florists' pots, as a garden annual in the temperate zone, and as a perennial shrublet in the tropics. It spread from tropic gardens of the British Empire to colonize hillsides and field edges and vacant lots from Jamaica to Singapore. Presumably, its murderous biochemistry armed the rosy periwinkle for conquest.

Local healers soon understood that this was no innocent invader. It became a miracle drug of folk medicine, prescribed by herbalists in every continent: South Africa, India, Australia, the Philippines, and incidently in Madagascar itself. It is said to cure

138

OPPOSITE: Madagascar periwinkle (*Catharanthus roseus*).

constipation and toothache, malaria and unwanted pregnancies. Dr. Noble, of Toronto, first scientifically tested rosy periwinkle extract because he heard that Jamaican healers prescribed it for diabetes.

Instead of a diabetes cure he found that the "unknown" plant arrested blood cancers. In 1958 he suggested that at last science might have found an effective treatment for childhood leukemia.[3]

Simultaneously Gordon H. Svoboda, of the Eli Lilly pharmaceutical company, was isolating the active principles. He succeeded through the content of vincristine, one of the most important therapeutic products, is only 0.00025% of the dried plant, and this must be separated from more than 40 other related, biologically active compounds. It took 12 tons of dried periwinkle to produce 1 ounce of vincristine sulfate.[4]

After Svoboda's biochemical triumph, doctors experimented more and more hopefully. Their first reports suggested 90% remission for leukemia.

Slowly it appeared that the hopes were too high. At the beginning of this decade, only 10% of children with acute lymphocytic leukemia might live for two years; now 75% can hope for two year's survival.[5] The side effects of the drugs, however, are as lethal as the disease: periwinkle extracts are only reprieve, not cure.

The Madagascar periwinkle does not selectively seek out diseased cells. It acts on one of the most fundamental processes of life. When a cell divides, its chromosomes double themselves and line up in the central plane of the cell like a procession of army worms. Two fans of microtubules connect each chromosome to two central points, one on each side of the cell. (The whole apparatus is called the "mitotic spindle.") At a chemical signal, the microtubules contract, pulling the doubled chromosomes apart and guiding them to each half of the cell like puppets on strings.

Periwinkle drugs unravel the strings.

Electron micrographs show microtubules magnified 20 million times. In periwinkle solution, their component strands of protein untwist into slack loops and curlicues like the end of frayed ropes.[6]

The rosy periwinkle arrests cancer because it stops cells dividing. It attacks similar tubules that aid nerve transmission, and thus leads to nervous degeneration. It attacks the microtubules that underlie amoebic movement, killing cancerous white cells but also blocking a patient's defense against other infection. And, trivially, embarrassingly, it attacks the fastest dividing normal cells of the body: hair root cells, which are wholly replaced every twenty-four hours. Sometimes an injection of periwinkle drugs makes all of a patient's hair fall out.

The Madagascar rosy periwinkle is going strong. Medically it is used in moderation and in combination with other drugs as one of the major weapons in the modern armory against cancer. Biologically, it lets us probe deeper and deeper into the structures of life. Chemically, new compounds are still being discovered, and the known compounds are so complex they defy artificial synthesis. As a chemical factory the weed is still ahead of the biochemists.[7] If you pick up any recent volume of the *Index Medicus*, the cubical dictionary-sized-list of medical articles, you are likely to find ten or a dozen papers each month on the nature and uses of the Madagascar periwinkle. After 300 years' cultivation and 20 years' intensive analysis, the rosy periwinkle remains partly an unknown.

Isalo massif.

Periwinkle roots, harvested for use in preparing
medicine, near Boerhinger warehouse.

What is this to do with the wild? Just this: six species of the same genus still grow only in Madagascar, each with its own secrets. The plateau periwinkle, a weed of the fire-swept grasslands, for instance, has at least five active compounds which are not among the forty-odd known from the rosy periwinkle, or indeed from any other plant.[8] But complete analysis peters out because the rarer species are rare. Tons of plants for biochemical research in the rosy periwinkle give way at the other extreme to the few collected specimens of leathery periwinkle. The leathery periwinkle grows in relict plateau woodlands and merits inclusion in the *Red Data Book of Endangered Species.*[9] One variety, the large-flowered oval periwinkle, grows only on the rock fortress of Isalo, whose ruined donjon keeps of sandstone rise out of the burning prairie, protecting a fauna and flora all their own from the besieging flames.

How do you value what you do not know is there? Twenty years ago the curative powers of the rosy periwinkle were a "superstition" of local healers. Twenty years from now perhaps we shall trace discoveries as important as the rosy periwinkle's to one of those related "unknown" species. At least, since Noble's and Svoboda's work, we can guess that the periwinkle species are unknowns which we may someday need. But what if a neighboring plant of the relict plateau woodlands or in a neighboring cranny of the Isalo sandstone might answer a need we cannot yet formulate?

Saving the wild is saving what we do not yet know: the drug untested, the genetic stock untapped, the species undescribed. It is saving what we do not yet love: indri or sifaka leaping in beauty like the spotted deer of our own childhood. It is saving what we do not yet understand: the working ecosystem.

SIDEWALK SORCERY

Monsieur Rakotosaka slept on a straw mat on the sidewalk of Tananarive. His white lamba was wrapped around him for bedsheet; his straw hat, crisscrossed with green plaits, lay over his face. Under his head for pillow, and in the crook of his arm, were two round, handleless baskets. The baskets exhaled odors that cut through the ranker smells of pavement and gutter—odors of varnish and resin, sage and indigo, and *Kaliphora madagascariensis*, which assaults the sinuses.

At five he rose, stretched, spat, unrolled his day-mat, and laid out his wares. The Malagasy names would seem as strange as the Latin ones: a bunch of *Phellolychium madagascariensis* to cure newborn-baby pimples, *Leptolaena fauciflora* for syphillis (one of an endemic plant family, the Sarcolaenacea), immortelle for bloody diarrhea, indigo for neuralgia, sage against evil luck. One plant he prescribes for diabetes or for hypoglycemia, saying scornfully that townsmen who can buy too much sugar can afford modern sugar diseases. Another, *Vernonia*, he sells frankly as a panacea.

The panacea, or general tonic, supports yet further links in the informal commerce of the marketplace. Monsieur Rakotosaka gathers herbs at his country village, searching the prairie and the rocks sheltered from fire. Every Thursday he boards a bush-taxi for Tananarive, to sleep on the pavement ready for Friday market. On Friday passers-by stop and haggle and compare, while the town-based tonic sellers purchase their weekly stock.

OPPOSITE: Herb seller in front of pharmacy (Tananarive).

Sidewalk display of medicinal herbs (Tulear). Chalk is for face-painting.

A tonic seller squatted by Rakotosaka's mat to finger the vernonia. The man carried a shiny aluminum jug, with a long spout like a gallon-sized watering can. A bunch of five little mugs hung at the end of the spout. The aluminum wares, of course, come from another part of the market, made and sold by yet more traditional craftsmen. The tonic seller bought Rakotosaka's vernonia, then brewed it into herbal tea. At ten in the morning, the tonic seller walked through the market and into the doors of office buildings calling out "Mangidy! Mangidy! Bitter! Bitter!" Many of the office workers drink a cup of bitter tonic every morning although there is no scientific proof that anything more than their own conviction is acting to improve their health.

The informal herbalist has strange links with the modern world. Rakotosaka sells *Haronga madagascariensis* to cure his client's stomachaches. German chemists have refined the active principles into a drug called harunganin, which is available now to dyspeptic Europeans. The best known of all Malagasy scientists, Dr. Ratsimamanga, shares the credit for refining a creeping weed of the rice fields, *Centella asiatica*, into the commercial wound-healer Madecassol. Dr. Ratsimamanga later became Malagasy ambassador to France. He was in part responsible for lifting the commercial restrictions on sidewalk herb-sellers like Rakotosaka. "It is obvious," he says, "that our people cannot pay Western prices for medicines. We must both use and develop our indigenous knowledge."

Rakotosaka the herbalist rolled up his mats in the slack hours of Friday afternoon and strolled along to the park at Tananarive Zoo. He brought a selection of herbs, tied in bunches, for Dr. Razafindrambao, Chief of the National Institute of Research into Medicinal Herbs. He spread them for display on the laboratory bench, near the bound volumes of the *Flora of Madagascar,* much as he had spread them on the sidewalk.

Dr. Razafindrambao gathered the plants to show his colleague Armand Rakotozafy for botanical identification just in case of surprises, but only one of the collection interested him for further testing. This the herbalist called mahaibé, "the wise one," a basil species. The herbalist said it treated bubonic plague.

Even under the biochemist's questioning the herbalist stuck to his story. He has seen a man with plague, and he himself has gathered the mahaibé which cured him. Dr. Razafindrambao once collected the same plant, and the same tale, from a herbalist 800 km away near Tulear. When men of different regions offer the same cures, there is slightly more chance that the cure is no local superstition but an effective drug.

Two French doctors, Gerard and Robic, developed the first modern plague vaccine at the Pasteur Institute of Tananarive. It would be ironic if the Malagasy had known all along a partial antidote for the Black Death.

A vast number of the medicinal herbs are already familiar and are indexed in published lists.[10] Many have already been tested for chemical and biological activity. Of course, there are many steps between first realizing that a product is active and its use as a modern drug. Rauwolfia, the Indian snakeroot, for instance gives us the tranquilizer reserpine. There are some indications that the Malagasy species of snakeroot works as well as the Indian one but without the depressive side effects.[11]

Traditional medicine also has its science. The most famous Malagasy drug is

Aloe capitata at Angavokely.

Clove-like tree commonly eaten by lemurs.

Lycopodium (at Angavokely), an opiate which gives courage to fighting cocks.

Euphorbia at Tulear.

Cerbera tanguin, the ordeal tree. It is a member of the Apocynacea family, like the Indian snakeroot and the Madagascar periwinkle itself. In the time of Radama I, if a person was acused of witchcraft, even by only one accuser, traditional laws prescribed ordeal by tanghin poison.

The surviving records of the king's sorcerers recount their incantations and procedures. Reading them makes it clear how hard men strive for science and justice, even while poisoning their fellowman face to face. The scientific spirit, like scientific knowledge, is not an all-or-none phenomenon of the past two centuries in the West.

A shaman opened the ordeal by chanting an invocation to the spirit of the tanghin tree. Chiefs and judges and even kings might be corrupted in a trial; they might be bound by spells; they might be simply unable to see past the surface of things. The shaman called instead on the all-seeing spirit of the ordeal tree to render abstract justice, not the partial justice of mankind.[12]

The accused squatted before the shaman on a mat inside a smoky hut, while witnesses watched to be sure that all was in order. It must have taken at least three or four hours of prescribed procedures before the accused actually swallowed his tanghin. It needs time and ritual to convert murder into execution.

One part of the ritual bore unpleasant similarity to the modern LD_{50}: the lethal dose for 50% of tested animals. By United States and European laws, pharmaceutical companies establish this dosage level for new drugs, food additives, and cosmetic components as an index of toxicity. The Malagasy shaman confined himself to a mere two experimental animals: two small chickens who were dosed with tanghin before the eyes of the accused. One chicken must live; the other died in paroxysms. If the dosage was not right, or even if the wrong chicken lived or died, the test was repeated with further birds until an LD_{50} was achieved, while the shaman prayed:

"It is not for vengeance, nor partiality, nor hate that we wish to kill this one, nor by particular favor that we wish to leave that one in life. We do not seek indulgent decisions nor pitiless ones, but a judgement which will not lie, will not cheat, will not deceive."

At last the accused squatted down before a clean mat with the objects of his execution before him. He ate a measured quantity of dry-cooked rice and three greasy morsels of uncooked skin from a fat chicken, both to help him live and as controlled conditions for the contents of his stomach. Finally he drank two grated tanghin pits mixed with water measured from a special spoon. (Of course, it was wise to reserve a particular spoon for tanghin—one would hardly want traces left in the daily rice.) After a time measured in minutes of chanting, witnesses began to feed him flour gruel. He either vomited quickly, returning the three pieces of chicken skin, flour, rice, and tanghin, or else he died, neither quickly nor painlessly.

Tanghin has been tested by modern drug firms for its reserpine-like effect. It may be a relief that the therapeutic dose is nearly the lethal dosage, so it seems unlikely that westerners will be fed extracts of the ordeal tree, at least in the near future. The tanghin poison is still stored in laboratory notebooks, against the discovery of future need. Meanwhile, present-day Malagasy use it only for murder or suicide.

PART 4

LEEWARD DOMAIN: WILDERNESS AND INDEPENDENCE

9

THE SPINY DESERT

THE MULTINATIONAL AND THE MOUSELEMUR

A 2-m aloe blazed like a red and yellow torch before the blue sea. Crown-of-thorns euphorbia, their gray strands tipped with crimson flowers, clung spikily in the fissures of granite. The sea-surge of milky azure crashed into rock clefts, foamed, sucked back to crash again.

We stood on the peninsula of Lokaro at the southeastern corner of Madagascar. Between us and Antarctica 5,000 kilometres southward, the waves and the soaring albatross endlessly circled the globe.

Inland the western skyline was a mountain range, ragged like the magnified edge of a razor blade. Those mountains, 2 km high and only 30 inland, are enough to force the moisture out of the trade winds, bathing themselves and the coastal strip in a rainfall of 2,500 m a year. Tomorrow night we would sleep on the other side of those mountains, in the village of Hazofotsy, 50 km away as the crow flies, where rainfall is down to 200 m.

Today, at Lokaro, we said good-by to moisture and lushness, to pawpaws and pineapples, to the easy, well-watered life of the coast. Ironically, having reached the last beachhead we stood among plants adapted to drought. The aloe and the crown-of-thorns survived on impervious crystalline rock, where the rain ran off at once into the sea: between rains they survive as though in a desert. *Stephanotis floribunda,* now naturalized in the world's flower-shops, also grows on the rock peninsulas. Few brides would picture the delicate white stephanotis of their bouquets rooted on Malagasy granite in the salt spray of the southeast trades.

Inland there is water but still little food for the plants. The Malagasy pitcher plant grows in acid, near sterile soil in the coastal bogs. Each leaf begins as a perfectly commonplace blade, then, at its tip, coils to a couple of loops twisted like a telephone wire, and then untwists into a conical death-trap for unfortunate insects. The red-lined lid attracts flies; the slippery lip and inner cup give them no footing; at the bottom waits

OPPOSITE: Giant aloe (*Aloe helenae*) on Lokaro peninsula.

Pitcher plant (*Nepenthes madagascariensis*).

Village on Lokaro peninsula.

a goblet of enzymes to digest the pitcher plant's victims. We found flies, grasshoppers, moths twitching as they dissolved. From one pitcher goggled a tiny tree frog with gelatinous green back and peach-orange paws. Its suckers held, unhindered, to the plant's waxy side. The little frog was apparently waiting to intercept a victim en route into the pitcher plant's maw.

Where the sterile white sand is better drained, coastal forest grows: some of the 40 endemic species of pandanus, beach orchids, and mangrove crabs. A little higher we found a vaccinium shrub whose white flowers and green berries are beloved by mouselemurs—small wonder, as vaccinium is also the genus of blueberries and cranberries.

This coastal forest is the start of our east–west journey: it was also the start of the first determined attempt by Europeans to settle in Madagascar. In 1642 a party of Frenchmen landed at Sainte Luce, the next peninsula to the north. They found the coastal forest "nearly impenetrable"; half their men died at Sainte Luce of fever. They were forced to the site of Fort Dauphin, a harbor whose present-day wrecks show that it still leaves something to be desired in the way of protection from on-shore gales.[1]

The new site was healthier but subject to attack by local Malagasy, whose attitude began with friendly trade and marriage but soured with the realization that the newcomers planned to trade only on their own terms, including the sale of Malagasy as slaves. Eventually Sieur Étienne de Flacourt arrived in 1648 to govern the disintegrating settlement. He survived attacks, treachery, and the indifference and bankruptcy of the company which founded the colony but died at last in 1660, when his ship was attacked by Barbary pirates and exploded in the combat. Final massacres left only a handful of fever-stricken settlers to beg their passage home in 1664.

The settlement of Fort Dauphin would be forgotten, insignificant as the earlier Portuguese garrison massacred at the nearby Bay of Galleons or the slightly later English foothold near Tulear, except for one thing: Sieur de Flacourt wrote a book. His *Histoire de la Grande Isle de Madagascar*, published in 1661, was the account of a keen, educated, and interested observer. He described people, language, history, plants, wild and cultivated, and Aepyornis, the elephant bird. He wrote of the "sifac," a white lemur "which often goes upon its hind legs"—and which no other naturalist noticed until Alfred Grandidier arrived more than 200 years later.[2] Flacourt did not even neglect to mention of the little gray squirrel-like Tsitsihy, or lepilemur, and the swaggering ringtail in its "troops of 30, 40, 50."

Among the mineral wealth of the island Flacourt listed iron, steel, silver, gold native and imported from Mecca, rock-crystal, topaz, garnet, amethyst, opals, aquamarines, bloodstone, agate, chalcedony, jasper. All are there today, but it is not the jewels of oriental splendor which bring today's wealth. Instead it is mica for electric components, thorianite ore rich in uranium, and perhaps now titanium.

When Flacourt's men landed at St. Luce they found half a dozen drunken sailors left from the crew of a Captain Goubert, sent specifically to look for a zinc mine. Flacourt surmised that Goubert's men, finding no mine, had simply scuttled their own ship and "then the merchandise they had brought served as largesse to the women of the country and to the Negroes, who brought them wine and honey from all sides, and so they lived in drink and debauchery, mocking the merchants who sent them."

United States Steel has far too long an arm for its employees to scuttle their ship and live on wine and honey in southern Madagascar, but the transnational corporation is the modern heir of those merchants who sent their ships across the world in search of minerals.

In the center of the Mandena forest station, in the patch of coastal forest where Bob Martin deciphered much of mouselemur social structure, stood a wooden tower: a pilot plant, or rather, a pilot machine. Its spiral conveyor belts rose and fell, while water washed the sand grains that slid to the inside of the spiral. For six weeks the belts washed white sparkling sand to the outside of the spiral, while heavy gray sand shifted to the inside—the dull gray color of titanium ore. For six weeks only the plant worked, then was dismantled and shipped back whence it came, leaving only excavated trenches in the north–south line of fossil and sand dunes to show where it had been.

Only a few trenches are left and a computer printout on the other side of the world, which records the concentration of ore from each trench, and, as important, the physical properties: titanium grain size as small as face powder would require sophisticated separation techniques, whereas grains nearer the size of the ordinary sand can be removed by weight fairly simply. Then, when the computer has dealt with the geological part (it took two years of mapping, marching, digging, building to reach this point) men will do the complicated calculations, the economic and political ones. If the figures look right and the Malagasy government agrees, U.S. Steel might eventually sieve through the dunes on a big scale with 12-m trenches. The excavated sand would be sent to factory ships (hard to nationalize) for extraction, and then the cleaned sand would be returned to the beach. The fact that the sand would also be cleaned of all vegetation and that the endemic coastal forest has no hope of recolonizing, seems a side issue to all concerned.

Giulio Raeder was engineer of the project, one of those men both born and trained to be pioneers. Raeder surveyed the fossil dunes and installed the separation plant, dealing one after the other with the resistance of nature, men, and machines. Raeder became defensive at once. "I can't stop you taking or publishing photographs. I checked to see if I could. This is Forest Station ground, so I can't."

He admitted that the last job he worked on was fouled up by conservationists. U.S. Steel had a titanium concession which included the highest sand dune in South Africa, as well as rare beach flora. "It gave the conservationists something to scream about. What the hell, we weren't going to touch *that* dune. And titanium mining is one of the cleanest extracting operations there are—all you get is a beach whiter than you started out with. But no, the conversationists managed to block the whole concession. At least in Madagascar I thought we'd be safe from meddlers. . . ."

"You mean, in Madagascar people cannot afford to take the view that a few trees here and there could matter more than cash in hand. Well, I think you are right. What matters very much more is the nature of the final contract—whether it puts cash in Malagasy hands or only in U.S. Steel's. Just possibly it could even help conservation if

Titanium-extracting plant, north of Fort Dauphin, owned by US Steel.

Waterfall at Manantantely.

the Malagasy bargained hard enough to get a fair share and then used the money for development, which allows people to take some of the pressure off the land."

"You're an odd conservationist."

"Well, it's a fact of life that poor countries aren't like rich ones. The one thing that bothers me, though, is why you had to put your pilot plant smack in the middle of natural woodland in amongst the mouselemurs, instead of on any of the miles of burned and barren dunes that have no other use than zebu pasture."

"Privacy. The forest station is government land. Nobody bothers us in the woods—and nobody here cares what we do in it."

THE WATERSHED

The road west from Fort Dauphin meanders through lush lowlands, past roadside stands with their pawpaws and beef-heart fruit, past an Antanosy tomb whose standing stones and crosses, carved boat for the soul voyage of the dead and carved lady carrying her Bible, catalogue the changing faiths of this land.

It rolls past Manantantely, the "village of wild honey" where the mountains' southern foothills shoulder almost to the road, covered with the white trunks and green canopy of eastern forest, where chestnut-colored lemurs grunt sleepily into their orange beards. The Waterfall by Manantantely falls west and south—already we were skirting the watershed: we had left the east coast behind.

It climbed to the col of Ranopiso, first home of the leukemia periwinkle and the only home of the three-cornered palm. Even in the tiny reserve set aside for this species, in the tiny relict of transitional forest, people hack off palm fronds for roof thatch. Why should people who rarely travel 10 miles in a lifetime know that the palm itself has a distribution of only 10 square miles?

Down from the col—there, at last, stretched out westward the sea of the spiny desert, the Didierea bush-land, spiked and spined, hostile and unrelenting.

Ten-metre spires of alluaudia rose up above the rest, giant's hands of bunched fingers raised toward the sky. Below them spread a gray-green tangle, close-set branches interlocking. Occasionally the colossal white trunk of a baobab stood clear, holding up its leafless branches, which are, according to legend, actually roots, for God by mistake planted the baobab upside down. Here and there the spire of a giant *Aloe helenae* rose like a red-tipped spear thrust through the gray—the only real color, and a menacing one, in the whole landscape. (*Aloe suzannae*, whose lemon yellow flower spike accounts for 2 m of its 6-m total height, is either too rare to see or simply extinct.) The only movement was a plume of dust, where an Antandroy herdsman followed his file of zebu on the long trek to water.

In the torrential rains of December and January the baobabs wear round crowns of green leaves proportioned like gigantic green-capped mushrooms. Line-storms stride over the land, swinging thunderbolts like a cane, trailing a coat of rain. Cyclones cross the mountains, the wind shrieking relentlessly hour after hour, uprooting trees, ripping off tin roofs like an old can kicked out of the way, and scattering wooden houses like handfuls of dry grass.

But we felt no rain: rain falls almost entirely in the summer months of December, January, February, and March. In September the dry season was nearing its peak, the brief cool of July already over. All but the hardiest trees stood leafless. In September the first flowers bloom: many trees of the spiny desert flower and fruit in the coming months, leaving seeds ready to germinate when the rains fall. This is winter, a winter of heat and dryness. A northerner from the snows can understand such winter, in spite of the heat shimmer over the land, because plants and animals have drawn into themselves. Like the winter of the snow the winter of drought is the land's death. But, like snowdrops and willow catkins blooming in frost, those blood-red aloe flowers herald the advent of spring.

Down we drove into the plain, turned north at the town of Amboasary, and circled back on a dirt track by the Mananara River. Only three hours' drive off the main road along the dirt track, with the dust lining our throats and fringing our eyelashes, brought us to Hazofotsy village, at the moon's edge.

Hazofotsy is an Antandroy cattle camp: bare, shadeless. Some of the tiny plank houses are no bigger than chicken coops; four, including Chief Tohimbinty's, are tall enough to stand up in.

Only one tree grows in the village, chiefly used to hang things on, though a great baobab guards the zebu corral in the sacred direction, to the east, while low thorn scrub more or less shields the unclean, or toilet, direction of the west.

"Do you remember me? I visited you five years ago when Alison Richard was staying here studying sifaka. You all came into Alison's house in the evening. A man played the lokanga, the one-stringed fiddle, and a girl tried to teach me to dance."

"Yes, of course we remember that evening. Of course you are welcome to stay here. Chief Tohimbinty will lend you his own house for your stay, the same one that Alison used when she lived here.

"And how is our Alison Richard, our Alisony? Tell her that Apelamary has a new daughter, Volamary has a daughter, Korosy has a daughter, and Tohimbinty sends his regards."

Again I am overwhelmed by the dignity and kindness of the villagers. In this prickly and inhospitable land, the sun beats down from the sky, the dust rises from the ground, and the plants reach out with fingers to claw as you pass. Then you come to a village of huts which seem thrown at random on the bare ground like a handful of knucklebones, and at the end you are greeted by proud and independent people in their own homes, who accept the wanderers benighted there as fellow humans.

FOREST OF NO SHADE

Hazofotsy lies beside the spiny forest, on the edge of one of the national wilderness reserves. This is a semidesert thick with trees that tear at you when you try to walk through. This is a forest of no shade where the sun beats directly onto the naked sand. There are leaves, a few leaves, even in the worst of September—but they are the fleshy lobes of alluaudia, set vertically to escape the noon light, or leaves which droop limply as the sun rises and extend only in the kinder rays of dawn and dusk. Many plants grow no leaves at all but consist of swollen green stems, like *Euphorbia stenoclada,* which can be milked for its latex to make glass cement or used in traditional fashion calk pirogues.

The light beats down and dazzles, and the heat shimmer rises. Although there are green plants, the thorn forest feels black, white, and gray. The white is sun, the black is the underlining of shadow, pure absence of light. The defensive vegetables are not colors but patterns—patterns of repulsion. Blunt thorns of *Alluaudia procera* twist in helices around the plants' gray 10-metre spires. The thorns of *Alluaudia ascendens* (a species confined to this valley) are studded all over its reddish bark like knobs on a mace. *Alluaudia dumosa's* thorns grow on branches of linked bulges; *Alluaudia antephora* has thin, branched thorny stems almost in the shape of a real tree. *Alluaudiopsis* grows directly from the rock in bouquets of thorn-studded whips. Almost needless to say, all these plants belong to an endemic Malagasy family, the Didiereacea.[3]

The other pattern, besides thorns, is the pattern of swelling. Baobabs, by their size, are noble, but commiphora bottle-trees, smaller and equally inflated, are merely gross, although an African commiphora produces the fragrant resin we call myrrh. The sausage tree has linked, leafless stems swollen like infected fingers. The elephants'-foot tree belongs to another genus of water-bottle plants, its engorged trunk topped with a ridiculous tuft of green leaves. This species bears triple thorns whose shadows intermesh in star patterns down the trunk. However, even these do not guard the tree. Men slash holes to reach the bitter fluid inside, which you can use for washing, or if desperate to drink.

The worst thorns of all are the harpoon burrs. Scattered through the forest grow small trees with golden yellow flowers, pretty as tree-born petunias, that rest the eyes among the endless bare thorns. The pretty petunias turn into burrs armed with tetragonal recurved hooks. The first that caught my shirt I pulled at casually—it came off sunk deep in my finger ends (the punctures lasted three days). As I freed it from my fingers, it settled into my trouser cuff. I kicked it off with my tennis shoe and found it clawing into the rubber. Thereafter I sat down and removed harpoon burrs by their one safe handle, with all the delicacy of a grooming monkey. Pity the zebu that tries to lick one off its flank with its tongue.

As usual, though, mechanical defense is less lethal than chemical arms: plants which do not scratch, poison. The laro, another of the leafless sausage trees, drips white latex that ulcers bare skin, or, in the eyes, can blind.

But why do the plants of the spiny desert need such armor? It is clearly defense against animals, and against fairly large animals: insects simply walk between the thorns. The pressure of browsing is probably as intense in rainforest with its thousands of interwoven species as it is in semiarid land, yet in rainforest a very low proportion of plants are thorny; here the majority. Rainforest plants have the option of simply outgrowing their predators, replacing browsed foliage as fast as it is removed. The arid zone plants presumably grow, or keep, a very closely calculated area of leaf during the dry season. With too much leaf too much water evapotranspires, so that the plants lack

Baobab and Didiereas along path into spiny desert (near Hazofotsy).

Alluaudia procera (Hazofotsy).

Latex tree (*Euphorbia laro*), sap of which causes blindness.

The human harpoon burr (*Uncarina grandidieri*).

Alluaudiopsis (Hazofotsy).

water; if they bear too little leaf they lack nutriment. If heavy browsing upsets the plants' calculations, they may be quickly brought below a critical minimum, and in the dry season it would be particularly difficult to find reserves for growth to restore the proper balance.

Defense of leaf area goes with defense of the water-storing trunk. In arid and semiarid regions the world over, plants develop thick, leathery, waterproof bark and often a waxy surface as well to reduce their water loss. Southern Madagascar again is one case of a general rule. Thorns arranged all down such a trunk, as in the elephants'-foot tree, may guard against wounds in the leathery skin, which threaten to tap the plants' vital juices. Quite possibly the greatest danger to desert plants is not simple browsing but hemorrhage.

Which animals could pose such a threat? In this forest you would expect formidable opponents for such formidable vegetables. Not man and his zebu: zebu are grazers by choice like other cattle and tackle Euphorbia only in times of famine. Besides, the plants evolved long before cattle arrived on the Malagasy scene.

It may be that the now extinct giant lemurs roamed this forest and that the plants still stand with lances raised against enemies defeated centuries ago. The modern browsers are at first sight ridiculously innocent: the fubsy gray lepilemur by night and the superb white sifaka by day. Either animal can seem everyone's instant imaginary pet: the large eyes, the muzzle long enough to be animal, not parody human but held downward so that you gaze into the eyes of a baby, and above all that soft fur, tooth-combed daily to perfect fluffiness, so that even in watching you can feel its caress on your fingertips, a visual antidote to the harpoon burr.

The plants, fairly evidently, react otherwise.

In early September the little gray lepilemurs concentrate on the flowers of the tall *Alluaudia procera*, climbing up to browse on the sea-urchin bouquet of inflorescences at the very tip of each arm. Later in the month they shift their attentions to the red-barked *Alluaudia ascendens*, browsing their way along emerging flowers that line the twigs. These two plants tide lepilemur over until new leaves begin appearing in October. At this critical season in September in a dry year lepilemurs dispensed about as much energy for their metabolism and their infrequent movements as they were consuming.[4] In short, both the animals and the food supply were on very narrow margins, though in other years and seasons they have a surplus of food.[5]

The other leaf eater of the forest, the white sifaka, was the goal of the morning's walk. We hoped to find one of the two groups which Alison Richard studied in 1970 and 1971 and revisited in 1974. Whenever we saw movement, far off through the branches, we walked toward it, hoping that it would materialize into white fur, black heart-shaped face, and lemon-yellow eyes watching us over the blunt muzzle. Alison Richard has told us what they eat: leaves and flowers of alluaudia like the lepilemur but also mature leaves of all the abundant species and most of the rare ones in the forest. The sifaka seem a good candidate for the total browser undiscouraged by thorns. Furthermore they eat bark. In September 1970 one group of sifaka spent 15% of their time chiseling out of the soft moist wood of *Operculicarya*, which is 80% water by weight.

Alluaudia procera (Berenty).

Alluaudia procera in leaf (Berenty).

In June they stripped the bark of the bitter-juice tree, apparently not for water, but for food or even medicine. Ernest Ranjatson, our forester guide, in between spelling plants' names for me in French, Latin, and Malagasy, hacked off strips of bitter-juice bark with a borrowed coupe-coupe. He explained that he promised some to a lady with a sick baby in Fort Dauphin. It is febrifuge, which cures malarial anemia.

(Later I learned it also flavors local rum, but such suspicions would belittle Ernest.)

"Sifaka!" cried Ernest. "Over there!"

We fanned out to try to see the sifaka group, but they fled at speed, white fur flickering through the alluaudia fingers.

The thorns formed patterns and dazzle patterns: the animals repeated the theme of black and white. The southern version of the Madagascar magpie robin showed up, pied black and white on his singing perch, as visible here as his eastern race was invisible in the rainforest of Hiaraka. The sickle-billed vanga, another of the Vangid family we first saw on Hiaraka, nested in baobab trees beside the white-headed vanga. Sickle-bills occasionally feed the young of the white-headed vangas, although this may be merely by mistake.[6] (The sickle-bill with its probing beak and the tiny coral-beaked nuthatch are the only Malagasy birds which take insects from cracks in tree bark, leaving a true woodpecker's way of life to the aye-aye.)

After the succession of black-and-white birds, the crested coua with its slate blue back and rufous bib looked positively garish. It squawked and postured in its usual obstreperous fashion, at home in the spiny desert as in all the other western woodlands. The crested coua may be the pride of an endemic Malagasy family but it is an egg-eating omnivore with the manners of a blue jay.

Then reptiles took up the theme of colorless pattern all over again: the antandroy radiated tortoise, its scales in Op-art dazzle pattern, blond stars on black scales instead of the black star-shadows of thorns on gray bark. The first tortoise we found was paint splashed as well. A forester had caught a man with 40 tortoises for sale, so he imprisoned the man and released the tortoises, paint marked for reidentification, here in the reserve. Forty tortoises is small-scale pilfering: in 1922, before they were protected animals, 16,400 kg of these tortoises was exported in one year to Mauritius and Reunion.[7] Fortunately, the radiated tortoise is taboo to most of the people in its home area—Tohimbinty's village will not simply recatch the released captives.[8] I am assured that the radiated tortoise is very good if marinated for a week in wine. I have tried only Malagasy-style tortoise stew with tomato and onion, which feels like boiled gray art erasers.

I much prefer Alison Richard's version: she was sitting watching her sifaka at high noon, while the sifaka drowsed in the shaded crotch of an alluaudia. Alison herself stayed awake only to fill in the minute-by-minute entry on her check sheets: resting—resting—resting. In the silence the sparse leaf-litter began to rustle. Her skin crawled as the rustling composed itself into footsteps: deliberate, heavy footsteps approaching. She was about to leap to her feet to confront the invisible giant striding through her forest when the tortoise's head poked up over a fallen log.

Lizards huddled in the shade of the fallen logs: one black with white polka dots

Radiated tortoise.

Underside of Radiated tortoise.

Lizard with pineal eye-spot (*Zoonosaurus hazofotsi*).

Spiny-tailed lizard (*Oplurus*). Iguanid lizards, like boid snakes, live in Madagascar and South America.

which we dubbed the guinea-fowl lizard. Another, a pale gray oplurus, bore thorns all down its tail like a fallen alluadia twig. The strangest lizard by far runs on the bare rocks that in the rains are stream beds. In the center of its head is a round black spot, for all the world like a "heaven-directed eye."[9]

The black spot covers the lizard's pineal eye, an outgrowth of the brain. In mammals like ourselves the pineal organ has sunk into the brain itself. This strange body seemed so discrete a part of the nervous system, and its functions so baffling, that Descartes considered it the point at which the soul influences the body. For Descartes the pineal was the principal reservoir of those "animal spirits" which he imagined flowing along the nerves to mechanically direct our movements. In man alone these spirits might be affected by perturbations in the mind or soul.

Only in the last ten years have scientists discovered the pineal organ's true function: it links the ebb and flow of bodily tides with the cycles of light and dark in the world around. The first vertebrate, the ancestor of fish and frogs and reptiles, apparently had an extra pair of real eyes in the middle of its skull which evolved into the later light-clock. In mammals, pineal hormones suppress sexual activity and may control the breeding seasons which are triggered by the changing length of day in spring or autumn.

Some lizards wear a transparent scale that serves as a real lens; our spiny desert lizard had a velvety black spot, far better suited to absorb infrared heat than visible light. Quite possibly the little lizard skittering over the sizzling rocks or shielded from the chill of the desert evening uses the heavenward eye to monitor heat as well as light.

Given the problem of heat defense, there must be great competition for shade. Lepilemurs nest in the rare tree holes; so do the little green Madagascar lovebirds. Eggs in open nests would soft-boil three minutes after sunrise. Where else to find shade? Under stones. I grabbed the nearest flat rock and tipped it over. Tohimbinty reached to stop me, then drew back.

Each flat stone sheltered one flat scorpion.

Squat, black, with crabclaws before and poison ejecting tail curled over behind, the scorpion clung upside down to its rock. As daylight hit it lowered its tail flat and streaked toward my hand. I dropped the rock and then, fascinated, looked again.

Each stone hid only one scorpion, except for one where a large black animal hunched over a pale greenish skeleton—either its own molted skin, or an intruder or a former owner sucked dry. Is this again a territorial system, in which each scorpion owns its stone, forays out at night, and retreats to cling underneath its castle at dawn?

"Sifaka!" Chief Tohimbinty called. We followed an apparently solitary individual, but again it fled at full speed and was lost in the Alluaudia. If we were starting a long-term study, we would persist. Alison Richard simply ran after her groups for three solid days, until they gave up leaping away—but that will not solve the immediate need to photograph willing animals.

Well, perhaps it is like the triple somersault at the circus: if you miss the first two times, people realize the trick is not so easy as it looks.

The third time it worked. I had no need even to say "sifaka." I just pointed. At last a sifaka group, deep in the branching bundle of an Alluaudia, stared calmly down at us with topaz eyes.

A male hopped a little higher on the thorny branches to peer down as we approached. He too was dark and white, pattern rather than color. His dark brown cap outlined his white brow in a widow's peak; the line of his black face had a jag up on the left side, his white cheeks were slightly shadowed with brown—individual quirks by which we could recognize him again and by which sifaka probably recognize one another.

Georges Pariente and Herb Gustafson have independently suggested that the sifaka's dark cap is for heat sensing, its function analogous to the black pigment of the lizard's third eye. Certainly the sifaka maintains its temperature by behavior. In the cool morning he climbs sluggishly into the sunlight and lolls back, arms akimbo, with sparsely furred black chest and belly absorbing the sun's rays. Later in the day he crouches so that his gleaming white back reflects heat and light; still later, by noon, he seeks shade.

The sifaka scattered, slowly, as we approached, each cooing in its throat like a dove as it began to leap. The male and a light-capped female jumped east of the trail, two more to the west. The cooing before motion and the scattering of the groups were not just due to us. Here in the spiny forest food resources are so sparse that family members commonly move and feed out of sight of one another, keeping track by soft noises as they go.[10]

Perhaps I should not say "family." The sifaka group usually has more than one male and more than one female, averaging five adults and subadults. It is by no means clear how closely they are related; it is clear that group membership can change, especially in the mating season. Sifaka have a highly synchronized mating season, perhaps only two weeks in any one forest, and a female is receptive for only about four days. During the mating season males roam, making long sorties through the forest and advances to females of other groups. To take one example, Fiona, one of Alison's females, mated with Fred and Polo from a neighboring group and with Intruder, a strange male, but with no males of her own group at all.

The sifaka's attitude differed toward each challenger. Fred, dominant male of the neighbor group, simply walked or rather leaped in and took over Fiona without opposition. Polo, Fred's subordinate, in contrast, spent two days chasing and being chased by Fiona and Fiona's own group male, Rip. Polo at last severely wounded Rip, gashing him with canines in face and limb, and chased Rip away bleeding red down his white fur. Fiona became a willing partner. By the next day, however, Polo had also vanished. Finally Intruder moved into Fiona's group with no opposition, taking over both Rip's former dominant position and Fiona herself.

The inference is clear that Rip, Fiona, and other members of their group knew all the neighborhood males as individuals: who was challengeable and who was not. It is also evident that a good deal of interchange takes place among groups. On other occasions females as well as males have moved, so the groups may not have even a fixed core of females and young.

One of the puzzling aspects of sifaka social structure is that sex ratio varies widely. Many groups have more males than females; others more females than males; there is no typical group composition. Alison Richard suggests therefore that a sifaka group is really a convenient foraging unit. The members of the foraging group are held by personal ties of current habit or even friendship: they may not be close kin, and they certainly are not necessarily sexual partners.[11]

How do they maintain the bonds of friendship? Partly by simply being together and sometimes in grooming and play. They groom simultaneously, the two heads moving piston-fashion as they lick and tooth-scrape each others' fur. They cuddle in a "locomotive" of animals, one boxed into the great jumping thighs of the next, like children playing train. They play: a juvenile or subadult solicits play with open-mouthed "play face" (like our own or any other primate child); adults respond and join in chasing or wrestling. Sifaka play achieves its hilarious effect in the habitual leaf-eaters' slow motion: both animals hang by their feet and fumble for a hold on each others' wrists, ears, noses, or else both sit face-to-face, trying to penetrate each other's guard to groom the other's genitalia. To us, with our quicker reactions, sifaka play seems a deliberately mimed parody: perhaps to a sifaka the human species seems in a state of constant fidgets. Wrestling of course offers far more opportunities with four hands each: players may end by seizing each other's ankles in their own great toes and playing the child's game of bicycle, the feet going slowly around and around in balanced opposition.

As we followed the sifaka eastward over the trail, we saw that one carried a baby, clinging with all four hands to the mother's back. The gnome face looked back at us, baby muzzle, oversized black ears, curious eyes. This jug-eared infant has little chance of surviving six months: it faces predation by fossas, constrictor snakes, harrier hawks; and disease, falls, and cold.

The mother paused, posed, inspected us. This group was clearly one of Alison's known ones, tame to scribblers in notebooks, tame to staring black-eyed lenses. I could not help wondering if this mother was Fiona and what she was up to during the last mating season. The gnome-like infant would be hard put to it to trace his paternity. Whatever the hazards to this particular babe, his species has evolved a level of activity, a pattern of foraging, a social structure, which lets them succeed in the spiny desert. The mother leaped off, white fur gleaming against blue sky, body extended in a straight line at takeoff, then turned with her hind feet before her, braced for landing 5 m away on a spine-studded trunk, while the baby clung like a living knapsack.

These animals are the other half of the equation of the spiny desert: the reason for the plants' defenses. These animals, with the sun's heat and the rain clouds that stop at the mountains, have formed the geometry of thorn and thorn-shadow, just as the plants have shaped the forces of sifaka muscle and bone and the trajectory of that gleaming leap.

ZEBU PEOPLE

We sauntered back toward Hazofotsy village, the sweat drying in the hot wind even as it formed, except when it actually fell in one's eyes.

We passed a signboard: Reserve Integrale no. 11ᵉ, fondé 1927. The region where we have walked is one of the twelve natural reserves founded with the ideal of total isolation from interference. Not even scientists are allowed in without a permit from the Eaux et Forêts, no hunters or loggers ever—in theory. The original conception of the forest reserves was to preserve true wilderness, 3,850 km² of it. The reserves were well chosen to represent all the major forest types of Madagascar and to be inaccessible—that is, to offer little prospect for exploitation. These are like the modern conception of wilderness parks in America, places for the naturalist and the hardy camper, with no amenities to tempt others.

For those who have seen East Africa's luxurious safari lodges, gin and tonic at the waterholes, it seems extraordinary that in Madagascar only Perinet has a lodging of sorts within walking distance of any wildlife. One is tempted to daydream that somehow Madagascar might skip a stage and keep its wilderness, while truly wild places become more and more precious, and not give in to so-called "development" until the Malagasy nation can make a conscious decision just what sort of development it really wants. Perhaps, if tourists could comfortably visit one or two wildlife areas, some money might be available to make sure the others are left alone. The reserves cannot, however, defend themselves.

The forest guard for reserve no. 11 lives at Amboasary town, 50 km from the nearest part of the reserve. The guard is responsible for 300 km², divided into three parcels: the stretch of spiny desert, a stretch that crosses the watershed into climax rainforest, and a third small area to include the triangular palm. He used to stay in the village of Ampahitsy on the reserve boundary, closer to his duties. The village lay across three major fords (I misjudged one, in 1963, and dropped a wheel of the Land Rover over a rock shelf underwater. It took three hours to assemble enough people to pull us out. Then they did a dance of triumph, an Antandroy conga line along the towrope. The reward they asked was the nylon rope to cut up for cattle leads.) On the whole the guard might as well live in Amboasary town, from which he can hitch a lift to the edge of any of the three parts of the reserve instead of starting inevitably on foot from one part. Besides, in Amboasary his five children can go to school.

One guard, in any case, can do little about supervising 300 km².

Before we reached the boundary sign, when we were well within the reserve boundaries, we passed a woodcutter with neatly stacked cords of alluaudia wood. Chief Tohimbinty said that a Chinese trader drives an ancient Mercedes truck biweekly from Fort Dauphin to collect the wood. He pays 15 francs here for a bundle of firewood and sells the same bundle for 35 francs in Fort Dauphin. Small-scale pilfering, small-scale entrepreneurship.

In 1958 there were about 29,000 km² of undegraded southern bush, less than half the 64,000 km² of eastern rainforest. There is no way to extrapolate to the present, given both the political and population changes which have taken place in intervening years. One difference is clear between the human uses of the two sorts of forest. The eastern zone contained a further 36,000 km² of degraded rainforest. In the east, felling for slash-and-burn agriculture has created vast areas of second growth, while in the south it

Zebu on dyke (Tananarive).

Tree near Ambovombe. The wind is from the sea.

is useless to fell the spiny forest unless the land can be irrigated, for nothing else will grow.[12]

Ironically, the southern bush protects itself from felling by being too poor to grow other crops, and from fire, the scourge of the western woodlands, by being too dry to burn. The plants with their thick bark and water-storing trunks do not ignite easily. Above all, no grass grows between the trees, and there is insignificant leaf litter from the grudging blobs of green that serve for leaves, so a fire cannot spread from one tree to the next.

The one real threat is the zebu, and even worse, the goat. Where forest is cleared, goats and zebu take care that no seedlings regenerate and also browse within the bush itself. These, and not the local people's need for a few twigs of firewood or 50 planks to build a house, are the real danger to the southern forests.

We reached the village to find that Volamary has anointed her little daughter's scalp with sticky green bark that she has pounded up in a mortar. This is *sanira*, a sapindaceus tree which is used everywhere in Madagascar as a ringworm preventative. Aside from medicinal plants and firewood, the people of Hazofotsy take very little from the forest.

I asked Chief Tohimbinty what his shotgun was for. Did all those sifaka flee from us because his people sometimes shot sifaka?

No, he denied firmly. Sifaka are *fady*, taboo to the Antandroy. His people do not kill sifaka. They would eat guinea-fowl from the forest, which is quite another matter, but you catch guinea-fowl in traps; you would not waste anything so expensive as a shotgun cartridge. And if ever marauding Tanosy tribesmen come hunting sifaka, the Antandroy beat them up and drive them away.

Tohimbinty's shotgun is for firing off at funerals.

A man's wealth is judged by the number of zebu which he owns and the number slaughtered at his funeral. Tohombinty himself is a man of substance: he has 200 zebu ranging up there in the foothills above the spiny desert.

Hazofotsy village itself is really a sort of cattle camp. The forty members of the village have other homes at Behara down the Mananara River, where they grow maize for their own food and rice for sale. During the rice harvesting season all able-bodied adults are at Behara, leaving only old ladies and children at Hazafotsy to mind the zebu. However, their hearts are here, not there. Whenever they are free, they walk 20 km upriver to stay at Hazofotsy, carrying maize and watermelons for food, for a person is really at home only with his cattle.

The village diet is exclusively maize, milk, and fruit. Rice is simply for sale to buy more cattle; they eat no, or virtually no, greens. Many Antandroy clear fields to grow their maize but generally near rivers or on sand: the harshest habitats are left to the forest. Tohimbinty himself ate a chicken once when he was ill, but that is all the available meat—except at funerals.

Alison Richard returned one day from Fort Dauphin to the sound of gunfire. Tohimbinty stood before his house, firing his shotgun, and apparently almost as afraid as Alison herself that the thing might explode. Beside him men were killing and dismem-

OPPOSITE: Tohimbinty, chief of Hazofotsy village, with senior and junior wives in the background.

Modern Mahafaly tomb near Behara, whose occupant once rode in an airplane.

Mahafaly tomb near Behara.

Traditional Mahafaly wood tomb carvings. No one is quite sure of the significance of carved wooden stelae (*alo-alo*)—possibly stylized human forms.

bering zebu. As they cut out each square chunk of flesh, they flung it onto a pile of meat, already buzzing with flies. By the end, the meat pile was higher than Tohombinty's house, with the butchers still hurling chunks upward to the top.

(A United Nations nutritionist told me: "There is practically no protein malnutrition in the south. A very healthy diet. You see, there are so many funerals.")

Just down the road from Hazofotsy stands the tomb of the richest man of the next village. Fifty zebu were slaughtered in his honor. People of the south do not disinter their family corpses like the plateau people, but the chief goal of life is a worthy death. The rich man's tomb is a painted cement house, with glass windows and iron bolts and hinges on the door. No living Antandroy throughout the valley can boast such a house—or would bother to have one.

The Antandroy are the despair of agricultural advisers, economists, even well-diggers. The most sympathetic adviser I talked to, Arne Fokkinga of the Lutheran Mission Agricultural School, summed up: "Well, why should you work in this climate? There is only a limited amount you can grow, a limited amount you can do with it. I teach them how to improve their chickens, how to raise a pig, but if they risk even so little capital as my methods need, well, they might lose it and be worse off. They have their own way of life." A plaintive United Nations report puts it even more succinctly. "We find it extremely difficult to introduce economic improvements, because the Antandroy seem to be happy."

The happiness need not be overstressed: Antandroy provide a major source of migrant labor for the nearby sisal fields or even for the sugar-cane plantations of far-off Nosy Bé. The commonest pattern is that an ambitious young man works in the cash economy, saves his money, and then returns to his village. He takes off his trousers and dons a loincloth. He can then achieve prestige in Antandroy terms and buy a wife. Above all he can buy zebu, the only true wealth, for his present status and future funeral.

Alison Richard went with Chief Tohimbinty to see his cattle, roaming wild in the foothills above the spiny desert. As Tohombinty and Alison came over each hill crest, he scanned the slopes beyond, identifying the members of his own herd unerringly at a distance where she needed binoculars to pick out even their markings. Some Malagasy dialects have upward of 140 words for the different colors of the "robes" of cattle. Decary recounts how one skeptical French administrator challenged an Antandroy to see if he could tell which cow the Frenchman had removed from his herd. The Antandroy looked over the 268 zebu in his corral and said at once, "You have taken a white heifer with a brown patch on the left eye."[13] The one Antandroy novelist remarks, "I have never known a man commit suicide if he lost his family, only if he has lost his zebu."[14]

SELF-RELIANCE AND THE PRICKLY PEAR

Boys splashed naked in the Mananara River. Sun-warmed ripples covered sun-gold sand, too warm for water, too cool for air, too clear to be anything but the heavy elements of light. Women filed down from the village to bathe and to fetch cooking water; later the men would bathe. Hazofotsy is a favored village by the clear river: in many parts of the south women walk 20 km or even more to fetch their water, and every two days men drive their zebu herds on dusty trails to the waterpoints to drink.

Eastward from Hazofotsy towered the hills of the Anosy chain, their slopes bare and glowing in the late light. Those are the slopes where the zebu pasture. Many have been burned clear within living memory.

At their crests, on most days, rolls a billow of cloud, cut off at the western edge as though with a knife. It is useless to regret the loss of the transitional forest of the western slope, to wish to see just how and where the white sifaka of the spiny desert might meet the black sifaka of the rainforest, how and where the ringtailed lemurs of the south would meet the orange-beared lemurs of the east. There remains few places where such a study could be done.

Again, the loss to the naturalist is far exceeded by the loss to the people. Where once the rainwater from a storm held back to flow for three or four days, now the floodpeak descends the river in a few hours. Where once the water flowed through the dry season, the water decreases year by year. The Mananara still runs, but the great Mandrare into which it flows can dry up in October until people of Amboasary town dig pits in the dampish sand of the river bed to find cupfuls of muddy fluid for themselves and their herds.[15]

We turned downstream through cathedral stands of alluaudia and pure bushy clumps of the poisonous laro. A fallen baobab made us detour—no, not fallen, but cut and hacked in two. Zebu chiseled the soft wood with their lower teeth, chewing it to squeeze out the water. Travelers used to tap the baobabs for water, simply poking in a hollow tube to collect the inner fluid. Other plants in the desert can be pounded in a mortar for juice.

In days past, women collected dew in the early mornings, tapping the bushes over a dish or sponging off the dew with a bit of wild cotton that they squeezed into a calabash.

The simplest answer for the people is to move from the driest regions to where there may be water, to give up the older way of life in order to farm at Ambovombe, where pumps tap the deep layer of water, or else around Behara, in the irrigated land.

At last, Ernest Ranjatson, our forester guide, showed us his real work, not merely his botanical hobby. He led the way across a canal that feeds the irrigation ditches around Behara, where Tohimbinty's people and many others have their rice fields.

At one point the irrigation canal lies only 10 m from an outer curve of the Mananara River. Ernest had been foreman of the work to stabilize the riverbank. First he graded the bank, then anchored it with wire netting, then planted bararatra, the widespread African reed-grass. On the inside curve of the river bararatra reeds grow naturally; on the outside curve they took root only with Ernest's encouragement. Where we would expect to see the river undercutting its bank, leaving the roots of the overhanging tamarinds dangling gray to show which trees would next collapse into the streambed, this bank shelves gently. Ernest's reeds have held even when cyclone floodwaters

OPPOSITE: The leaf-tailed lizard of Nosy Mangabé. This is one of six species in a Malagasy genus of geckos.

The scarlet frog lives only in a small region by the Bay of Antongil. Females like this one are 10 centimeters long, males less than half their size. All 150 Malagasy frogs are endemic.

The flame tree (*Hildegardia erythrosiphon*) of the deciduous west flowers at the end of the dry season. Like many trees of the dry forest, it flowers on leafless branches before leaves and fruit grow in the rains. It dominates the remaining unburned forest, buzzing with tiny black bees. This genus is unique to Madagascar.

Zebu chewing baobab tree felled for them to get water.

Bare slopes of Anosyennes Hills east of Hazofotsy.

Sisal plantation (Berenty).

Sisal factory (Berenty).

Drying sisal (Berenty).

Ernest, Morris, and Dickon on irrigation canal, which is protected from typhoons.

Digging for water in dry bed of Manambovo River.

rushed down from the denuded Anosy hills. The irrigation canal, on which so many farms depend, is relatively safe from the river.

"I have worked on windbreak plantation at Tsiampona, on stabilizing the sand dunes of Lake Anony, on guarding the river banks above the high bridge at Amboasary," boasted Ernest. He is one of the people who, under both colonial and postcolonial administrations, has tried to help build a Madagascar where nature can work with man.

It is necessary. The irrigation, the canal, the dam at Behara, and the area where we picnicked are not just new-fangled and alien intrusions into Chief Tohimbinty's way of life. They are not even just an attempt at improvement on the traditional ecology of the happy Antandory. Traiditional human ecology disappeared in the year 1928—or, to go even further back, it appeared, out of Mexico via Reunion, in 1769.

In 1768 the Count de Modave refounded a French settlement at Fort Dauphin, a century after Flacourt's men had abandoned the site. Modave was a philosopher, a correspondent of Voltaire's, an idealist who planned to "leave the local chiefs the peaceful exercise of their rights and their authority over their own subjects. I shall hold them in a dependence which they will not even notice." Within three years Modave was selling slaves like everyone else at the time. The colony promptly ended in a massacre of reprisal by those same local chiefs.[16]

Modave's lasting contribution was not a book but a plant. He imported the Mexican prickly pear from the botanical garden of Reunion "to embellish the sea-ward face of the fort, and by this means make it impenetrable." Modave's variety of prickly pear bore 10-cm spines, tennis-racquet-shaped leaf-lobes, purple, edible fruits, and was capable of growing as a solid wall 4 m high. It spread through the spiny desert, wild and planted. On the most favorable red calcareous clays it replaced the local vegetation. In other areas it fringed paths, clearings, and villages, its bayoneted barriers not so much difficult to penetrate as impossible. Many Malagasy towns and settlements are still named *Beraketa* ("Many racquet cactuses").[17]

When the French reached Antandroy country in 1900, every village was encircled by walls of raketa, like rolls of barbed wire in trench warfare. Many of the sinuous desert paths were lined with the cactus, defying any escape.

Decary describes "pacification" of the south in 1900.

The French troops struggled, after a fashion, against the Antandroy-cactus alliance, in the course of truly blind marches without any possible advance patrols. They pushed slowly through nearly waterless country, by unknown pathways abruptly blocked, sometimes for a hundred meters, by cut heaps and piles of thorns. The paths then had to be cleared under a hail of spears and gunshots fired by invisible warriors, to whom one could not reply and whom one was incapable of pursuing. We confirmed the truth of the old local proverb, *Longo Tandroy sy raketa:* "The Antandroy and the prickly pear are relatives."[18]

The cactus hedges were not originally planted as defense against the French but against

ABOVE: Herd of zebus and goats on traditional path through Berenty Reserve. Mohair goats, which were introduced to the south, contribute to both overgrazing and industry.

Prickly pear cactus used as a living fence.

cattle thieves. An Antandroy in the old days did not consider himself a man, or fit for marriage, until he had carried out a successful raid on the zebu of a neighboring clan. By night, raiders crept up to cut through the raketa hedge which formed the corral. They led the cattle away silently through the breach. Sometimes, however, a village on the alert gave battle in defense of its herd. A guardian in the fields might attempt to fight off a daylight raid, fail, and be left with his feet horribly riddled with cactus spines to prevent pursuit. In Africa or among the Malagasy Bara tribes cowherds are usually little boys, who whack their patient beasts along with sticks and shouting, but even today in Antandroy each file of zebu that comes to the river to drink is herded, and guarded, by an adult man with a spear.

The prickly pear did not serve only for defense. Its fruit was a chief stay of hunger, its leaves were a chief source of water in the drought. Zebu and humans alike lived off the insipid fruit and juices pounded from leaves and trunk. Bare-torsoed women picked the pears with a long stick with a nail on the end, rolled them rapidly underfoot in the sand to remove some of the hairlike spines, and then peeled them with the aid of another flattened nail. Meanwhile, men cut the branches, piled them together with dry grass, and set fire to the heap, which removed enough of their spikes for the zebu to chew. Decary calculated that in his district of Tsihombe alone, 15 tons of cactus pears was consumed each day of the dry season.

There remained risks in this food even after singeing or peeling. Decary learned that Antandroy zebu's tongues should be avoided because they were full of embedded spines. People's tongues also picked up the fine, maddening fruit hairs, but people had solved the problem: most carried a pair of small iron tweezers on a string around their necks. After a meal, one would stick out one's tongue and ask one's neighbor to groom out the nearly microscopic prickles with one's own iron tweezers.

All this is past. In 1925 the cochineal beetle of Mexico was deliberately introduced to Tulear. The cochineal is the source of our familiar crimson cochineal dye—it is also the natural enemy of the prickly pear. By controlling the cactus the French hoped to control the people.

The cochineal multipled. In 1928 it spread from Tulear across the south to Antandroy. Whirling eddies of flying males hindered the traveler's way. One Frenchwoman who grew up in the south told me of early car-journeys: "Swarming clouds of cochineal would hit the car and the windscreen and be crushed—the automobile seemed drenched in blood."

The cochineal does not attack spineless prickly pear. Resistant strains of the cactus have been reintroduced to Antandroy, although they have never spread so widely as the old, bayonet-armored raketa. Ernest found us just one plant of the old variety, struggling to survive under white-fluffed sucking cochineal larvae, soft beetle grubs almost inextricable from their tangle of white excretion. They smashed under our fingers into crimson dye.

Meanwhile, the Antandroy died. Years of exceptional heat and drought had always brought famines. Losing the raketa meant an extra turn of the screw. The great famine of 1931 followed directly on the destruction of the prickly pear. In some districts half the population died or emigrated, starting the Antandroy habit of migrating as laborers to other areas. In 1943 and 1956 famine struck again: you can still meet people on the coast who were children of 1943 bartered away by their parents, and named "Exchanged for corn."

The story of the prickly pear again illustrates the interdependence of man and nature. The spiny desert, apparently the most inviolate of Malagasy habitats, and the Antandroy, the most independent of Malagasy people, cannot be understood without knowing the role of a paddle-leaved cactus from Mexico—or the Mexican beetle grub which seems no more than crimson smears on a shriveling leaf.

Cochineal beetle larvae and pupae on prickly pear cactus pad (Fort Dauphin).

Zebus in Mandrare River.

Ground cover and kily tree in drier part of Berenty forest.

THE BALANCE OF NATURE

RINGTAIL AND SIFAKA

High noon. The wide Mandrare curves lazily, circling back toward the mountains which gave it birth. Ripples glitter white over pale sand. An Antandroy and his zebu are black silhouettes on the sand plains of the far bank. The eye contracts in the glazed light; the spearman becomes a Giacometti stick-figure, attenuated to black verticals. Light envelopes him, curving in past his thigh and calf, narrowing his silhouette to the vertical essence of humanity leading the silhouetted black essence of his herds.

The near bank rises dark green, tamarind woodland masses against light and water. Against the burning sun of winter and the cyclone-fed floods of summer, the trees of Berenty defend 100 hectares of soil and the pyramid of life of a Malagasy river forest. So great a difference to make with inside and outside curve of the river, looking toward or away from the sun—on one bank the abstraction of the idea, humanity naked and alone on naked sand, with the zebu his chattels. On the other bank, the complexity of living nature, the green and murmurous world in which we evolved.

The bark of the kily tree is warm and rough on my back. My toes burrow into soft dust pitted with the traps of ant-lions. Cicadas hum the lullaby of forest noon; black and white swallowtails flit through the speckled sunshadows.

Birds and mammals, though, are still. Even the malachite kingfisher has abandoned his lookout snag on the river; a sleepy female toulou-bird settles in the leaf litter.

The lemurs siesta as well. They lie curled up together in furry balls on a branch, ringed tails thrown over like feather boas, or, hot, elongate on a horizontal loop of liana with chin flat and all four feet and tail dangling down on either side.

A peacock-tail curtain of lianas shelters their sleeping place—overlapped leaves gleaming emerald on the side toward the sunlit glade, malachite on the shadowed woodland side. The massive bole and outstretched arms of a kily, majestic as a northern white oak, spread over the little lemurs, holding the liana curtain of their repose.

185

They are safe here. The Berenty reserve has been set aside, fenced, and guarded by the de Heaulme family. Monsieur Henry de Heaulme, his son Jean de Heaulme, and daughter and son-in-law M. and Mme. Du Pray have preserved the hundred hectares at Berenty and several thousand hectares at Morondava as parcels of the richest, most unique natural flora. In times to come, that family should stand among the greatest benefactors of the Malagasy heritage.

"Now show *me*. You have seen the sacred lemurs of Lavalohalika. It is your turn to show me the lemurs of Berenty."

"Right, Guy. We just walk in the gate, down the main trail, but I am sure that you will show me something new, instead. When Marguerite came, she straight away pointed out sifaka feeding in an introduced tree species down on the lower riverbank, where I had never seen them before."

"How many scientists have worked here, in all?"

"I did the first detailed study of lemur behavior in 1963 and 1964, following the Petters' general survey of all the lemur species. Norm Budnitz and Kathy Dainis spent 1972 and 1973 on ringtail ecology, Jay Russell and Lee McGeorge studied lepilemur and mouselemurs in 1974. Lee tape recorded everything which makes noises, day and night, and showed how each species uses different frequencies or different times of day like radio stations parceling out the air waves. Ann Mertl studied ringtail scent-marking in 1975, while Herb Gustafson followed up sifaka territory sizes. Quite a respectable list, without counting many shorter visits, not to mention a whole series of television teams—Guy, there's your first lemur."[1]

Guy Ramanantsoa stared at the lepilemur. The lepilemur glared back, a rolled up handful of gray fur, oversized thighs, limpid brown eyes, the pupils contracted to pinpricks in the daylight. It sat at the doorway of its hole in the "lepilemur tree," as it (or a predecessor) sat by that hole in 1970 for Marcel Hladik to photograph, and still sat in 1974 blinking at Lee and Jay. Guy approached the lemur one foot at a time, ever more gingerly. Finally, he found his breath to ask, "Why isn't it afraid?"

Guy had already taught me something new. He had worked at every level from local forester to chief of the forest service; he has visited and walked over every official natural reserve in Madagascar. He had never seen Malagasy animals which were used to people, yet unafraid, except in his island of sacred lemurs. What is commonplace for tourists in other countries, Yellowstone bears lolling by the roadside or Nairobi lions drowsing in the shade of the Volkswagen bus, is virtually unknown in Madagascar. The tame wild animals of Berenty are almost unique.

I found my own wits to tell him, "Oh, they are very blasé here. Ringtail groups grow so used to having their pet scientist that they meow when you get up to leave—the same contact call they make when the troop itself splits up. . . . Now, here is a sifaka boundary; only a hundred meters from the gate we are leaving the first territory for the second. Those two kily trees that touch over the trail form a crossing point, where a sifika group can traverse without coming to the ground, and where they can watch up and down the trail for possible rivals. This is a natural place for a territorial boundary."

"Is this one of the boundaries that are still the same after twelve years?"

Sifaka at a "crossing point" (Berenty).

Refuge entrance to Berenty Reserve.

Lepilemur in nest hole (Berenty).

"Yes, it is—My Blaze Nose troop came up to these kilys, and no farther, just as Herb's Troop A did this year. Of course, we don't really know what happened during the years between, but it was right under these two kilys that Herb and Anne and I started cooking up the paper that you and I now have to finish."

Guy flew to Berenty in part to see the animals for himself, and in part to finish a summary article on its scientific importance to present to the Academie Malgache.[2] Each of the scientists who have worked here "discovered" Berenty independently, as a reserve with animals who would consent to intensive study. There was no reason to try to build on one another's work. In fact it would have crippled later, more sophisticated analyses to stick to the crude measures of my early description. Oddly, it was not until Herb and Anne and I found five of the sifaka boundaries in the same trees where they had been, that we realized we must at last take stock of all the studies together.

The extraordinary fact about Berenty is that the ringtail and sifaka populations seem to be nearly unchanged over the last twelve years, about 100 sifaka and 150 ringtails in the 97-hectare reserve. Furthermore, there has not been any obvious degradation of the forest. Perhaps here, in this small reserve, we actually have an equilibrium situation, the golden age where all the species' populations can continue indefinitely in balance with one another. Guy and I were asking each other, Is the stability real? If so, how do they do it? And if we find out how the lemurs do it, what are the implications for other species, other reserves, even for the human animal?

Primates, including lemurs, are long-lived animals, slow to mature. A mother ringtail is pregnant for 4½ months and in the wild does not breed until she is 2½ years old. (A cat of the same size is pregnant for 2 months and breeds at 9 months or 1 year of age.) Zoo lemurs have lived in captivity for over 20 years.

The generation time of an animal to a great extent determines what you can find out about it. Fruit flies in bottles, with a new generation every two weeks, can reveal the principles of genetics and evolution. Gorillas and elephants, instead, tell us how a complex creature with a life span near our own adapts to its complex environment. The lemurs are in between—social, complicated, primates, but somewhat shorter lived—and here we had one of the earliest studied wild primate populations right under our hands (or, more accurately, over our heads).

How do they manage? There are only three possibilities: birth control, migration, and death. Birth control is not so funny as it sounds. Many mammals, when overcrowded, do not conceive, or they abort or even eat their own litters. There is no sign of such pathological behavior at Berenty, but not all the females give birth each year, and there may well be some social influences on the proportion which do. One clear difference from lemurs in captivity is that laboratory female ringtails have conceived at less than a year of age. Here in the wild, with normal light and climate, they first mate at two-and-a-half.

Migration in and out of the reserve is another possibility. The ringtails are essentially isolated. They can go out of the reserve across a cattle drove; but beyond that is only degraded woodland full of zebu, and eventually bare riverbank. The sifaka who tolerate the truly dry forest can escape across an isthmus of spiny desert, which still connects to uncleared lands of the south. It would be relatively simple to monitor that desert corridor just to see which individuals turn up in which troops.

The question we can begin to answer already is how the animals partition the habitat within the reserve itself.

Ringtails are fluid. As they swagger from season to season and from year to year, their troop ranges expand, contract, fission, overlap. Before the mating season, in April, troops roam, doubling their normal range.[3] The males lift their black muzzles to coyote-howl from troop to troop. They scent-mark, males and females pressing their gentials to branches, or the males gouging upright saplings with the scented spurs of their forearms. Males of a troop indulge in stink-fights, perfuming their tails by drawing them between the spurs, then standing up to quiver the scented tail at their enemy like an outraged feather duster.

At last, in May, the females come into estrus, over only two weeks in any one forest. Each female is receptive for only a few hours in one year.[4] The males fight around her—physical fights where antagonists leap into the air to gain height for the downward canine slash like raking a nail through the skin. The female withdraws branch by branch with the winner, although he must tear off, or out of, her as much as twenty times to confront his pursuers. At last the consort pair leaves the troop for the few hours when the female is receptive, leaving the losing males to lick 3-inch gashes in limbs or flank.

At the end of the two-week orgy, the whole troop is exhausted. Ringtails lie blinking in the sun. Males limp around the food trees; former antagonists groom each others' noses. Females withdraw to one anothers' society, taking priority for food over the males as always. The troop ranges contract to half their premating size.

However, this is not the end of the story. As the dry season progresses, the troops again begin to wander. They fragment. The subordinate males, or Drones Club, lag farther and farther behind. Troop ranges again overlap, and stink fights begin again. At last, in November, as many as one-quarter of the males may change troop. Dominants change as well as subordinates, so they are working on some calculation of their relative status in the neighborhood. The males can recognize and respond differentially to the scent-posts of neighbors. They go beserk if presented with the scent of a total stranger from the opposite end of the reserve.[5]

Ringtails change their behavior not only by season but by year as well. In 1963–64, relatively lush, wet years, they seemed to maintain exclusive territories. In September 1970, at the end of three years' drought, their ranges overlapped so completely that they shared access to food and drinking sites on a time plan, like sharing a computer.[6] In 1975 a troop of 40 animals foraged together for a month, apparently a temporary alliance of smaller groups.[7]

In short, the ringtails change pattern as if to keep their pursuing primatologists on the hop. However, the core of each range, and the total population, stays much the same. Arguably, they are showing the resourcefulness of highly adaptable creatures. Compared to congeneric brown lemurs, ringtails range farther, eat a more varied diet, travel more on the ground, and use scrubbier forest.[8] If the ringtails are adapted to

Sifaka "on the branch where we left him" (Berenty).

Ringtailed lemurs—watchful (Berenty).

Ringtailed lemur (*Lemur catta*) at Berenty. Note wrist spur.

Leaping sifaka (Berenty).

LEFT: *Lemur catta* genital-marking a tree (Berenty). Large trees that were spur-marked as saplings can be permanently scarred. RIGHT: Tree marked by *Lemur catta* (Berenty).

Sifaka (Berenty).

Ringtailed lemurs in Berenty Reserve. Troop members often use tails to communicate.

OPPOSITE: A male ringtailed lemur scent-marks a broken sisal stem. H
sniffs the branch, which is often a traditional spot marked by othe
lemurs before him. Then he mixes the scent from his forearm witl
scent from glands on his breast and gouges the branch with perfume
forearm spurs.   Photo by Alison Joll

The tiny crab spider matches the flowers of a butter-gold tree. The tree is a Malagasy species of a widespread African genus. It is one of the few kinds of trees that survive in the fire-raked grasslands. Photo by Alison Jolly

Two ringtails touch noses in the ancient mammalian gesture of greeting and reassurance. The seated ringtail is a one-eyed, battle-scarred male who limped behind the troop with dragging tail. When he stopped to rest, another male turned back from the troop to touch noses. Photo by Alison Jolly

sparser woodland than other lemurs, and above all to more unpredictable resources in wet and dry years, their ranging patterns may help them cope with changing habitats and give them the elasticity of behavior that lets them keep a stable population.

The Berenty sifaka are a total contrast. Not only do some of their troop boundaries remain after twelve years. Much more important, the core areas of most troops have stayed put. There is, and there has been, one troop based at the first trail crossing, one at the second, one at the third. The maps show only crudely what all the sifaka watchers feel: we could walk into Berenty tomorrow and see a sifaka on the branch where we left him at the end of our studies.

Not all those sifaka would be the same animals. Herb said, "The houses are the same, no matter who lives in them."

Males at Berenty, as at Hazofotsy, change troop in the mating season. Even out of season, sifaka can shift alliance. The 1975 death of an old male called Tramp triggered a chain migration. At least half the males and one-fifth of the females in five adjoining troops shifted group, one to the next, within three days.[9]

Troop boundaries shifted too, and a new group formed between—but the new one in fact occupied an old "house." I had known a troop in just that position during both 1963 and 1970, even with part of the same boundary line. It looked as though the sifaka follow precedent as meticulously as a lawyer with his brief.

How do they do it, and why? The why is not too hard. Sifaka eat many mature leaves, and Berenty seems rich and stable enough to make it worth defending small, year-round territories. How? In part by territorial battles, a sort of arboreal chess game. The two groups of white knights face each other, then leap toward each other in close formation. They scent-mark the trees, males with throat gland and urine, females with genitalia. They mix, leaping apparently at random. You wait to see individuals confront each other, but like chess, the game is to occupy spaces, facing outward from one's own base, to threaten and force retreat. Opposing champions may even land back to back on a single branch, each facing in his own direction. When the battle is played out, the sides retreat to their own ground still glaring and scent marking, having reaffirmed but hardly ever shifted a boundary.

In short we have at Berenty almost a living model. The animals themselves have made all the simplifying assumptions. When you write a text or formulate a theory, you start out with the simplest case: suppose the population is stable, suppose the habitat is undegraded, suppose the animals mark out a perfect mosaic of territories. Or, suppose that you have your control groups already given by nature: two species to compare in the same forest and two comparable forest types, wet and dry. All these ideal simplifications actually exist at Berenty.

Of course we lack all sorts of knowledge. No matter what studies have been done, it is only a start. There is far more to learn about these two species alone. Then, we must put these together with Jay Russell's data for lepilemurs. Then someone should start on the birds and above all on the one large fruit-eater we have not even touched.

There is one region of Berenty that the ringtails and sifaka do not enter. As Guy and I approached, piercing squeals and bickering assaulted us, and then the rank smell of guano, even before we saw the first of the dozen bat trees. It is sheer numbers which bewilder you at first, huge part-denuded trees, crawling with life, hung with many thousands of bats in clusters on every branch and twig, harems loosely grouped, nipping one another, jostling, jabbering, scrabbling with the claws of their wings. Then suddenly, you see their size—nightmare bats of 3-, 4-, even 5-foot wingspan, for these are flying foxes, the Malagasy species of the giant fruit bat. At last, though, if you look, you see them as animals, and see that they are beautiful. Their fur is red as any fox, red-golden in the sunlight. They have long muzzles and large dark eyes, and black wings to fold like a cape over their gleaming fur.

Guy clapped his hands—the whole swarm took fright and circled into the air. The sun shone through their outspread alae, outlining the skeleton of the elongate fingers. The huge translucent membranes made them as improbable in flight as creations of Leonardo da Vinci, whirling in their thousands overhead, russet and black against blue sky.

If so small a reserve as Berenty really does maintain stable populations of its mammalian species—ringtails and sifaka and lepilemur, the thousands of flying foxes and the pair of fossas—perhaps we can take hope for conservation in Madagascar. If Guy and his students find out how it is done, they may even have lessons to teach other continents.

BIRTH CONTROL AND DEATH CONTROL

About 20 sifaka babies are born each year in the censused part of the reserve; about 50 ringtails. Only half reach one year of age. They die from falls, from disease, probably from predation by swooping harrier hawks or fossas. None of us has actually seen a baby caught, but the lemurs themselves proclaim their predators. When the ringtails find a menace on the ground they gather round, yapping in synchrony like 20 ill-mannered little terriers. A group of sifaka may join them, chorusing "shi FAKH" in their throats and noses. But if it is not a ground, but an aerial, terror, lemurs waste no time in mobbing. As the harrier hawk stoops, ringtails scream and sifaka roar, fleeing downward under cover, while all the other troops in earshot cock their ears and look toward the alarm.

The pattern of early infant deaths is common to most forms of life, to all mammals. It was common to man until the advent of modern medicine. When we know enough about lemurs to make a life table, we will also recognize a way by which people do *not* want to keep themselves in equilibrium. Our love for our children is part of our mammalian heritage, a heritage which makes us treasure each separate baby.

Whatever the pros and cons of development, whatever the threat of world over-population, very few people can consciously endorse the "natural" or "underdeveloped" solution: to deny all 20th-century medicines and let half the children die.

If we cannot accept this form of population control, we shall need to consciously consider alternatives. Biology throws some light even on this question. For all species but our own, it is an evolutionary decision, not a conscious one, how many children to raise and how to share the benefits of parental care among the family's offspring.

A populated bat tree (Berenty).

Young fruit bat nicknamed "Dorian" (Berenty).

Giant fruit bats (*Pteropus rufus*),
or flying foxes (Berenty).

Where a species' environment is closed and highly predictable, each offspring will have to compete for a limited set of resources. The parents' best strategy, then, is to invest as much as possible in each single offspring, to make it strong and healthy enough to compete successfully. This usually means a small number of children who are given a good start in life by any means at hand from large, yolky eggs to parental care. Other species do not share human scruples about their means to channel parental investment into the fortunate young. On the one hand we have the "altruism" of the worker honeybee, who gives up all possibility of reproduction herself in order to raise her siblings. At first sight it seems as though such a system ought never to evolve by natural selection. How could an individual gain by reproducing less, or how could a mother gain by sterilizing the majority of her daughters? The answer in selective terms, is that if the sister honeybees cooperate to rear their mother's brood, they actually produce more offspring carrying their own genes than would each one attempting to rear her own larvae.[10]

On the other hand behavior mildly called "spite" also appears among insects. Several parasitic wasp species which lay eggs in beetle larvae have evolved as cannibals—fratricidal cannibals. Their growing young molt several times inside their prey, the living beetles. One of these molts leads to a form with massive jaws. The first wasp to reach this stage turns on the other wasps growing from the same batch of eggs inside the beetle. It kills and then consumes its brothers and sisters.[11]

This cannibalism has evolved at least five times among five different kinds of wasps. It is clearly an evolved response to the cramped food supply: the fact that one beetle grub can support only one wasp. It is, in fact, only a form of family planning in a limiting environment.

The opposite case from the predictably limiting environment is those species whose environment fluctuates wildly and unpredictably. If they happen on a good season or into a field already planted fence-to-fence with their favorite food, all their young may survive. If they happen on a bad year or fall on barren ground, little that their parents can do would help them. The best strategy for these species is to bear as many young as possible and broadcast them to take their chances in an uncertain world.[12]

These strategies are evolved through the ruthless power of natural selection, not, in any species but our own, by conscious choice. Even dandelions can make such caluclations. Two dandelion races in the United States are weeds of weedy fields and weeds of lawns. The lawn weeds are opportunists. They grow and mature as fast as possible, bear many seeds per head, though puny ones, and disperse these seeds to grow as best they can. The lawn dandelion's environment is unpredictable; its chief competitor is a lot of browbeaten grass, its chief control the man with the mower who may or may not sleep late on Sunday and let that week's dandelions rush past him to fruition. In contrast, the field dandelion has a relatively predictable set of vigorous competitors and less chance of arbitrary mowing. It grows more strongly and slowly among the ragweed and clover, and it bears only a few large seeds, each equipped in turn for strong vegetative growth.[13]

People make the same choices consciously but apparently on much the same lines as the dandelions. The trend of all recent research suggests that only when people feel that the future is predictable do they control their family size. If you have some confidence in the future and foresee limited resources to divide, you may say, "Well, we shall have only two children and send them both to law school." In developed countries family size has dropped to about two children. However, if chance diseases are likely to kill half your children before they are five, to inflict droughts or large-scale wars or other catastrophes out of all control, it generally seems better to have as many children as possible, in hopes that some will find a raft to carry them through the possible shipwreck of the family.

What can the Berenty lemurs tell us about population control? They, like other primates, have few children cared for over long periods. They are already part of the trend which one can trace for living primates, and which presumably derives from our common ancestors. Lemurs have only one baby a year, baboons one every two years, chimpanzees a four- or five-year birth interval. The children of higher primates are physically dependent on their mothers for longer and longer times, as you study animals closer anatomically to man. With the longer generation times, the likelier is a period of stress—drought or famine—to fall within each generation rather than decimating one generation and sparing another. We are the ultimate among living primates as long-lived creatures in a predictable environment—one which we have learned to predict and in large part to control.

Biologically, women are adapted to bear a family of 12 children each, at a lavish scale of well-nourished American Hutterites who believe in breast-feeding but not contraception and do not marry until around 22.[14] If nourished like a !Kung bushwoman, with perfectly adequate protein but a dearth of fat, the birth interval rises to four years and the average family is down to five, with no woman bearing more than seven children. !Kung figures are probably near the human norm for most of our evolution up until the agricultural revolution. This is not just because the !Kung are hunter-gatherers, like early man. Mankind at large may have had richer hunting grounds than the Kalahari desert, and especially as we ranged northward we may have eaten plenty of fat. (I picture cave-bear, for instance, as eminently greasy.) The functional reason for wide birth spacing, however, is that it is hard to carry a baby and a toddler for any distance together, even if you have already invented baby-slings. Nomadic women simply could not afford to have a second child until the first could walk the needed distances, unless their band was so coherent that fathers and aunts would carry the extra young.[15] A large number of hunting tribes practice infanticide, killing babies born too close to a sibling, with some mutual agreement that such a child never really lived.[16]

Agricultural peoples can afford to breed up to their capacity, from the point of view of women's work. Even the !Kung, when they settle on agricultural lands, bear a child every two years. Agricultural peoples, on the whole, are not so healthy as surviving hunter-gatherers, for settled life is more conducive to epidemic disease. Disease culls the extra children instead of the tribal wise-woman, while a woman tries to bear her twelve babies if she can.

If we now choose to limit ourselves from the potential twelve live births down to two, or none, small wonder we need women's lib—women need a career to do something with our extra energy! And small wonder that we shall need to rework a great deal of our social attitudes to invest more care in fewer offspring. If we are now to guide consciously what, for all our evolution, we have achieved by following biological urges, we shall need all the self-understanding we can find.

The Berenty lemurs will not tell us anything directly about the choices before us. They can only illuminate the choices our ancestors made in the past. They already have made the choice to have fewer children than most other mammals so that those children might survive and compete in their mosaic of leafy territories.

LEARNING TO BE A LEMUR

The great ground coua waddled in the shade, its head balancing back and forth like a pheasant's. The rufous breast glowed warmly, the shading of cream throat and dove-gray back feathers delicately cool. Only a surrealist would equip such a bird with its scarlet and turquoise eyepatch, the jeweled eye of a Byzantine golden cockerel set into the soft feathers of a living bird.

Paradise flycatchers fluttered and warbled, eight males in a single sapling. One was the black and white form, showier even than the russet and black, the two trailing white streamers of his tail twice the length of head and body. He postured and twittered and flicked himself from branch to branch, his tail semaphoring his movement to the other males. A flock of Madagascar lovebirds circled one another, shouting and squawking before they separated into pairs to nest. Although the pairs flock together to feed in winter, they are commonly maintained for life. The squawks matter. A mated lovebird, caged away from its spouse, does not accept a new mate so long as it can hear the voice of its own.[17]

This was September spring. Dry winter would end in the first storms of November. (The Malagasy word for summer is "thunder-time.") The displaying birds were warming up to the prologue of mating.

Horrible squawks assaulted the woodland. This was not the lovebirds, but bigger, like a barn door in a tantrum. A Vasa parrot, drab gray of plumage and awkward of movement, crashed into the upper branches with the grace of a thrown dinner plate. The parrot was not calling to a mate but to ten-year old Margaretta.

Margaretta sat cross-legged on the sand of the Berenty path, among the conical pit traps of ant lions and the meandering traces of last night's 8-inch flatworms. She squinted at a bit of music paper in her lap and blew into her school recorder.

She complained, "Herb promised that parrots would answer me if played their song, and there's only something screeching so I can't concentrate."

"Well, look up."

"Ohhh—it's a parrot!"

Margaretta had not recognized the bird's song, but the bird knew. Herb had given her a key to a behavioral lock.

The pitch, and something in the recorder's timbre, were essential, for whistling or

OPPOSITE: Ground coua (*Coua gigas*).

Ringtail with young clinging to breast (Berenty).

Lemur catta. Female grooms infant riding on mother's back.

singing the same call gains no response. Tempo, at least within wide limits, did not matter: Margaretta played at quarter speed what Herb rendered as a grace note or the parrot as a squeak in its syrinx.

Much innate behavior shares this characteristic: the animal responds to a few, striking qualities of a stimulus and reacts to a very simple model that has only those essential qualities. The parrot's song may not necessarily be innate, or wholly innate. Some birds learn their species notes from hearing adults sing. Even those birds, however, have innately directed learning. They learn the "right" song much faster and more accurately than "wrong" songs. Such innately guided behavior underlies many of the actions of birds, as well as fish and reptiles, above all in those situations where communication between species members leads to reproductive success: in gaining a mate and in rearing young.

Mammals, on the other hand, have much more latitude for learned variations of their behavior, which allows for a range of actions effective in a wide variety of situations. We humans with our own versatility are only the culmination of a long evolutionary trend toward relying on learned knowledge and inventive cleverness.

As primates go, the lemurs are relatively stupid in learning about objects. In many sorts of formal problems and in their initial lack of curiosity about objects, they seem hopelessly outclassed by most of the New and Old World monkeys.[18]

Lemur social systems, on the other hand, are fairly complex, like those of monkeys and of apes. It is true that we have as yet no standardized measures of social subtlety. In this domain we ourselves rely on intuition and operate largely in the same nonverbal fashion as any other animal. Although we can put our fingers into the kaleidoscope of social relations, our understanding still depends more on the mental craft of the tinkerer than on any objective or scientifically replicable methodology. Therefore, we cannot say that lemurs are socially more or less complex than other primates. We can say only that lemurs, like other social mammals, including monkeys, maintain a network of learned individual relations that influence most of their actions, even where they feed and how they sleep, and certainly with whom they mate and how many young they can raise to prolong their genes.[19]

This is the speciality of primates, above all other mammals. Our social matrix allows us to learn in safety and compels us to learn if we are to find our individual roles in a complex society.

From a lemur's birth, from our own, the reflexes built into nerve and muscle interplay with a system capable of learning to make body and mind. It takes time to form an individual in this laborious manner. The birds are courting to celebrate spring—their eggs will be laid, then their young fledged, in the rich summertime of rains. Spring for the ringtails is not the season of mating but of birth. Each of the Malagasy lemur species gives birth at a time which lets its young mature to weaning during the rains.[20] The big sifaka are born first, in July, then the middle-sized lemurs in September, last the little mouselemurs at the beginning of November.

The giant ground coua padded slowly across the trail by Margaretta. It circled and crossed under a low kily full of ringtails—and there was the season's first infant. He clung lengthwise on his mother's white belly fur, very new, still damp, almost certainly born in the night or early morning. (Almost all diurnal primates are more likely to be born at night, as are humans if you add up statistics for a few hundred normal births.)[21]

The baby was about three inches long. Its head was almost spherical, like a Ping-Pong ball with black eye-and-muzzle spots painted on and tiny pointed ears with white ear tufts. Beside the head, his body was insignificant, legs and arms folded up like gray pipe cleaners. The tail dangled in a minute corkscrew, its black and white stripes like a dashed line drawn in soft pencil. What to call him? Harlequin, for the face-mask? No, Harlequin is far too clever, with too sharp a nose—something else about a disguise. Domino! A little masked domino with three round spots for eye, eye, muzzle.

The mother sat back on her haunches. Domino clung with hands alone, his feet almost helpless in her fur. Development proceeds from front to back. Domino could suckle, could lift his head, although he did so rarely, could pull himself with his hands toward the nipple. In a few days the nerves would function better down the length of his spine, he would cling and push more strongly with his hindlegs, and his tail would curl into a prehensile belt around his mother's waist.

Domino did not look like a human infant, yet many of his reflexes were the same as our own. Newborn babies, like newborn primates, can clutch with their hands and push with their arms and often lift their heads, as long as they are placed with tummy against something—our ancestors' position of ventral contact to the mother. They can root for the nipple and suckle it, they can turn their face with its unfocused eyes toward a mother's moving head or voice. If you let a newborn's head drop sharply or slap its mattress, its arms and legs flap wildly toward the midline and its hands clutch in midair. This is the Moro reflex, used for centuries by doctors to test babies' coordination. Not until the 1960s did we realize that the Moro is the ancient clutching of a primate infant for his mother's belly fur when she jerks into movement.[22]

And the mother's response to all these fixed gestures of groping, holding, nursing? The human beams at her child; the mother ringtail dropped her chin on Domino's head and licked his tufted ears. So begins the process of learning and teaching. With every action and reaction, mother and child are creating a new and personal bond out of the raw material of their nervous systems. The newborn's repertoire of movements are "the reflexes of love."[23]

Other ringtails approached to nose the infant, first two females, then a male. A juvenile came and sat against the mother—probably last year's infant, for family bonds presumably last for life, as in other primates. The mother put her arm around Domino to adjust his position. The baby cradled inside the crook of her forearm and elbow just as a human baby would. Of course, it is primate to hold things with open hand and arm, not with the inturned forelimb of the terrestrial quadruped. It is just another example of the gesture, the trick of movement, which can persist across evolutionary time and species distance as surely as the molding of bones and perhaps even the bases of emotion. And of course it is my own background that brings the gesture home to me, an observer trained to concentrate on detail, a mother, a female. Females of every social primate species are fascinated by one another's infants. Is it possible to sort out the layers of experience or of intellectual justification that amplify and modify my interest in little Domino, from that social emotion which predates all human cleverness and goes back to the common ancestor of ourselves and the ringtails?

Leave them there, with that gesture of maternal protection. Little Domino has only half a chance of reaching one year old, when he may be a mischievous juvenile wrestling with his peers. He has perhaps a quarter of a chance of reaching two years old, to strut around the older males as they fight in the mating season. Domino's likely death preserves the environment for those few infants who survive.

Lemur catta with newborn (Berenty).

11

SUICIDE BY FIRE

FLOWERING SEASON

We have one major Malagasy habitat left to visit: the dry deciduous woodlands of the west. Looking at this final region, will it again be clear how a human way of life is interwoven with the forest's past and with its future?

I hope so, because Rachel Rabesandratana, teacher of botany at the University of Tulear, will join us to show me her flowers and look at my lemurs.

"After all, Alison," she said as she smiled, flashing most unprofessional dimples, "if you can park your children for this part of the trip, so can I. My husband will just pay a little less attention to his Marine Research Station for the next few days, and a little more to Haja, Hary, Naina, Noro, and Hobilalao."

One of Rachel's students, now an agricultural officer, suggested that we travel to a rosewood forest near the little Bara village of Bekily. There are hundreds of Bekily towns and hamlets in Madagascar. The name simply means "many tamarinds." Where many tamarinds grow there must be water and rich soil, a welcoming homestead for human beings.

Drive north on the main highway from Tulear. You climb again through spiny desert. The west has even less rain than Hazofotsy, and its calcareous or sandstone rocks swallow what rain there is. The land is pocked with sinkholes; springs and artesian wells unexpectedly bubble out again, depositing rococo crusts of travertine on their fountain basins. It is a hydrologist's delight, for there are vast underground reservoirs. However, inept boreholes can break through the lower strata and drain the whole reservoir into inaccessible depths.[1]

The plant species here are the true survivors, adapted to even more dessicated soil than the spiny desert of Hazofotsy on its waterproof granite base. *Alluaudia comosa* funnels out from the ground like a vegetable tornado. *Didierea madagascariensis* makes the forest's colonades, its spikes in crosses of four, the longest one at the bottom

Limestone sinkhole in dry brush north of Tulear.

Rachel Rabesandratana gathering medicinal plants near Tulear. I am at left.

Barleria with its thorny leaves.

Colonial flattid bugs (flower-mimics).

growing 10 cm long. An infant Didierea begins as no more than a fistful of flesh inside its mesh of spikes, a sea urchin of the land.

This is the season of flowering. Trees of both desert and dry woodlands flower in September, so their seeds can germinate with the first November rains. Flowers were everywhere: *Jatropha mahafaliensis*, the female flower the color of dried blood at the tip of a cluster surrounded by creamy green male flowers with red guide-lines. The species is unique to Madagascar and to the calcareous Mahafaly region; the genus is pantropical, a euphorb used nearly everywhere to purge or to poison friends and relatives.

Here was the mattress mint, whose dry flower heads stuff mattresses throughout southern Asia. I remember my delight at first learning that in Madagascar you do not buy pillows, you pick them. Rachel pointed out that the mattress plant again has no true petals but furry bracts in their place. At last she finds a real flower, complete with pistil, stamens, and periwinkle-blue petals. It was a *Barleria*, of the Acanthus family. It had armed itself at every leaf base and along the sepals with yet another set of thorns.

As Rachel showed off the western desert and asked for photos for lecture sides, I began to suspect her of a botanical crime comparable to a zoologist's sympathizing with animals—like any mere gardener, she actually likes flowers.

But the commonest one escaped her interest—a fluffy white cluster, which when breathed upon lifts an erectile bustle of petals and hops off its twig. This colonial flatid bug is only a flower mimic.

Then among the western species of thorn and the Moringa bottle-trees we stopped, stared, at one little leafless tree. At the branch tips perched five-petaled flowers as large as the spread fingers of a woman's hand, waxy and white like stars, with deep creamy yellow throats and a yellow pistil. Each flower lay so heavy, so unblemished, it seemed stupidly artificial. One would dismiss those blooms in a florist's shop as some crossbred creation, a too perfect version of the ideal.

Heavy in the dry air, as out of place as a mirage of hothouse dance corsages, hung the scent of wild gardenia.

As you climb from Tulear, the spiny desert gives way to deciduous forest. Then you top a rise, some 150 km inland, and the woodland stops. Before you lies only rippling savanna as far as the eye can see—unbroken for 500 km as the crow flies to Tananarive.

Not all those hundreds of miles of prairies are the same. In this western country much of the grassland is fertile pasture, dominated by *Hyparrhenia* and *Heteropogon*, whose close-set stems and heavy seed heads nourish most of the Malagasy national herd of 11 million zebu. As we drove on the grass following oxcart tracks toward Bekily village, about 20 km from any road, the standing hay shimmered gold, with odd dense spots around every termite hill. (I do not know if this termite effect is the result of greater fertility or some mechanical protection.)

Where this sort of grassland is abused by overgrazing, by fires, or by natural poverty of the soil, the pasture grasses give way to tougher and less nourishing varieties. The end point is pseudosteppe, more and more common as one mounts toward the plateau. *Aristidia* is the dominant genus of pseudosteppe, a bunch-grass that propogates itself by underground rhizomes, well sheltered from fire and also guaranteed to offer virtually no accessible nourishment to hungry cattle. Aristidia is at once a triumph of nature, which can flourish on crumbling bedrock that contains no organic nutrient at all, and a condemnation of human management, which has brought much of Madagascar into this condition. On true steppes dry or cold climate limits plant life. In the pseudo-steppes of Madagascar, by contrast, it is sheer poverty of the soil that reduces vegetation to such tough and grudging grasses.[2]

The western savanna, like the pseudosteppes of the plateau, resulted from the fire which cleared four-fifths of the dry Malagasy forest. Still today, yearly fires attack the pasture grasses, pushing them a little farther toward Aristidia pseudosteppes, and yearly the fires gnaw at the forest edges. It has been estimated that one-quarter of Madagascar's surface burns in each dry season.

The zone that was once the deciduous woodland stretches north from Tulear all the way to the northernmost tip of Madagascar, near Diego Suarez and the Montagne d'Ambre. The woodlands, of course, are no longer continuous over this vast area. They are pockets, islands, which totaled about 26,000 km² as of 1956, as opposed to the more continuous 64,000 km² of rainy eastern forest and 29,000 km² of southern thornbush. The deciduous forest has only about 5,000 km² of degraded or second-growth formations; dry second growth burns.[3]

Let us not exaggerate. The surviving woodlands have maintained themselves already for many centuries in the face of the fire. Where forest still exists it is growing on deep sandy or clay soils, where water seeps down to tree roots, out of reach of grasses. It is not surprising that even where forest has once been cut for shifting cultivation, it may regenerate as before.[4]

The forest edges regenerate with second growth composed of seedlings of the woodland trees themselves. Again there is a marked contrast to the east, whose degraded, bushy savoka is largely foreign species and where the trees of the high rainforest rarely seem to replace the savoka before it is burned or razed for new crops. The forest trees of the west, used to drier conditions and more sunlight within mature, climax woodland, apparently could recolonize at least parts of the savanna—if only they did not meet a frontier of fire.

It is, again, a question of balance. If there are the right number of cattle, they find rich hay in the western savannas and feel no need to invade the forest. In the dry season they live on the "green bite" (the new grass shoots that spring up when fires pass). Some fire, and some green shoots, are clearly necessary in a balanced cattle economy.

This is, however, a fragile equilibrium which can be destroyed by human population increase, by increase in the cattle herds, and by some forms of increase in the market economy. As usual, all the factors relate to one another. More people want more cattle and more cash. Cash crops in this region mean shifting cultivation of peanuts and therefore cutting the forest for fields, or else irrigated cotton on black alluvial soil in the streambeds. In turn the cotton fields involve keeping the cattle out of what was once rich pasture and forcing the displaced herds to put still greater pressure on the drier grass and woodland.

The only time I have seen men controlling a grass fire in Madagascar: a step forward? (near Betioky).

Flowering butter-gold trees (*Acridocarpus excelsus*) in Jarindrano.

Erosion west of Tananarive.

Grazing pasture changes the composition of the vegetation. The grasses that zebu prefer are selectively destroyed, especially along the forest edges where the zebu seek shade at noonday. Within the forest the cattle take shoots of favored tree species, and, in time, the whole woodland becomes sparser, drier, sunnier. It is then more susceptible to fire, which can roll back the boundary tens or hundreds of metres in a year. Koechlin calls this a retreat by stages. He measured aerial photographs of a region north of Bekily village and found the forest edges had changed little over the past 20 years, but periods of relative equilibrium have in the past and will in the future alternate with periods of brutally sudden change in the habitat.

The loss of woodland in the long term affects the water supply and drainage, so cattle and people may find themselves in a tightening trap as a consequence of their own attempts at expansion.

The glinting grasslands near Bekily village gave no hint of such degradation. Out of the straw-gold waves stood isolated butter-gold trees. Rachel and I buried our noses in their peony-scented blossoms. One flower in the tuft, about 4 inches from my left eye, politely moved over, wriggling its legs. The tiny butter-yellow crab spider may spend its whole life cycle on a single tree, awaiting the moment of golden blossom.

THE SUFFICIENT VILLAGE

The track diverged. A very old, toothless lady appeared, carrying her water bucket on her head, her mud-colored dress sagging from the remains of shoulder straps.

"Which way to Bekily?" Rachel asked.

The old lady swung around, water bucket and all, to point the way.

There, tucked into a shoulder of hill, with its rice fields in a cup of a valley below, stood Bekily, blending with the hillside, for its square mud houses are made from a clay pit in the village itself.

A white-haired and dignified grandfather strode to meet us, with two other old men, three old women, about five each of the younger men and women, and countless children. We asked for the uncle of Rachel's student to see if he might guide us on to the forest.

"He is down in his rice field, working. Will you not accept our hospitality while we send a messenger for him?"

The villagers installed us in their headman's house on three real Western-style folding chairs. The house was bare of other furniture except an iron bedstead with mosquito net in one corner and a fine straw mat on the floor. The room was clean, however. In this region, among people of the Bara tribe, they build storehouses and kitchen in an attic, so there was no cooking smell or grime of soot. The men arranged themselves to our right, women and children to our left.

They questioned us straightaway about our official status. They were much relieved when Rachel said we had already made courtesy calls on the Chef de Province in Tulear and the sous-préfêt of Sakaraha. Their village council was responsible for policing this area; they were glad that they did not have to deal with unaccredited foreigners wandering through and that, in fact, we are properly vouched for.

Rachel in turn asked them about the forest. They described all their lemurs with precision: ringtails, the white sifaka and the brown ones, red lemurs and yellow red lemurs, and even the markings on each variety.

"Do the lemurs come down and damage your crops?"

"No, they stay in the forest. On the contrary, we eat the lemurs. Not sifaka, or the forked lemur that wakes up at night. They smell horrible and taste worse. However the red and yellow ones taste very good indeed."

"How do you catch them?"

"They are not worth bullets. The best way is to have many people surround a tree. Then, we shake the trees and shout Oo-lu-lu-lu! The lemurs fall down, then we just catch them with our hands."

"Lemurs bite!"

"Not if you clamp round the neck, just behind the head."

As Rachel questioned further about her own interests in medicinal herbs, a buxom girl in an orange dress, who had been answering questions along with the men, went out the door and then returned to bow and say our meal was ready: Would we be pleased to eat?

Rachel feigned amazement, knowing that we must be fed, according to village hospitality anywhere in the world. She had already told the village we must leave quickly for the forest, to forestall them killing a chicken for us. They had hastily prepared a minimum: white rice and whole bananas, with "silver water," a smoky tea made by boiling water with the burned rice grains at the bottom of the cooking pot.

We moved to an adjoining house to eat, our three chairs brought after us, and sat down at a table made by a competent carpenter. The windows were squared off by an equally competent mason; clothes hung from a board nailed to the wall, with neatly beveled detail between the pegs. Rachel asked who made all these things. It was the headman's son, the man who was building a house as we came in. He was not the only craftsman in the village—women worked in straw, making intricate articles like the woven mat that framed the chief's shotgun on the wall.

"Do you make everything that you need?" Rachel asked the headman.

"Nearly everything."

"Do you grow everything that you need?"

"We have rice, manioc, bananas, chickens, greens. We buy salt and nails, but very little else. Why should we?"

"When did your ancestors come here?"

"Long, long ago. The grandfather of the grandfather you met was born here. This village is all one family. Only two men who came with the forest logging concession have asked leave to settle here and to marry into the village. Our village council met. We gave them leave to stay and assigned them land. The village council decides whose land we shall work each day. As the village is also a family, the decisions are not difficult."

"What about the future? What do you want? A road? A school?"

"No, we do not need a road, with the little that we trade. And what would our children learn in school that is of use in a village? They would only grow away from their family."

"All the same," Rachel persisted, "you should send one or two of your children to school. Then that child could help the village to deal with the world outside."

The headman was silent, since courtesy forbade him to disagree. He changed the subject.

"Look at our fields. You see, we have enough for ourselves."

We looked out at the cupped valley: green rice fields, with a backdrop of the *Medemia* palms that mean water in plenty here among the hoed lands just as they do by woodland streams. In this landscape, on the sedimentary rocks, the springs bathe the low lying pockets, while the high land has only the golden grasses of the endless pasture.

Is this at last the happy village of the ecologist's dreams—self-sufficient in its economy, confident of its past and its future, in balance with its environment?

Even here man has changed the primeval landscape. The most ancient village sites of inland Madagascar are only a little north of Bekily in the same sort of ecology. Their inhabitants in the 15th and 16th centuries had cattle and crops and forged iron. The people of the 15th century village, like those of Bekily, ate lemurs and other wild things when they could, leaving behind in their middens the bones of western hapalemur as well as fossas and the fat spiny tenrec, which people still eat today, baked in mud to remove its prickles as English gypsies cook hedgehogs.[5]

Even in those days villagers were not wholly isolated. Among the tenrec bones and the local pottery lie Indian beads, shards of a brown Chinese jar, and Islamic celadon ware. Only a little later, around 1650, the first great Sakalava kingdom sprang from this western area to spread the ideas of centralized kingship from here to the north. Perhaps the idea of kingship derived from the same surge which produced the Central African empire of Zimbabwe. Although scholars usually insist on the Indonesian origin of Malagasy customs, much came from Africa or from multiple crossings of the Mozambique Channel by an Indonesian–African stock.[6] The African-looking Bara as a group, like any other tribe, have a history that includes invasions and wars; each village has its own history, which can only approximate the ideal of Utopian balance or self-sufficiency.

What we have finally learned today is that the balance is not, and never has been, inevitable.

Most biological systems have some buffering, some homeostasis, such that they return to a point of equilibrium if only slightly disturbed. Beyond certain limits, though, if one part of the system is too much disturbed it starts irreversible changes that kill the organism or destroy the ecosystem until it settles again to a new, usually much simplified equilibrium.[7]

The 15th century villagers and their predecessors went too far. A nearby prehistoric site is filled with bones of the giant subfossils and the little hippopotamus.[8] They had apparently already died off by the 15th century. Now, today, even the forest where villagers used to hunt fossas and lemurs is gone as well.

Casual hunting did not lead to extinction, but forest clearance did, and the drainage patterns which changed with the loss of the trees. The prehistoric pond of Ampoza was apparently a little clay pan in the woods, without organized source or exit. Elephant birds drank there, and the pygmy hippopotamus wallowed in its oozy mud. It was like many surviving ponds within the dry woodland set with purple water lilies, where grebes and Meller's duck swam among the animals long since gone just as they swim today. It was like the cup of the Bekily rice fields, now turned to human uses instead of water lilies.

Rene Battistini, doyen of geographers who have written about Madagascar, believes that after the early deforestation of this western region with the increased runoff from the cleared lands, those little cups began to erode and to flow into one another. The river systems ramified, captured the isolated ponds, and drained the country of the water which is life.

We looked at Bekily's fertile valley: a fortunate valley which is still isolated from any river and still largely isolated from the market economy.

Rachel lapsed from her scientist's stance to ask, "Do you have rice to sell me? You probably know that there are many problems with rice distribution in the city of Tulear, and it would be very useful if I could buy a few kilos for my family."

"Of course we have extra rice. How much would you like?"

They grouped in the shade of a spreading kily, while a grandmother measured the rice into Rachel's basket. The old woman's hands wove rhythmically as a shuttle in the measuring gesture which every Malagasy uses: plant the measuring tin or woven straw cup in one's own rice basket, then two hands together for the first scoop, tossing rice to fill the straw cup, two hands together for the second scoop, trickling grains into a heaped cone on top of the cup while the extra falls back in one's own basket, then one hand to toss the laden cupful into the buyer's basket, and start again.

How Malagasy, how generous, that the measure for sale or cooking should be the heaped cup, fairly piling on every grain the cup can hold. How different, in spirit, from the leveled teaspoon or the weighed-out grams of western purchases.

I wondered if this scene was a last relic of the past or a prophecy of the future: the city woman in her formal white lamba buying surplus rice from the village grandmother. I wondered who really knew the right path: Rachel and I with our university educations, our travel to many continents, our juggling of children and intellectual career, or this old woman whose grandchildren tilled the fields of her grandfather, so that her generous hands might fill our cups.

FORKED LEMUR

Rachel, Russ, and I set up camp in the lovely woodland near Bekily. Rachel wandered through the glades, secateurs in hand, clipping spring flowers. All the woodland was in flower, from the lobster-clawed sprays of the *Chadsia* tree to the little yellow sepals along the twining liana. High against the skyline, a dome of rose madder abuzz with tiny black bees, rose the crown of a Madagascar flame tree.

Russ lay immobile beside a tiny clear streamlet, where infrequent zebu had left

OPPOSITE: Swampy forest near Bekily with palms and other evergreens.

Charaxes (Jarindrano).

Butterflies (*Anapheis antsianaka?*) in Jarindrano.

Lobster claw plant (*Chadsia*) near Sakaraha.

Fly (Jarindrano).

muddy hoofprints on the bank. He photographed five species of butterfly which settled on the wet mud, including a leaf-winged charaxes, one of the most treasured of Malagasy lepidoptera. "Even the most minute variants of leaf-wing find themselves dignified with a name... the rarity and difficulty of capture add to many species' value,"[9] while the antenor swallowtail, large as a man's hand, glided 12 feet overhead.

Beside the hoofprints at the tiny ford were rows of little lemur handprints, where the ringtails came down to drink.

It was hard to remember that the handprints were ringtails' not racoons, that the swallowtails and leaf butterflies and gray-trunked rosewood trees were endemic species, not the trees and butterflies we know. This seemed an ordinary deciduous woods in early spring, although the spring came after a winter of dry heat, not wet cold.

Dusk fell over the lovely campsite. I pitched my orange nylon tent, which Rachel would share. Russ hung his mosquito net and staked up his aluminum-framed rucksack as a backrest, to Rachel's admiration. If we could travel northward in the dry forest to the sculptured Karst plateaus, to the home of the noble Western baobab ("mother of the forest"), and the rare and ridiculous jumping rat, the cumulative effect of new plants and animals would shake us again into a sense of wonder. However, that night recalled only scout camps and family cookouts and student hikes. The evening bird trills blended with the burbling stream and the cozy bubbling of cookpots over the campfire.

Rachel began to giggle. "If only the children could see me really camping. This is the first night I have ever slept in a tent."

"Didn't you even camp in Europe?"

"Of course not. My husband and I traveled all over France, Frankfurt, Tübingen, Rome, but we slept in youth hostels like other foreign students. We visited cathedrals, not forests. Here, it would be considered impolite if not insane to refuse village hospitality to sleep out among the ghosts and the wild boars, dragging one's own house like a snail. Besides, we have no such luxurious equipment as tents and sleeping bags. But I assure you, I enjoy this life."

Rachel had again neatly punctured the bubble of our provinciality. "Everyone's" memory of camping out is only a Western memory. If our own enthusiasm for the wild began with the 19th century Romantics, access to the wild began to spread with Lord Baden-Powell and Ernest Thompson Seton and Henry Ford. The wild as a separate place, nature as a separate entity to "go back to," is the cumbersome Western concept. For the villagers of Bekily, the fabric of nature is the backdrop of their lives.

Then, just as the last color left the darkening trees, the soft camp noises were cut off by a chorus of amplified squawks like a parrot turned pop star.

The upper third of the trees around our little clearing exploded with squawking: more of the same voices answered every hundred metres down the stream. We seized headlamps while two of the squawkers conversed, in accents with some structural resemblance to a sifaka's cooing contact call but shouted as though to a deaf aunt.

"It must be phaner, the forked lemur. No one makes more noise than phaner!"

The squawk changed to a series of pitched clicks, testing the loudspeaker by spitting into it.

We focused the headlamps. A pair of small orange eyes glared back at us from a high branch. Then, instead of hopping from vertical to vertical and staying put, as a lepilemur would, or scuttling and pausing, as a mouselemur or dwarf lemur would, those eyes launched themselves in a straight line through the treetops like a horizontal shooting star.

"*That's* phaner! After it!"

We chased that phaner until it doubled back and lost us. We craned our necks at two who groomed each other and played like little sifaka, hanging by their feet and sparring, almost out of sight in a 30-m rosewood tree. We swore back at a phaner who camouflaged itself, swearing at us, among crisscross branches.

They were everywhere, insulting or serenading, until one decided to hang beneath the branch of a low tree to browse on flowers and ignore us.

Phaner is blond, honey gold like a kinkajou, with a deep brown or black stripe up its back that forks to bisect each eye. Its long, dark-plumed tail would do justice to a diurnal lemur. It runs on branches like a proper leaping quadruped, not with the hunched, short-armed build of the other nocturnal forms. It also operates visually, most active at dusk and dawn and in full moonlight.[10] It feeds largely on flowers, nectar, and resin and an exudate of flower-mimic bugs, at least in these months of the springtime in the flowering woodland.[11]

I once asked Pierre Charles-Dominique, who knows more than anyone else about the lives of nocturnal prosimians, if phaner might be the most sociable of night-living primates. After all, they click and squawk at each other, hourly, all night long.

Pierre was doubtful. "We just notice phaner's social signals because we can hear them. With other nocturnal prosimians, you have to smell them. It is true, at least, that males are permitted to follow females, chasing through the female's territory, and that several neighbors may gather at a corner of their territory for shouting concerts."

I still like phaner. I would rather hear it than smell it, and I would just love to pat it.

Little chance though, for that. Phaner lives and browses on nectar and shouts in the night only within the Malagasy western woodlands. I have yet to see one in any zoo.

BOA IN THE BARROOM

We were all too excited to sleep much between the moonlight and the hourly chorus of phaner. Dawn in the woods cool and dewfresh, with neither the closeness of rainforest dawn nor the chill of the desert.

We climbed a bank, away from the green trees of the streambed. At once the bushes are dry and leafless, entwined with the permanently leafless creepers of endemic Malagasy vanilla vines. At first sight unpromising. Yet from such dry Malagasy forests, on calcareous cliffs, comes one of the most famous of tropical trees—the flamboyant or royal poinciana. Climb 5 or 10 m from streambed to stream bank; you travel from green to gray, from evergreen swamp trees to dry, twisted, winter woods. This is, of course, the same difference in height and ecology as that between Bekily's fertile rice fields and the dry golden pasture.

Downstream our brook ended in a little pond, which had no outlet but simply seeped away into the ground. Cattle egrets and the cosmopolitan glossy ibis minced along its borders, with the Malagasy variety of the pretty little three-collared plover. Behind the pond rose a backdrop of dark green western pandanus and fruiting palm trees of the two western species.

Even here there were signs of people: zebu with notched ears drinking at the pond, and a runway of earth and leaves leading to a vine noose which is a trap for ground couas. A little pile of feathers showed that the trap had worked at least once. Another pile of feathers, brown and white banded, large enough for a turkey, belonged to a bubuka, the Madagascar cuckoo falcon. Cuckoo falcons sit motionless for hours on end, perched on trees at the forest edge. Possibly this one succumbed to no more subtle hunting than clever stalking and a flung stone.

Among the Medemia palms stood other evergreens including trees whose fruits stick out like balloons from its trunk—a phenomenon common in wet forests, rare in dry woodlands.

Rachel and I followed the little watercourse to its head, a small swampland where the water oozed from under the higher ground before gathering itself together into the stream. We had traced the streamlet from end to beginning, a seam of water that opens and closes in sedimentary stone.

I was hoping that we should find the *akohoanala,* the crested ibis. I told Rachel about the bird, a mismatched child's cutout. It stands half a metre high, with heavy, pheasant-brown body, a long iridescent green crest, a down-curved ibis's beak (the only bit that is zoologically appropriate), and then the whole affair is mounted on a pair of red chicken legs. I have twice before seen the crested ibis in just this sort of woodland.[12]

But no, no ibis. A springing in the trees instead, where a troop of sifaka bounded away among the green swampland foliage. Two of the sifaka were white with brown caps—the common *Propithecus verreauxi* we had seen throughout the spiny desert. Three more gleamed chocolate brown and cream with eagle wing patterns on arms and legs, dark breasts, dark chocolate backs.

Georges Randrianasolo and I have a standing argument about those dark sifaka. Georges maintains that they are a distinct race, *Propithecus verreauxi majori.*[13]

I protest that there are mixed troops of the "extinct subspecies" with normal white ones. This is only a color variant.

Guy, when I showed him mixed troops over the de Guiteaud's plantation house near Berenty, offered an olive branch. Perhaps this color variant is a subspecies in the course of formation or in the course of absorption back into the main race—one of those genetic differences which show in the fur and can mark transitions between populations. Instead of arguing about their significance, we should study them.

But there is so much to study, and so little time. The sifaka over the plantation house were trusting, tame, after 30 years of hopping unmolested over the de Guiteaud's lawn. If any amateur had kept track of those two troops' members, we would know all about sifaka color inheritance and most of what we want of sifaka behavior.

In 1977, three months after the last Frenchman left, the last of those tame sifaka has been eaten.

There is so much left to study that we may never have time to see. The afternoon drew on; sleepy grunting in a fig tree above us meant that rufous lemurs are waking from their prolonged siesta. It was so familiar—that grunting. I knew before looking up. There would be a male or so, gray with plumed black tail and rufous orange mane; there will be a female like my pet Calomella, red-brown with white clown eyebrows painted above her lemon eyes and black nose.

Wrong. There was a female with white clown eyebrows and black nose and proper rufous-lemur grunts bubbling up in her throat. She was, however, the wrong color. Where she should have been glowing red, she was muddy yellow all over. The tiny male baby, wrapped transversely around her like a belt, was the right color: his sprouting tufts of mane grew properly reddish orange, but there was no denying his mother was frankly jaundice hued.

When we stopped in Bekily village, the villagers had listed the lemurs of their forest. They knew the white sifaka and the variant brown sifaka. They knew the red lemurs and added that they knew yellow red lemurs, which trooped with the red ones as brown sifaka trooped with white. I had never heard of a yellow red lemur—but there she was, stretching her rump high and hands and arms straight before her, working the kinks from her fingers. A quick sniff and groom of the baby, then she bounded away. An orange-maned male, even sleepier, followed after.

There is so much still to learn. There is a new species of lepilemur, discovered by its chromosomes on a microscope slide.[14] The leech-filled forest of the Montagne d'Ambre holds a population of albino mongoose lemurs.[15] Ian Tattersall and Bob Sussman found two distinct color forms among the mongoose lemurs of Ankarafant-sika, a forest station on the main road to Majunga, where every mammalogist has studied before them.[16] Perrier's sifaka, wholly black in a tiny isolate forest between the ranges of two white forms, was only discovered in 1931 and may be extinct by 1981.[17] *Hapelemur simus* was discovered, then "lost" for a hundred years, until Petter and Peyriéras found it again in 1972. Jean-Jacques Petter is still looking for *Allocebus*—for a second specimen, alive, to prove that the single skin from 1875 was not the last of these mammals on earth.

And then there are even wilder tales which return and return.

Last Saturday we drove at sunset from Sept Lacs to Tulear with Rachel, Rabe, and their children, Haja, Hary, Naina, Noro, and little Hobilalao. The day had been thrilling for the children—their first view of lemurs and sifaka, for dependents are not permitted to use government transport, so they had never been in the field with university expeditions. They paddled in the travertine pools of a limestone spring; they watched sifaka in their creamy white coats spring onto the creamy arms of a fig tree; they gorged on kilys from a tamarind tree, wantonly burned down so that it fell across the track, to their elders' annoyance.

The sun set over Table Hill behind Tulear, a posed sunset, red halfway up the Table, blue to silhouette the top. Headlights on the tarmac highway. Haja, Hary, Naina, Noro, and even Hobilalao chorused a temperance song, "Abjure, Abjure, Abjure!"

Russ jammed on the brakes and made the swiftest U-turn ever performed by that

Propithecus verreauxi, brown form.

Brown sifaka (*Propithecus verreauxi majori*) with normal member of the same troop on de Guiteaud concession near Berenty.

Russ with Amie, the boa constrictor, at the hotel bar in Tulear.

Land Rover, as children squealed and adults babbled. He leaped out into the roadway, while a taxi bore down in the opposite lane. Russ pounced on a long, straight, whitish stick, which was crawling headfirst in front of the taxi. The taxi driver in turn jammed on his brakes—he seemed to have no inhibitions about hitting Russ but nosed down in horror as the stick turned into 4 feet of coiling boa constrictor.

The boa was white below, with flat transverse scales beneath. On the paved road, with no humps in the ground or leaf litter to allow sideways wriggling, it inched forward in a straight line by peristaltic waves passing down those transverse scales. Above, it shaded to a light gray and dark brown dazzle pattern, with 30-odd transverse bars that did not meet properly in the midline, as though the back seam had been sewed up crooked. Its small head was decorated with a black moustache line, beneath which the tasting tongue flickered in and out. The shortness and bluntness of its tail, posterior to the anogenital opening, indicated she was probably female. In most ways she resembled the boa which we found on the island of the sacred lemurs, but this western form was much lighter in color. This is a general phenomenon. Many of the nocturnal lemurs of the west and south are light gray, while their eastern forest counterparts are dark brown or even rufous. The color differences relate directly to the differences in illumination.[18] The western forests are sparse and moonlit; wet eastern forests are darkly shaded. Of course, camouflage relates to the senses of nocturnal predators and prey, not to our own, diurnal eyes. Nocturnal animals in general do not see red, so the rufous eastern lemurs appear as deepest gray in a dark gray background, neither black, which would show up too darkly, nor gray, which would be too pale. As for the western boa, to any eyes she was a stick of mottled moonlight.

Boas bear their young alive, having incubated their eggs past hatching inside their bodies. Females can store sperm as well. Russ's captive might bear young up to two years later, producing several litters of 20-odd snakelings when she does so.

Home to drop off the tired children, who were wriggling more than the boa. Russ exulted over his serpent while Rachel more practically admired Russ for going on family picnics equipped with double-sewed snake sacks.

Back to the hotel recommended by the upright, churchgoing Rabesandratanas as being nearest their home. Perhaps they did not realize that the hotel has the highest concentration of girls per barroom, and presumably per bedroom, in Tulear. It was Saturday night. In rooms over the bar there seemed little prospect of rest. Russ suddently decided to try a little popular education in his own fashion, wrapped the boa around his neck, and sauntered into the bar.

Pandemonium. It was more like birds mobbing an owl than any human behavior. Men and girls oscillated around a 4-foot distance from the snake, fascination and fear keeping balance. Hands reached out and shot back, eyes opened wider and wider. Snakes are held in fear and horror here, the boa, the dô most of all. They are wholly taboo and never appear on tomb paintings, only in the secret rituals of sorcerers. There are no truly poisonous snakes in Madagascar, so this horror can have no basis in common sense avoidance. Either it is a legacy from ancestors who came from lands of cobras and puff adders and mambas or else Freud is right that the mere shape of a snake makes it supernatural.

The burly bartender was the most courageous. Bare except for shorts and apron, his muscles announced that he was bouncer for the establishment as well as tapster. Egged on by his diminutive girl friend, he asked if he could put the snake around his own neck. As the crowd inched in, Russ showed him how to hold the boa and how to touch her, bringing a hand slowly up from underneath (after all, she was used to crawling over sticks) not frightening her by grabbing down from above.

I was as frightened as the bartender, for different reasons. A boa bites nastily and hold on to its prey as it laps its coils around. No one was in danger of being squeezed by so small a snake, but if the placid animal finally bit, we could find ourselves in a barroom brawl that would have us evicted from Tulear—perhaps even, if the military governor of the province took our clowning amiss, from the country.

Russ began to explain "C'est votre amie!" over and over. He found his French so fluent he surprised himself, to say that she eats rodents and small birds, that "votre amie" protects people's crops.

"You don't like rats, do you? Well, then, the snake is on your side! C'est votre amie!" Here, Alison, hold Amie a minute, while I buy some beer."

A history student from Tulear University, wearing purple sunglasses, and three high-school biology students come to talk. (You find students in all sorts of places.)

"Is it really a Malagasy snake? We have never seen one. Aren't there any snakes at all like this in Africa?"

Purple-shades challenged me: "Why do you say there are none in Africa when we have learned that most Malagasy animals come from Africa?"

So, yet again, I sat down to explain about Gondwanaland and the origin of Malagasy boas to the very people who should have been telling me. Purple-shades and his friends should have been able to thump the table and declare, "Here in the Malagasy Republic, even our biology is nationalist!"

Russ retrieved Amie. Even the girls began to pat her now, explaining that they have been brought up to be afraid and wonder why.

Three Indians at a table asked me over. They were worried that we were taking pictures to make fun of people. I told them about this book, saying this was a rather exceptional Saturday night.

"If you are interested in lemurs as well as snakes," said Mr. Asgaraly, "please join us. Please tell me about a strange lemur which I kept at my farm at Beroha. We have sifaka, red lemurs, and ringtails there, but this one was different.

"It was black all over in the shadow, but in sunlight deep reddish brown. Its face was flat, not pointed like other lemurs, but more like the guenon monkeys of Africa. It often walked on its hindlegs but with one foot before the other, not hopping with two feet like a sifaka. The old lady I bought it from told me that the young of this species are born in December, so it was five months old when I bought it in early June. At that time it sat about 25 cm high. I presume the adults are somewhat larger. I kept it for two months, then it died. No, I do not know where my servant buried the skeleton."

I sat with my mouth open. We have asked whether you need to save forest to preserve a rare species. We have asked whether you need forest to preserve all the rare species of a climax habitat. We have asked whether you need forest to guard the eco-

I hold Amie for high school students. Purple-shades is the one in the hat.

nomic advantages of the future. But how much do you need to discover a species of primate unknown to science?

A new primate, a black, monkey-faced lemur in a forest where no such thing should be. . . . Perhaps, in spite of all the centuries of scientific study Madagascar remains an unknown world.

Russ coiled up the flaccid Amie and slipped her into her snake bag. "That is one very tired boa constrictor," he told his disappointed audience, the barroom full of new friends who had been educating us.

FOREST FIRE

One-quarter of Madagascar burns each year. Fires crackle across the grasslands, driven by the prairie wind. Fires necklace the hillsides, chains of scarlet jewels in the night. Fires invade the plantations of pine and eucalyptus, destroying years of foresters' toil.

The fires are set deliberately, then burn uncontrolled, stopping only when the wind drops or when a cliff face or patch of bare soil checks their course.

After the fires, small green shoots poke upward from the charred tussocks of grass—survival for the zebu, which are the peasants' pride.

As we emerged with Rachel from the forest near Bekily, a few ribbons of woodland rose out of the golden savanna, relics of the forest that once covered the west.

Rachel pointed across the shimmering heat waves of the prairie. "Look at the smoke. That fire has reached the trees!"

Edges of flame still spread through the grasslands, east and west. Red-winged locusts sprang out of the tussocks and flew before the blaze. One fire-resistant tree stood alone on the charred savanna, replete birds of prey perching on its smoke-blackened branches. Kestrels and larger hawks circled before the advancing flames, waiting for insects, lizards, and rodents to choose between death by fire and death by beak and talon.

The fire was deep in the forest edge, the frontier of second growth, while high primary forest stood behind, hidden in smoke. A red glow crawled through the litter of dead leaves, charring them into blackened ash like paper ash. It mumbled around the roots of bushes and trees, sometimes passing on between live trees still standing, sometimes settling to pick the bones of a fallen log.

Where the fire stayed long enough in dead logs and twigs, in dried zebu pats or piles of leaves beneath a bush, the living bark of trees began to curl and scorch. Low, dry, bushy twigs made kindling, leading the fire up into the branches. Heat ascended standing trees, ever more intense, from the fire at their base and the crackling bushes below. A tree screamed as its sap began to boil, and the gasses burst from fissures in its bark. At last, all at once, the tree burst into a torch of flame, scarlet for 15 m against the sky.

"Fireworks!" said Rachel, smiling, but her smile was ugly.

The fire moved deeper and deeper into the forest: black leaf ash and white wood ash on the ground, then sudden, isolated scarlet torches, springing now near the edge, now deep inside the boundary woodlands, as individual by individual, the trees succumbed.

The sight of it was deliberate, advancing menace, but the noise and heat of it

Hawk waiting near fire for prey.

Fires spread on the plateau until stopped by a road, flooded paddy, or cliff face. Pasture grasses and firewood have no protection.

engulfed one: the continuous crackling of burning leaves, the flap of wind as the heat billowed forward, above and through the fire noises the kestrels whistling. And then, again, that shriek of a tortured tree.

"Look at the ground," Rachel called. "The zebu eat the forest edge so it is drier year by year, then even add their own fuel. You can see, those zebu crottes keep burning and hold the heat for long enough to set still more trees on fire. You can see the future, year by year, with still more fires and more zebu."

Rachel stood, her white lamba around her shoulders, facing the burning woodland.

"I have taught for fourteen years," she said, "in school and university. Every year I tell the students, 'We are laying waste our own lands.' Every year they say 'Yes, ma'am' to their teacher. And look, just look. Every year the land burns over and over again. It makes you want to give up trying, to say if this is all they want let them burn it all. Only a fool could still believe it is worth the battle."

"Rachel, you won't give up!"

Rachel turned away, the forest behind her blue gray with heat like an open kiln, slashed by the scarlet towers of flame.

"You are right, I can't give up. Not the scientists, not the politicians, not the people. We shall somehow save Madagascar from suicide by fire, and from our own indifference. We shall all, somehow, preserve our land, in the way it ought to be."

Fire poster near Fianarantsoa.

PART 5
OUR OWN WORLD

12

OUR OWN WORLD

Is there hope? It all depends.

It depends on whether we have the wisdom to conserve *our* future.

I could conclude with cheery optimism. For all our doom-mongering, we conservationists tend to optimism. We believe that our species need not reduce the planet to a desert of starving cattle and dying children. We even believe that we will not reduce the world to a point where all remaining protoplasm is divided into pests or producers, defined only in relation to our own rapacity.

However, wilderness could die, and many people would not miss it. Like the people of the Malagasy plateau, we would still have poets and presidents, mothers who nurse their children, and farmers who cultivate their fields. Each nation must make its own decision between the claims of agricultural land, of forest managed for timber, and of climax wilderness, actively preserved as the heritage of the future.

Then it is the whole world's decision whether to support that choice.

UNESCO already lumbers slowly toward acting upon this truth. UNESCO's World Heritage Convention is a group of nations that have pledged themselves to jointly finance sites of outstanding natural or cultural importance. However, most of us are only beginning to realize that everyone can share in the beauty of the Parthenon or the Amazon, Krakow's historic center or the Galapagos Islands—just as everyone can share in their neglect and destruction. Above all, powerful nations are only beginning to see that they have a selfish interest in preserving these wonders *in situ*, not merely in bringing chunks of the Parthenon frieze to London or a diorama of stuffed Amazon birds to New York.

The world has become a finite reserve for the human species. Whatever is left of wilderness must be preserved by active policy decisions that draw boundaries to the human reserve, coupled with the political will and financial support to keep those boundaries.[1]

OPPOSITE: The only survivor of a burning, the *Sclero Caraya caffra* tree, whose thick bark protects it from the flames.

The first step is to get rid of the sentimental belief that we can somehow slip back to a golden age in passive equilibrium with nature.

In the golden age, ever since we were lemur-like beasts, half our babies died, as lemur babies die at Berenty. Because we have evolved the depth of primate parental love, we will never again voluntarily accept population control by the death of young children. As with population control, so with resource control. No society today willingly lives in cold, or hunger, or even the uncertainty of the future that has always been a peasant's lot. We may not need the obesity of Northern riches, but we are not going to return to bare subsistence by choice.

Even within apparently traditional societies there is rarely long-term equilibrium with nature. On the contrary the people we have met in this book share a long history of ecological change. They, as much as any other frontier people, exploit their capital of land. They, like the rest of us, gain and lose from an economic system that stretches far beyond their villages.

In Hiaraka, Jean and Emmanuel live by virgin rainforest by a perfect beach. Far from being a static paradise, their part of the east has been for five centuries the domain of pirates, traders, slavers. Their most famous tribal king fought not just for land but to gain control of the slave trade with Europe. Now the region grows vanilla, coffee, and cloves for sale in world markets. Jean's bid to make his own independence, when he turned his back on the search for a city job and went off to plant clove trees in the forest, put him instead at the mercy of international commodity markets (or lack of them) and the relative price of synthetic clove oil in New Jersey.

In Lavalohalika, island of sacred lemurs, there has also been change. The whole population of the island fled and returned during wars between Malagasy tribal kingdoms. The recent change in ecology is obvious to all: forest degraded, soil eroding. The people's resource again is trade, not this time in the international sector but with the mainland peasants. Islanders barter tortoiseshell and rum for the rice which no longer grows on their crumbling land.

In Hazofotsy, Tohimbinty and his family seem archetypal cattle people, proud in spear and loincloth among their well-loved herds. Again, however, their habitat has changed with the spread and the destruction of the Mexican prickly pear, their dry season staple over 150 years. They now depend for food on government-irrigated lands. They buy their cattle with money gained not through trade but by exporting themselves as migrant labor.

Finally, there is Bekily. The villagers of Bekily say, "We have enough." They demand no road, no school, with the wisdom to know that such benefits would destroy the pattern of village life. Their minimal trade links provide a few luxuries from the sale of their surplus food. They seem at last to be truly the people of the golden age.

Yet even there we know from archeological records that the forest has been pushed back and that the drainage patterns have ramified as fires cleared the land. The Sakalava kingdoms rose and fell; the rosewood loggers came and went. Bekily's current position is perhaps an ideal which other villages could aim to achieve. It is not, however, an inevitable or accidental achievement that some built-in feedback mechanism keeps at an optimum or that no outside influences can reach. It is maintained, instead, by conscious choices at every level from that of village council to that of the central government, which fixes the price of rice.

Such a village is not merely flotsam left aside by the main economy. It has riches enough because its agricultural products are reasonably priced and because the present Malagasy government has abolished the "fiscal minimum" head tax of about $20, which is trivial to any bourgeois and was designed only to harrass peasants into joining the money economy.[2] Neither is Bekily a pocket of political ignorance but an organized village council whose first act was to check whether our visit had official approval.

The self-sufficient village is an ideal, but it cannot be reconstructed by going backward in time to the 19th century, before head taxes and hut taxes and conscript labor, before DDT and antimalaria pills.

We cannot go back. We can instead choose the future we would like to share.

The Malagasy peasant can choose to maintain woodlots not because they are unaccountably precious to central government but because his own children need fuel, house timber, and protected watersheds. He can also respect the wilderness areas but only if financial benefits flow to surrounding communities. Occasional tips to guides and porters are not enough. Neither are exorbitant hotel bills paid in Tananarive, which never reach the peasants.

The Malagasy government can choose to put resources into its 6,704 km² of national reserves and parks. These were originally set aside by farsighted Frenchmen in 1927. (France did not create its own first national park until 1965). In total the Malagasy Reserves amount to only 1% of the whole land area, far less than many other countries. Still, they represent the best habitat of the various biotopes, so financial support to safeguard them must be a priority of the newly created World Wildlife Fund— Madagascar, and its director, Barthelmy Vaohitra. Such support, though, should harmonize with educational and economic development. Malagasy know that wilderness lives not by biology but by human economics.

The international community can choose to support both Malagasy nature and the Malagasy people by trade agreements that recognize the importance of primary resources. It can do so grudgingly, forced backward step by step in the economic confrontation of North and South. It can do so willingly, working toward solutions which benefit both sides. It can choose, as well, to support WWF—Madagascar, for the rich can afford longer-term investment than the poor, in a factory or a tree. The choice is difficult even in rich countries to save an Alpine valley or a redwood grove. But it is a choice that we make, just as we have not turned the Louvre into office blocks or the Lincoln Memorial into a parking area. How much more is it in our interest to preserve the biological diversity of a finite planet. Even far-off Madagascar is our own world.

We have asked how much wilderness is needed to save a species, how much to save a climax community. We have asked if it is worth saving medicinal plants whose uses we have not yet guessed or forms of life, long since evolved, whose existence we never suspected. How absurd to think we must put a price on an alternate world of evolution—the island-continent of Madagascar—before deciding whether it is worth preserving.

But these are still only small questions, with small answers. They are the equivalent of reasons a medieval monk would give for laboriously copying out a text of Plato. He could murmur that he saved a great and ancient treasure. He could not dream that he sowed the seeds of the Renaissance, the scientific revolution, the transformation of man's estate.

How much wilderness do we need to save for new ideas—to interpret ecology and evoluation at a new level of understanding? How many alternate worlds do we need on our finite earth to inspire the theory or the social creativity that succeeds Darwinian evolution, embracing it as relativity embraced Newtonian physics?

The conservation of nature is not simply the conservation of our past—that which we did not create. It is also the conservation of our future. It is conservation of all the forms of life that have not yet evolved, and of the understanding that we have not yet achieved, which may one day become mankind's reality.

RESERVES OF THE MALAGASY REPUBLIC

		Area (km²)	
1.	Betampona	22	East coast rainforest
(2.	Masoala)	(210)	(Masoala peninsular rainforest, declassed 1964)
3.	Zahamena	731	Escarpment rainforest
4.	Tsaratanana	486	Low and high altitude forest, lichen forest, heath
5.	Andringitra	312	High altitude forest and heath
6.	Lokobe	7	Sambirano rainforest
7.	Ankarafantsika	605	Deciduous woodland
8.	Soalala	217	Deciduous woodland, caves and cave fauna
9.	Antsalova	1,520	Deciduous woodland, karst landscape
10.	Tsimanampetsotsa	432	Calcareous desert flora, flamingo lake
11.	Andohahela	760	Southern rainforest, desert flora on granite, and transition between these extremes
12.	Marojejy	601	Eastern forest from 100 to 2,100 m altitude
	Total	5,694	

NATIONAL PARKS OF THE MALAGASY REPUBLIC

1.	Montagne d'Ambre	182	Isolated rainforest mountain
2.	Isalo Massif	815	Ruiniform sandstone masses
	Total	997	

SPECIAL RESERVES

Analamazaotra or Perinet	8	Reserve for indri inside forest station
Nosy Mangabé	5	Island reserve for aye-aye
Grand total	6,704	km², or 1% of total land area of Madagascar

EPILOGUE

GOD'S FIRST DEFEAT:
A TSIMIHETY LEGEND

In ancient times, they say, all wild animals walked in peace during the day and during the night. Birds of the night, even the ill-omened owl, crossed the paths of men at noonday, with the crocodiles, mongoose-cats, serpents, and wild boars. God made no distinction between men-with-hair-at-the-top and any other creature.

Those-with-hair-at-the-top soon became sly. They began to slaughter their fellow beings. The animals complained of those-with-hair-at-the-top. These animals demanded divine interdiction, for it was a matter not only of life but of liberty and of equal status of all living beings.

God spoke to the plaintiffs. "Let all that breathe come up to Mount Ampitsonjoana, west of the village of Vohimarina, next Friday. Watch out, fellows. I shall have a few revelations to make."

On the appointed day, all the animals ran to the meeting place, except men, who stayed below in their fields. The crocodiles with rocky backs, the slow and apprehensive tortoises, the chameleons who count their steps wherever they go, all were there.

God said, "Let each one speak his complaints against men!"

Before any animals replied to him, he threw down a fearful thunderbolt; he unloosed a furious tempest. The swollen clouds billowed out into monstrous forms and colors.

Men, although frightened, climbed to the meeting place, wearing loincloths and armed only with coupe-coupes. They brought with them wooden bowls, half filled with water. They sprinkled the surroundings; they chanted "Malemy, Malemy": Be gentle, be sweet.

Quickly the thunder ceased, the wind calmed. God was for a moment powerless.

"See here," said God to the plaintiffs. "These men-with-hair-at-the-top are already grown much too strong. They do not listen to me nowadays. They openly defy my laws.

I recommend that you animals start running away from them. Do not come out in the daytime any more, if you can manage it. At least I shall make sure that these people never grow a fine sense of smell, nor very sharp eyes either. As for you, crocodiles, take yourselves off and hide in the water." (Before this, crocodiles lived in gullies which the Tsimihety still call crocodile holes.)

That happy moment marked God's first concession to man; since then man rules supreme over all other animals. Still, today, whenever God's thunder and lightning attempt to restore his ancient power, older Tsimihety are careful to repeat their soft, troubling charm: "Malemy, Malemy."

From Rabearison, *Contes et Légendes de Madagascar* (Imprimerie Luthérienne de Tananarive, 1967).

SPECIES MENTIONED IN THE TEXT

Scientific names are followed by English, French, and Malagasy, where known, and by family and class.

An asterisk indicates an endemic Malagasy species or family. A dagger indicates an extinct species.

*Acrantophis dumerilii	Western boa constrictor Boa de l'ouest Dô	Boidae, Reptilia
*Acrantophis madagascariensis	Madagascar eastern boa constrictor Boa malgache de l'est Dô	Boidae, Reptilia
*Acridocarpus excelsus	Butter-gold tree Arbre doré Sariheza, moramena, etc.	Malpighiaceae, Angiospermae
*Adansonia grandidieri	Western baobab, mother of the forest Baobab de l'ouest "mère de la forêt" Raniala	Bombaceae, Angiospermae
*Adansonia za	Antandroy baobab Baobab antandroy Za	Bombaceae, Angiospermae
*Aepyornis maximus	Elephant bird Oiseau-éléphant Voron-patra	* †Aepyornithidae, Aves
Afromomum angustifolium	Wild ginger Gingembre sauvage, longouse Longoza	Zingiberaceae, Angiospermae

*Afzelia bijuga	Hintsy Hintsy Hintsy	Leguminosae, Angiospermae
*Agapornis cana	Madagascar lovebird Iseparable à tête grise Sarivazo, karaoka	Psittacidae, Aves
*Allocebus trichotis		*Lemuridae, Mammalia
*Alluaudia antephora	Alluaudia Alluaudia	*Didiereaceae, Angiospermae
*Alluaudia ascendens	Alluaudia Alluaudia Songo bé	*Didiereaceae, Angiospermae
*Alluaudia comosa	Alluaudia Alluaudia Sony	*Didiereaceae, Angiospermae
*Alluaudia dumosa	Alluaudia Alluaudia Rohondra	*Didiereaceae, Angiospermae
*Alluaudia procera	Alluaudia Arbre pieuvre Fantsilo hitra	*Didiereaceae, Angiospermae
*Alluaudiopsis fiherenensis	Alluaudiopsis Alluaudiopsis	*Didieraeceae, Angiospermae
*Aloe helenae	Giant or Helen's aloe Aloë d'Hélène	Liliaceae, Angiospermae
*Aloe suzannae	Giant or Suzanne's aloe Aloë de Suzanne	Liliaceae, Angiospermae
*Anas bernieri	Bernier's duck Canard de Bernier	Anatidae, Aves
Anas erythrorhynca	Red-billed duck Canard à bec rouge Rahaka, menamolotro, etc.	Anatidae, Aves
*Anas melleri	Meller's duck Canard de Meller Kaka	Anatidae, Aves
*Angrecium sesquipedalum	Comet orchid Orchidée comète	Orchidaceae, Angiospermae
* †Archaeolemur edwardsi	Archaeolemur Archaeolémur	*Indriidae, Mammalia
* †Archaeolemur majori	Archaeolemur Archaeolémur	*Indriidae, Mammalia

*Ardea humbloti	Madagascar giant heron Heron de Humblot Vano Humblot	Ardeidae, Aves
Arenaria tricollaris bifrontatus	Madagascar three-banded plover Pluvier à triple bandeau Vorombato	Charadeidae, Aves
*Aristidia multicaulis	Aristidia bunch grass Herbe aristidia Bozaka	Graminae, Angiospermae
*Asio madagascariensis	Owl, Madagascar horned Hibou malgache Vorondolo, hanka	Strigidae, Aves
Asplenium nidus	Bracket fern Fougère nid d'oiseaux	Aspleniaceae, Filicineae
*Avahi laniger	Woolly lemur Avahi avahi Avahy, fotsifé	*Indriidae, Mammalia
*Aviceda madagascariensis	Madagascar cuckoo-falcon Baza malgache Bubuka, endrina	Falconidae, Aves
*Barleria sp.	Barleria Barleria	Acanthaceae, Angiospermae
*Barringtonia butonica	Bishop's-bonnet tree Bonnet d'évêque Fotabé	Lecythidaceae, Angiospermae
*Borassus madacascariensis	Western Borassus palm Rônier Dimaka, etc.	Palmaceae, Angiospermae
*Brookesia minima	Chameleon, lesser Brookes's Chamoeleon de Brookes	Chamoeleontidae, Reptilia
Bubulcus ibis ibis	Egret, cattle Héron garde-boeufs Vorompotsy	Ardeidae, Aves
*Canarium madagascariensis	Ramy Ramy Ramy	Burseraceae, Angiospermae
Carcharodon carcarias	Grcat white shark Grand requin blanc Akihofotsy	Squalidae, Chondrichthes
Caretta caretta	Loggerhead turtle Tortu couanne Fano mamy	Chelonidae, Reptilia

Casuarina equisetifolia	Filao, horsetail tree Filao Filao	Casuarinaceae, Angiospermae
*Catharanthus coriaceus	Leathery periwinkle Pervenche coriace	Apocynaceae, Angiospermae
*Catharanthus ovalis	Oval periwinkle Pervenche ovale	Apocynaceae, Angiospermae
*Catharanthus roseus	Madagascar or rosy periwinkle Pervenche malgache, pervenche rose Vonenina, salotsa	Apocynaceae, Angiospermae
*Cedrelopsis grevei	Bitter-juice tree Arbre jus-amer Katafa, katrafay	Meliaceae, Angiospermae
Centella asiatica	Centella Talapetraka Talapetraka	Umbelliferae, Angiospermae
Centropus toulou toulou	Madagascar coucal, toulou-bird Coucal malgache Toloho	Cuculidae, Aves
*Cerbera tanghin	Ordeal tree Tanghin Tangina	Apocynaceae, Angiospermae
*Ceriops boviniana	Madagascar mangrove Mangrove malgache	Rhizophoraceae, Angiospermae
*Chadsia grevei	Chadsia tree Arbre chadsia Sanganakolahy, etc.	Papilionaceae, Angiospermae
*Charaxes sp.	Charaxes butterfly Papillion charaxes	Nymphalidae, Insecta
*Cheirogaleus medius, C. major	Dwarf lemur Cheirogale Hataka	*Lemuridae, Mammalia
Chelonia mydas	Green turtle Tortue franche Fano zato	Chelonidae, Reptilia
*Chrysiridea madagascariensis (or Urania ripheus)	Urania moth Urania Lolonandriana	Uraniidae, Insecta
Colea sp.	Colea Coléa	Bignonaceae, Angiospermae
*Commiphora monstruosa, and other spp.	Commiphora bottle-trees Arbre-bouteille commiphora	Burseraceae, Angiospermae

*Copsychus albospecularis	Madagascar magpie robin Merle dyal, merle à miroir blanc Fitatra, fitatr'ala, todia	Turdidae, Aves
*Coracopsis vasa	Vasa parrot Grand perroquet vasa Siotsabé, boeza bé	Pittacidae, Aves
Corythornis vintsoides	Malachite kingfisher Martin-pêcheur malachite Vintsy	Alcedinidae, Aves
*Coua caerulea	Blue or caerulean coua Coua bleu Taitso manga, mariha	Cuculidae, Aves
*Coua cristata	Crested coua Coua huppé Tivoka, tsiloko	Cuculidae, Aves
*Coua gigas	Great ground coua Coua géant Eoke	Cuculidae, Aves
Crocodilus niloticus	Crocodile Crocodile Voay	Crocodilidae, Reptilia
*Cryptoprocta ferox	Fossa Fossa Fosa	Viverridae, Mammalia
*Cyathea sp.	Tree fern Fougère arborescent	Cyathaceae, Filicineae
*Cycas thouarsi	Madagascar cycad Cycas, sagoutier Fatio, fatra	Cycadaceae, Gymnospermae
Cypsiurus parvus gracilis	Madagascar palm swift Martinet des palms Manaviandro, tsiditsidina	Apodidae, Aves
Dactylopius coccus	Cochineal beetle Coccinelle	Coleoptera, Insecta
*Dalbergia spp.	Rosewood Palissandre Manary	Leguminosae, Angiospermae
*Dasogale fontoynonti	Pseudohedgehog Hérison malgache	*Tenrecidae, Mammalia
*Daubentonia madagascariensis	Aye-aye Aye-aye Ha-hay	*Daubentoniidae, Mammalia

*Decarynella gracilipes	Cave-dwelling daddy longlegs Moissoneur ou opilion des cavernes	Opilionidae, Arachnida
*Delonix regia	Flamboyant tree or royal poinciana Flamboyant	Papilionaceae, Angiospermae
*Didierea madagascariensis	Didierea Didiéréa Sony	*Didiereaceae, Angiospermae
*Didierea trolli	Staghorn didierea Didiéréa à tiges horizontales Sonibarika	*Didiereaceae, Angiospermae
*Diospyros perrieri and other spp.	Ebony Ebène Pingo, hazomainty	Ebenaceae, Angiospermae
*Discophus antongilii	Antongil scarlet frog Grenouille vermeil d'antongil	Ranidae, Amphibia
Dugong dugon	Dugong, sea-cow, manatee Dugong Lamboharano, lambondriaka	Dugongidae, Mammalia
*Echinops telfairi	Pseudohedgehog Hérison malgache Sora	*Tenrecidae, Mammalia
Eretmochelys imbricata	Hawksbill turtle Tortue caret Fano hara	Chelonidae, Reptilia
Eubalaena australis	Southern right whale Trozona	Baleinidae, Mammalia
*Euphorbia laro	Laro Laro	Euphorbiaceae, Angiospermae
*Euphorbia milii	Crown-of-thorns euphorbia Couronne d'épines	Euphorbiaceae, Angiospermae
*Euphorbia oncoclada	Sausage tree Arbre saucisse Famata betondro, etc.	Euphorbiaceae, Angiospermae
*Euphorbia stenoclada	Euphorbia Euphorbe Famata-botrika	Euphorbiaceae, Angiospermae
*Eupleres goudotii	Eupleres Euplères Fanaloka	Viverridae, Mammalia
*Euryceros prevostii	Helmet bird Eurycère de Prévost Siketribé	*Vangidae, Aves

*Galidia elegans	Galidia Galidia Vontsira	Viverridae, Mammalia
*Gardenia spp.	Gardenia Gardenia	Rubiaceae, Angiospermae
Grevilea robusta	Australian silky oak Chêne d'Australie	Proteaceae, Angiospermae
*Gymnogenys radiata	Madagascar harrier hawk Polyboroide rayé de Madagascar Fitiaka	Falconidae, Aves
* †Hadropithecus stenognathus	Hadropithecus Hadropithecus	*Indriidae, Mammalia
*Hapalemur griseus	Hapalemur Hapalémur Alokosy, bokombolo	*Lemuridae, Mammalia
*Hapalemur griseus occidentalis	Western hapalemur	*Lemuridae, Mammalia
*Hapalemur simus	Hapalemur simus	*Lemuridae, Mammalia
*Haronga madagascariensis	Harungana Harongue Harungana	Hypericaceae, Angiospermae
*Helichrysum gymnocephalum	Immortelle Immortelle Rambiazina	Compositae, Angiospermae
*Hemicententes semispinosus	Pseudohedgehog Hérison malgache Sora	*Tenrecidae, Mammalia
Heteropogon contortus	Heteropogon grass Herbe polisson Danga	Graminaceae, Angiospermae
*Hildegardia erythrosiphon	Madagascar flame tree Boaloaka	Sterculiaceae, Angiospermae
* †Hippopotamus lemerlei	Pygmy hippopotamus Hippopotame nain	Hippopotamidae, Mammalia
Hyparrhenia rufa	Hyparrhenia grass	Graminaceae, Angiospermae
*Hypogeomys antimena	Madagascar giant jumping rat Rat géant de Madagascar Votsotsa	Cricetidae, Mammalia
*Hypositta corallirostris	Coral-billed nuthatch Sittelle malgache Sokididy	*Vangidae, Aves

Hypsipetes madagascariensis	Madagascar bulbul Bulbul malgache Horovana, tsikoroana	Pycnonotidae, Aves
*Indogofera compressa	Indigo Indigotier Zavila, kifafatahy	Papilionaceae, Angiospermae
*Indri indri	Indri Indri Babakoto	*Indriidae, Mammalia
*Ispidina madagascariensis	Madagascar hunting kingfisher Martin-chasseur malgache Vinsty-ala, vinsty-mena	Alcedinidae, Aves
*Jatropha mahafaliensis		Euphorbiaceae, Angiospermae
*Kaliphora madagascariensis	Kaliphora Kaliphora Kipantrizoma, ranaindo, etc.	Cornaceae, Angiospermae
*Lemur catta	Ringtailed lemur Maki Maky	*Lemuridae, Mammalia
*Lemur fulvus albifrons	White-fronted lemur Lémur à front blanc Varika	*Lemuridae, Mammalia
*Lemur fulvus collaris	Orange-bearded lemur Lémur à barbe rouge	*Lemuridae, Mammalia
*Lemur fulvus fulvus	Brown lemur Lémur fulvus Vary, gidro	*Lemuridae, Mammalia
*Lemur fulvus rufus	Red lemur Lemur rouge Vary	*Lemuridae, Mammalia
*Lemur macaco	Black lemur Lémurien noir Akomba, gidro	*Lemuridae, Mammalia
*Lemur mongoz	Mongoose lemur Lémur mongoz Gidro	*Lemuridae, Mammalia
*Lemur (varecia) variegatus	Ruffed lemur Lémur variegé Vary	*Lemuridae, Mammalia
*Lemur (varecia) variegatus ruber	Red ruffed lemur Lémur variegé rouge Vary mena	*Lemuridae, Mammalia

Lepidochelys olivacea	Olive ridley turtle Tortue olive Mindroy	Chelonidae, Reptilia
*Lepilemur mustelinus	Northeastern lepilemur Lépilémur Fitikily, boengé, tsitsihy	*Lemuridae, Mammalia
*Leptolaena fauciflora	Leptolaena Leptolaena	*Chlenaceae, Angiospermae
*Leptosomus discolor	Madagascar cuckoo-roller, or Kirombo coural Coural Vorondreo, kirombo	*Leptosomidae or Coraciidae, Aves
*Leptoteris viridis	White-headed vanga Artamie à tête blanche Tretreky	*Vangidae, Aves
*Limnogale mergulus	Pseudo-water-shrew Musaraigne nageur, pseudo-	*Tenrecidae, Mammalia
*Lophotibis cristata	Madagascar wood ibis Coq des bois, ibis huppé Akohon'ala	Threskiornithidae, Aves
*Mantidactylus brevipalmatus	Water-wing frog Grenouille à bouée	Ranidae, Amphibia
*Mantidactylus cowani	Sucker-mouth frog Grenouille succeur	Ranidae, Amphibia
*Mantidactylus leavis	Torrent frog Grenouille des torrents	Ranidae, Amphibia
*Medemia nobilis	Medemia palm Palmier noble, sâtre Satre	Palmaceae, Angiospermae

* †Megaladapis edwardsi
  M. grandidieri
  M. madagascariensis
	Megaladapis
	Mégaladapis
		*Lemuridae,
		Mammalia

Mentha javanica	Mattress mint Vony fotsy	Labiacea Angiospermae
* †Mesopropithecus pithecoides	Extinct quadrupedal lemur Lémurien quadrupède éteint	*Indriidae, Mammalia
*Microcebus murinus	Mouselemur Microcèbe Tsidy, tsitsihy	*Lemuridae, Mammalia
*Mugil macrolepsis	Endemic mullet	Mugilidae,

	Muge endemic Zompona	Pisces
* †Mullerornis	Gracile elephant bird	* †Aepyornithidae, Aves
*Myzopoda aurita	Sucker-footed bat Chauve-souris myzopode	*Myzopodidae, Mammalia
*Nelicurvius nelicourvi	Nelicourvi weaver Tisserin nélicourvi Fody-sahy	Ploceidae, Aves
*Neodrepanus coruscans	Wattled sunbird Souimanga caronculé Soymanga	*Philepittedae
*Neodypsiis decaryi	Three-cornered palm Palmier triangulaire, palmier de Fort-Dauphin	Palmaceae, Angiospermae
*Nepenthes madagascariensis	Pitcher plant Nepenthe	Nepenthacae, Angiospermae
Numida mitrata	Helmeted guinea-fowl Pintade mitrée Akanga	Phasianidae, Aves
Nymphaea stellata	Water-lily Nénuphar étoile Tatamokirano, etc.	Nymphaeaceae, Angiospermae
*Ocimum spp.	Mahaibé, basil Basilique Mahaibé	Labiaceae, Angiospermae
*Operculicarya decarii	Operculicarya	Rubiaceae, Angiospermae
*Oplurus (6 endemic spp.)	Oplurus Oplure	Iguanidae, Reptilia
*Oryzorictes O. hova O. talpoides O. tetradactylus	Pseudomole Taupe tenrec Antsangy	*Tenrecidae, Mammalia
*Pachypodium lamerei	Elephants'-foot tree Pied d'éléphant Vontaka, hazo tavoahangy	Apocynaceae, Angiospermae
*Papilio antenor	Antenor swallowtail butterfly Papillon antenor	Papilionidae, Insecta
* †Paleopropithecus ingens	Paleopropithecus Paleópropithèque	*Indriidae, Mammalia

Periophthalmus papilio	Mudskipper Periophtalme Kitrantra	Gobiidae, Pisces
* *Phaner furcifer*	Forked lemur Lémurien à fourchette Volovy, tantana	Lemuridae, Mammalia
*Phellolychium madagascariensis	Phellolychium Phellolychium	Umbelliferae, Angiospermae
*Philepitta castanea	Asity, velvet Philépitte veloutée, merle doré Asity, soy-soy	*Philepittedae, Aves
Phragmites mauritianus	Reed-grass Roseau à canne Bararatra	Gramineae, Angiospermae
Plegadis falcinellus	Glossy ibis Ibis falcinelle Doaka, famakisifortra	Threskiornithidae, Aves
* †Plesiorycteropus madagascariensis	Madagascar fossil aardvark Aardvark	Orcteropodidae, Mammalia
*Pletodontohyla tuberata	Burrowing frog Grenouille fouisseur	Ranidae, Amphibia
*Podiceps pelzelnii	Madagascar little grebe Grèbe malgache Vivy, kiborano	Podicipitidae, Aves
Potamochoerus porcus	African bushpig, wild boar Sanglier Lambo mena, lambo hova	Suidae, Mammalia
*Propithecus diadema	Diademed sifaka Sifaka à diadème Simpona	*Indriidae, Mammalia
*Propithecus diadema edwardsi	Southern black sifaka	*Indriidae, Mammalia
*Propithecus diadema perrieri	Perrier's sifaka Sifaka de Perrier Simpona	*Indriidae, Mammalia
*Propithecus verreauxi	White sifaka Sifaka Sifaka	*Indriidae, Mammalia
*Propithecus verreauxi coronatus	Crowned sifaka Sifaka couronné Sifaka	*Indriidae, Mammalia

*Pteropus rufus	Madagascar fruit bat or flying fox Chauve-souris grand, or renard volant Fanity	Pteropodidae, Mammalia
*Raphia ruffia	Raffia palm Raffia Rafia	Palmaceae, Angiospermae
*Rauvolfia concertiflora	Malagasy snakeroot Rauwolfia	Apocynacea, Angiospermae
Rauvolfia serpentina	Indian snakeroot Rauwolfia	Apocynacea, Angiospermae
*Ravenala madagascariensis	Traveler's palm Arbre des voyageurs Ravenala	Musaceae, Angiospermae
*Rhacophorus goudoti	Sarobakaka frog Grenouille sarobakaka Sarobakaka	Ranidae, Amphibia
Rhipsalis cassytha	Cactus Rhipsalis Vatilotso	Cactaceae, Angiospermae
*Salvia leucodermia	Sage Sauge	Labiatae, Angiospermae
*Sclerodactylon macrostachyum	Dune-grass Herbe des sables	Graminacea, Angiospermae
Scylla serrata	Mangrove crab Crabe des mangroves	Canceridae, Crustacea
*Stephanotis floribunda	Stephanotis Stephanotis	Asclepiadaceae, Angiospermae
Sterna bergii	Mascarene swift tern Sterne huppé Samby	Sternidae, Aves
*Strongylodon madagascariensis	Strongylodon liana	Leguminosae, Angiospermae
Tamarindus indica	Tamarind, kily Tamarinde Kily	Leguminosae, Angiospermae
Tchitrea mutata mutata	Madagascar paradise flycatcher Gobe-mouches de paradis malgache Tsingitry	Muscicapidae, Aves
*Tenrec ecaudatus	Tail-less tenrec, pseudohedgehog Tenrec Tandraka	*Tenrecidae, Mammalia

* †Testudo grandidieri	Madagascar giant tortoise Tortue géant de Madagascar	Testudinidae, Reptilia
*Testudo radiata	Antandroy radiated tortoise Tortue radié Sokake	Testudinidae, Reptilia
*Tylas edwardsi	Tylas vanga Bulbul à tête noir Kinkimavo	*Vangidae, Aves
*Uncarina grandidieri	Harpoon-hook burr Harponier Farahetsa	Pedaliaceae, Angiospermae
*Uroplatus fimbriatus	Leaf-tailed lizard Uroplate Tahafisaka	Gekkonidae, Reptilia
Vaccinium spp.	Vaccinium shrub Vaccinium	Ericaceae, Angiospermae
*Vanga curvirostris	Sickle-billed vanga Vanga écorcheur	*Vangidae, Aves
*Vanilla spp. (endemic)	Madagascar leafless vanilla Vanille sans feuilles de Madagascar	Orchidaceae, Angiospermae
*Varecia or Lemur variegatus	Ruffed lemur Lémur variegé Vary, varika	*Lemuridae, Mammalia
*Vernonia trinervis	Vernonia Vernonia Ambiaty	Compositae, Angiospermae
*Zoonosaurus (10 endemic spp.)	Black-spot lizard Lézard au tache noir	Cordylidac, Reptilia

NOTES

CHAPTER 1

1. A. Jolly 1972a; Attenborough 1961.
2. Milon, Petter, and Randrianasolo 1973.
3. Andrianampianina 1971.
4. IUCN 1972.

CHAPTER 2

1. Smith 1976a, b.
2. Embleton and McElhinny 1975.
3. Smith and Hallam 1970.
4. Matsuda, pers. communication; Brenon 1972.
5. Wegener 1920.
6. McKenzie 1972; McKenzie and Sclater 1973.
7. Cracraft 1973, '74, '75; Sauer and Rothe 1972.
8. Raven and Axelrod 1974, 1975.
9. Blanc 1972.
10. Richards 1972; Aubreville 1949.
11. Stearn 1971.
12. Whitmore 1975.
13. Martin and Wright 1967.
14. Tattersall and Schwartz 1974.
15. Millot 1952.
16. Nelson et al. 1973.
17. Battisini 1972; Humbert 1954; Perrier de la Bathie 1921; F. le Bourdiec, Battistini, and P. Le Bourdiec 1969.
18. Koechlin, Guillaumet, and Morat 1974; Good 1964; Moore 1972.
19. Millot 1972; Paulien 1972.
20. Peyriéras 1976.
21. Keiner 1963; Keiner and Richard-Vindard 1972.
22. Blanc 1972; Brygoo 1971.
23. Blanc 1972.
24. Paulian 1961; Guibé 1948.

25. Milon, Petter, and Randrianasolo 1973; Dorst 1972; Moreau 1966.
26. Dorst 1974a, b; Peterson 1975.
27. F. Petter 1972.
28. Eisenberg and Gould 1970; E. P. Walker et al. 1966.
29. Albignac 1972.
30. Hill 1953; Tattersall 1973a.
31. Bourlière 1973.
32. Moreau 1966; Cartmill 1974b.

CHAPTER 3

1. Perrier de la Bathie 1939–41.
2. Milon, Petter, and Randrianasolo 1973.
3. Land 1975.
4. Catala 1940.
5. Moynihan 1960.
6. Griveaud and Albignac 1972.
7. Grandidier 1875, 1890–96.
8. Battistini and Verin 1967, 1972.
9. Koechlin, Guillaumet, and Morat 1974.
10. FAO 1975.
11. Ibid.
12. Chauvet 1972.
13. Blaug, Jolly, and Colclough 1977.
14. Aziz 1977.
15. Nelson et al. 1973.
16. Bureau International de Travail 1972.
17. Chenery et al. 1974.
18. INSRE 1968/69.
19. Lipton 1977.
20. Ward 1976.
21. Boserup 1965.
22. Fosberg 1972; Greenland 1975.
23. Eckholm 1975, 1976a.
24. Eckholm 1976a, 1976b.

25. Grandidier 1903–1920, from Purchas 1625.
26. Bulpin 1968.
27. Labatut and Raharinarivonirina 1969.

CHAPTER 4
1. Whitmore 1975.
2. Leigh 1975, personal communication.
3. Ibid.
4. Ibid.
5. Whitmore 1975.
6. Whittaker 1975.
7. Montgomery and Sunquist, 1975.
8. Koechlin, Guillaumet, and Morat 1974; Geertz, 1968.
9. Roederer 1972.
10. Perrier de la Bathie 1921.
11. Koechlin, Guillaumet, and Morat 1974.
12. Whitmore 1975.
13. Forcier 1975.
14. Perrier de la Bathie 1921.
15. Leigh, personal communication.
16. Odum 1963, 1969.
17. Moore 1972.
18. Lovejoy 1975.
19. Petter 1962; Martin 1972, 1973; Russell 1977; McGeorge, 1978; Andrianatsiferana and Rahandraha 1973a, 1973b, 1974.
20. Cartmill 1974b.
21. Thorington 1968.
22. Martin 1972, 1973.
23. Petter-Rousseaux 1962.
24. Andrianatsiferana and Rahandraha 1973a, 1973b, 1974.
25. Charles-Dominique and Martin 1972.
26. J. J. Petter and Peyriéras 1970.
27. MacArthur and Wilson 1967.

CHAPTER 5
1. Ramanantsoa 1975.
2. Noël, in Labatur and Raharinarivonirina 1969.
3. Hughes 1975; Frazier 1975.
4. Perrier de la Bathie 1921.
5. Bloch 1975.
6. J. J. Petter 1962.

CHAPTER 6
1. Labatut and Raharinarivonirina 1969.
2. Tronchon 1974.
3. Battistini 1972.
4. Koechlin 1972.
5. Cabanis, Chabouis, and Chabouis 1970.
6. Pollock 1975, 1977.
7. A. Jolly 1966, Richard 1978.
8. Griveaud 1959.

CHAPTER 7
1. Bishop 1963.
2. Labatut and Raharinarivonirina 1969.
3. Sibree 1880.
4. Labatut and Raharinarivonirina 1969.

5. Sibree 1880.
6. Decary 1950; Paulien 1961.
7. Domergue 1971.
8. Decary 1969.
9. Bloch 1971.
10. Mayer 1971.
11. FAO 1975.
12. Geertz 1968.
13. Ibid.
14. Bloch 1971, 1975.
15. Bloch 1971.
16. Le Bourdiec 1972.
17. Boiteau 1958.
18. Dox, in Labatut and Raharinarivonirina 1969.
19. Raybaud 1902; G. Grandidier 1905; Standing 1908. Lamberton 1934.
20. Battistini and Verin 1967.
21. Tattersall 1973a.
22. Mahé 1972.
23. Berger et al. 1975.
24. Battistini 1971b; Battistini and Verin 1972.
25. Flacourt 1661.
26. Polo 1295 (1875).
27. A. Walker 1967.
28. Tattersall and Schwartz 1974; C. J. Jolly 1970; Tattersall 1973.
29. Andrews, personal communication; A. Walker 1967.
30. Zapfe 1963.
31. Tattersall 1972.
32. A. Walker 1967.
33. Decary 1950.
34. Flacourt 1661.
35. Patterson 1975.
36. Martin and Wright 1967.
37. Razarihelisoa 1973a.
38. Perrier de la Bathie 1921, 1939.
39. Leigh 1975, personal communication.
40. Razarihelisoa 1973b.

CHAPTER 8
1. Boiteau 1972.
2. Stearn 1975.
3. Kreig 1965.
4. Svoboda and Blake 1975; Aikman 1974.
5. DeConti and Creasey 1975.
6. Warfield and Bouck 1974.
7. Abraham 1975; Creasey 1975.
8. Tin-Wa and Farnsworth 1975.
9. IUCN 1972.
10. Debray, Jacquemin, and Razafindrambao 1971.
11. Razafindrambao, personal communication.
12. Rabearimanana 1975.

CHAPTER 9
1. Deschamps 1961.
2. Milne-Edwards and Grandidier 1890–96.
3. Rauh 1963.
4. Charles-Dominique and Hladik 1971.
5. Russell 1977.

6. Milon, Petter, and Randrianasolo 1973.
7. Decary 1950.
8. Juvik 1975.
9. Eakin 1970.
10. Richard 1974*a*.
11. Richard 1974*b*; Richard and Heimbuch 1975.
12. Koechlin, Guillaumet, and Morat 1974.
13. Decary 1969.
14. Dreo 1976.
15. Aldegheri 1972.
16. Deschamps 1961.
17. Decary 1947.
18. Decary 1969.

CHAPTER 10
1. A. Jolly 1966*a*; J. J. Petter 1962; Petter-Rousseaux 1962; McGeorge 1978; Russell 1977; Mertl 1976, 1977; Gustafson, in preparation.
2. A. Jolly et al., in press.
3. Mertl-Millhollen et al., 1979.
4. Evans and Goy 1968.
5. Mertl 1875, 1977.
6. A. Jollyu 1972c.
7. Bomford, personal communication.
8. Sussman 1975, 1977.
9. Gustafson, personal communication.
10. Lack 1954; Hamilton 1970; Wilson 1975.
11. Wilson 1971.
12. MacArthur and Wilson 1967.
13. Gadgil and Solbrig 1972.
14. May 1978.
15. Kolata 1974; Howell 1976.
16. Birdsell 1977.
17. Dilger, personal communication.

18. Cooper, personal communication; A. Jolly 1964*a*, 1964*b*.
19. A. Jolly 1966, 1972*a*.
20. Petter-Rousseaux 1968.
21. A. Jolly 1972*c*, 1973.
22. Prechtl and Bientema 1964.
23. Blauvelt and McKenna 1961.

CHAPTER 11
1. Domergue 1971.
2. Koechlin 1972; Kroechlin, Guillaumet, and Morat 1974.
3. Chauvet 1972.
4. Koechlin, Guillaumet, and Morat 1974.
5. Verin 1971.
6. Kent 1970.
7. Hutchinson 1953; May 1977.
8. Battistini 1971*a*.
9. Paulien 1951.
10. Pariente 1974.
11. Petter, Schilling, and Pariente 1975.
12. Keith, Forbes, and Turner 1974.
13. Hill 1953.
14. Rumpler, in press; Jungers, in press.
15. Ramanantsoa, personal communication.
16. Tattersall and Sussmann 1975.
17. Befourouack 1975.
18. Pariente 1974.

CHAPTER 12
1. "The human reserve": T. Eadey, personal communication.
2. Boiteau 1958; Fremigacci 1975; R. Jolly, and Raberinja 1975.

BIBLIOGRAPHY

Abraham, D. J. 1975. Structure elucidation and chemistry of the bis Catharanthus alkaloids. In W. I. Taylor and N. R. Farnsworth, eds. The Catharanthus Alkaloids. Marcel Dekker, New York. 125–40.

Aikman, L. 1974. Nature's gifts to medicine. Nat. Geogr. 146: 420–40.

Albignac, R. 1972. The Carnivora of Madagascar. In R. Battistini and G. Richard-Vindard, eds. Biogeography and Ecology of Madagascar. Junk, The Hague. 667–82.

———. 1973. Mammifères Carnivores. Faune de Madagascar 36. ORSTOM, Paris. 206 pp.

Aldegheri, M. 1972. Rivers and streams on Madagascar. In R. Battistini and G. Richard-Vindard, eds. Biogeography and Ecology of Madagascar. Junk, The Hague. 261–310.

Andrianampianina, J. M. 1971. La Protection de la Nature à Madagascar. Background document for the United Nations Conference on the Human Environment, Stockholm 1972.

Andriantsiferana, R., and Rahandraha, T. 1973. Variations saisonnières de la temperature centrale du microcèbe (Microcebus murinus). C. R. Acad. Sci., Paris 277: 2215–18.

———. 1973. Variation saisonnières du choix alimentaire spontané chez Microcebus murinus. C. R. Acad. Sci., Paris 277: 2025–28.

———. 1974. Effets du séjour au froid sur le microcèbe (Microcebus murinus, Miller 1777). C.R. Acad. Sci., Paris D278: 3099–3102.

Attenborough, D. 1961. Zoo Quest to Madagascar. Lutterworth Press, London. 144 pp.

Aubreville, A. 1949. Climats, forêts, et désertification de l'Afrique tropicale. Soc. d'Editions Géographiques, Martimes et Coloniales, Paris.

Aziz, S. 1977. The Chinese Approach to Rural Development. Macmillan, New York. 168 pp.

Battistini, R. 1971a. Conditions de gisement des sites de subfossiles et modifications récentes du milieu naturel dans la region d'Ankazoabo. Taloha, Revue de la Musée d'Art et d'Archéologie, Université de Madagascar 4: 19–28.

———. 1971b. Conditions de gisement des sites littoraux de subfossiles et causes de la disparition de la faune des grands animaux dans le Sud-Ouest et l'extrème Sud de Madagascar. Taloha, Revue du Musée d'Art et d'Archéologie, University of Madagascar 4: 7–18.

———. 1972. Madagascar relief and main types of landscape. In R. Battistini and G. Richard-Vindard, eds. Biogeography and Ecology in Madagascar. Junk, The Hague. 1–26.

———, and Verin, P. 1967. Ecologic changes in protohistoric Madagascar. In P. S. Martin and H.

E. Wright, Jr., eds. Pleistocene Extinctions. Yale University Press, New Haven and London. 407–24.

————. 1972. Man and environment in Madagascar. In R. Battistini and G. Richard-Vindard, eds. Biogeography and Ecology in Madagascar. Junk, The Hague. 311–38.

Berger, R.; Ducote, K.; Robinson, K.; and Walter, H. 1975. Radio-carbon date for the largest extinct bird. Nature 258: 709.

Birdsell, J. B. 1977. Spacing mechanisms and adaptive behavior of Australian aborigines. In F. J. Ebling, ed. Population Control by Social Behavior. Institute of Biology, London. 213–44.

Bishop, M. 1963. Petrarch and His World. Indiana University Press, Bloomington. 399 pp.

Blanc, Ch. P. 1972. Les reptiles de Madagascar et des îles voisins. In R. Battistini and G. Richard-Vindard, eds. Biogeography and Ecology of Madagascar. Junk, The Hague. 501–614.

Blaug, M.; Jolly, R.; and Colclough, C. 1977. Education and Employment in Africa. UN/ECA, Addis Ababa.

Blauvelt, H., and McKenna, J. 1961. Mother–neonate interaction: capacity of the human newborn for orientation. In B. M. Foss, ed. Determinants of Infant Behavior. Methuen, London, 3–28.

Bloch, M. 1971. Placing the Dead. Harcourt Brace (Seminar Press), London. 242 pp.

————. 1975. Property and the end of affinity. In M. Bloch, ed. Marxist Analysis and Social Anthropology. Malaby Press, London, 203–28.

Boehrer, J. L.; Solar, S.; Rabesandratana H.; and Coulanges, P. 1974. Arch. Inst. Pasteur Madagascar 73: 245–50.

Boiteau, P. 1958. Contribution à l'Histoire de la Nation Malgache. Éditions Sociales, Paris. 431 pp.

————. 1972. Sur la première mention imprimée et le premier échantillon de Catharanthus roseus (L). G. Don. Adansonia sér. 2, 12: 129–35.

Boserup, E. 1965. The Conditions of Agricultural Growth. George Allen and Unwin, London. 124 pp.

Boulding, K. E. 1973. The economics of the coming spaceship earth. In H. E. Daly, ed. Toward a Steady-State Economy. W. H. Freeman, San Francisco. 121–32.

Bourlière, F. 1973. The comparitive ecology of rain forest mammals in Africa and tropical America: some introductory remarks. In B. J. Meggers, E. S. Ayensu, and W. D. Duckworth, eds. Tropical Forest Ecosystems in Africa and South America: A Comparative Review. Smithsonian Institution Press, Washington, DC. 279–92.

Brenon, P. 1972. The geology of Madagascar. In R. Battistini and G. Richard-Vindard, eds. Biogeography and Ecology of Madagascar. Junk, The Hague. 27–86.

Brygoo, E. R. 1971. Reptiles: Sauriens: Chamaeleonidae, Genre Chamaeleo. Faune de Madagascar 33. ORSTOM, Paris. 318 pp.

Bulpin, T. V. 1968. Islands in a Forgotten Sea. Books of Africa, Cape Town. 346 pp.

Bureau Internationale de Travail. 1972. Rapport au Governement de la République Malagasy sur les problèmes de l'Emploi. BIT, Geneva. 227 pp.

Cabanis, Y.; Chabouis, L.; and Chabouis, F. 1970. Végétaux et Groupements Végétaux de Madagascar et des Mascareignes. Bureau pour le Développement de la Production Agricole, Tananarive. 4 vols., 1,345 pp.

Catala, R. 1940. Variations expérimentales de Chrysiridia madascariensis Less. [Lepidoptera, Uraniidae]. Arch. Mus. Nat. Hist. Naturelle, Paris, ser. 6: 17: 1–262.

Cartmill, M. 1974a. Daubentonia, Dactylopsila, woodpeckers and klinorhynchy. In R. D. Martin, G. A. Doyle, and A. C. Walker, eds. Prosimian Biology. Duckworth, London. 655–72.

————. 1974b. Re-thinking primate origins. Science 184: 436–43.

Charles-Dominique, P., and Hladik, C. M. 1971. Le lépilemur du Sud de Madagascar: écologie, alimentation et vie sociale. La Terre et la Vie 1: 3–66.

———, and Martin, R. D. 1972. Behaviour and Ecology of Nocturnal Prosimians. Zeitschrift für Tierpsychologie, suppl. 9. 90 pp.

Chauvet, B. 1972. The forest of Madagascar. In R. Battistini and G. Richard-Vindard, eds. Biogeography and Ecology of Madagascar. Junk, The Hague. 191–200.

Chenery, H. B.; Ahluwalia, M. S.; Bell, C. L. G.; Duloy, J. H.; and Jolly, R. 1974. Redistribution with Growth. Oxford University Press, London.

Clarke, A. C. 1966. Voices from the Sky. Victor Gollanz, London.

Clawson, M. 1979. Forests in the long sweep of American history. Science 204: 1168–74.

Cracraft, J. 1973. Continental drift, paleoclimatology, and evolutionary biogeography of birds. J. Zool., Lond. 169: 455–545.

———. 1974. Continental drift and vertebrate distribution. Ann. Rev. Ecol. Syst. 5: 215–61.

———. 1975. Historical biogeography and earth history: perspectives for a future synthesis. Ann. Missouri Botan. Gard. 62: 227–250.

Creasey, W. A. 1975. Biochemistry of dimeric Catharanthus alkaloids. In W. I. Taylor and N. R. Farnsworth, eds. The Catharanthus Alkaloids. Marcel Dekker, New York. 209–236.

Dasmann, R. F. 1976. National parks, nature conservation and "future primitive." Ecologist 6: 164–67.

DeBray, M.; Jacquemin, H.; and Razafindrambao, R. 1971. Contribution à l'inventaire des plantes médicinales de Madagascar, Paris (Travaux et Doc. d'Orstom). 150 pp.

Decary, R. 1947. Époques d'introduction des *Opuntias monacantha* dans le Sud de Madagascar. Rév. Internat. Botanique Appl. d'Agr. Trop. 27: 455–60.

———. 1950. La Faune Malgache. Payot, Paris. 236 pp.

———. 1969. Souvenirs et Croquis de la Terre Malgache. Éditions Maritimes et d'Outre-Mer, Paris. 248 pp.

De Conti, R. C., and Creasey, W. A. 1975. Clinical aspects of the dimeric Catharanthus alkaloids. In W. I. Taylor and N. R. Farnsworth, eds. The Catharanthus Alkaloids. Marcel Dekker, New York. 125–40.

Deschamps, H. 1961. Histoire de Madagascar. Mondes d'Outre-Mer. Éditions Berger-Levrault, Paris. 348 pp.

Domergue, C. A. 1971. Les grands traits de l'hydraulique à Madagascar. Madagascar Revue Géographie 19: 7–47.

Dorst, J. 1947a. Les chauves-souris de la faune malgache. Bull. Mus. Nat. Hist. Nat., Paris. 306 pp.

———. 1947b. Essai d'une clef de détermination des chauve-souris malgaches. Mem. l'Inst. Sci. Mad. A: 1: 81–88.

———. 1948. Biogéographie des Chiroptères malgaches. Mem. l'Inst. Sci. Madagascar A: 1: 193–98.

———. 1972. Evolution and affinities of the birds of Madagascar. In R. Battistini and G. Richard Vindard, eds. Biogeography and Ecology of Madagascar. Junk, The Hague. 615–28.

Dreo, P. 1976. Pélandrova... Éditions du CEDS, Montvilliers. 401 pp.

Eakin, R. M. 1970. A third eye. Amer. Sci. 58: 73–79.

Eckholm, E. P. 1975. The deterioration of mountain environments. Science 189: 764–70.

———. 1976a. Losing Ground: Environmental Stress and World Food Prospects. Norton, New York.

———. 1976b. The other energy crisis: firewood. Ecologist 6: 80–86.

Eisenberg, J., and Gould, E. 1970. The tenrecs: A study in Mammalian Behavior and Evolution. Smithsonian Contributions to Zoology 27. 138 pp.

Embleton, B. J. J., and McElhinny, M. W. 1975. The paleoposition of Madagascar: paleomagnetic evidence from the Isalo Group. Earth Planet. Sci. Letters 27: 329–41.

Evans, C. S., and Goy, R. W. 1968. Social behavior and reproductive cycles in captive ring-tailed lemurs (*Lemur catta* L.) J. Zool., Lond. 156: 181–97.

FAO Statistics Series. Production Yearbook 1975. Food and Agriculture Organization of the United Nations. 555 pp.

Flacourt, Etienne de, 1661. Histoire de la Grande Ile de Madagascar. Publié à Troyes, chez Nicolas Oudot, et se vendent a Paris, chez la vesue Pierre l'Amy. 471 pp.

Forcier, L. K., 1975. Reproductive strategies and the cooccurrence of climax tree species. Science 189: 808–10.

Fosberg, F. R., 1972. Temperate zone influence on tropical forest land use: a plea for sanity. In B. J. Meggers, E. S. Ayensu, and W. D. Duckworth, eds. Tropical Forest Ecosystems in Africa and South America: A Comparative Review. Smithsonian Institution Press, Washington, DC. 345–50.

Frazier, J. 1975. Marine Turtles of the Western Indian Ocean. Oryx 13: 164–75.

Fremigacci, J. 1975. Mise en valeur coloniale et travail forcé: La construction du chemin de fer Tananarive-Antsirabe (1911–1923). Omaly sy Anio (Hier et Aujourd'hui), Université de Madagascar 1–2, 75–137.

Gadgil, M., and Solbrig, O. T. 1972. The concept of r- and K-selection: evidence from wild flowers and some theoretical considerations. Amer. Naturalist 106: 14–31.

Geertz, C. 1968. Agricultural Involution: The Process of Ecological Change in Indonesia. University of California Press, Berkeley. 176 pp.

Good, R. 1964. The Geography of the Flowering Plants, 3d ed. Longmans Green, London. 518 pp.

Grandidier, A. 1875, 1890–96. Histoire physique, naturelle, et politique de Madagascar. Paris.

———. 1903–20. Collection des ouvrages anciens concernant Madagascar. Paris, Comité de Madagascar et de l'Union coloniale. 9 vols.

———. 1905. Recherches sur les lémuriens disparus et en particulier ceux qui vivait à Madagascar. Nouv. Arch. Mus. Hist. Nat. Paris (4 sér.) 7: 1–142.

Greenland, D. J. 1975. Bringing the green revolution to the shifting cultivator. Science 190: 841–44.

Griveaud, P. 1959. Insectes: Lepidoptères: Sphingidae. Faune de Madagascar 8. 161 pp.

———, and Albignac, R. 1972. The problems of nature conservation in Madagascar. In R. Battistini and G. Richard-Vindard, eds. Biogeography and Ecology of Madagascar. Junk, The Hague. 727–40.

Guibé, J., 1948. La répartition géographique des Batraciens de Madagascar. Mem. l'Inst. Sci. Madagascar A: 1: 177–79.

Guichon, A. 1960. La superficie des formations forestières de Madagascar. Rev. forest. français 6.

Hardin, G. 1973. The tragedy of the commons. In H. E. Daly, ed. Toward a Steady-State Economy. W. H. Freeman, San Francisco. 133–48.

Hamilton, W. D. 1964. Selfish and spiteful behaviour in an evolutionary model. Nature 228: 1218–20.

Hill, W. C. O. 1953. Primates: Comparative Anatomy and Taxonomy. V. I. Strepsirhini. Edinburgh University Press, Edinburgh. 798 pp.

Howell, N. 1976. The population of Dobe Area !Kung. In R. B. Lee and I. DeVore, eds. Kalahari Hunter-Gatherers. Harvard University Press, Cambridge, Mass. 137–51.

Hughes, G. R. 1975. Fano! Defenders of Wildlife 50: 159–63.

Humbert, H. 1954. Les territoires phytogéographiques de Madagascar. Leur cartographie. Les Divisions écologiques du monde. CNRS 195–204. Paris.

———, and Cours-Darne, G. 1965. Carte Internationale du tapis vegetal, Madagascar. French Institute of Pondicherry.

Hutchinson, G. E. 1953. The concept of pattern in ecotogy. Proc. Acad. Nat. Sci. Philadelphia 55: 1–12.

_____. 1965. The Ecological Theater and the Evolutionary Play. Yale University Press, New Haven. 139 pp.

INSRE. 1968/69. Enquêtes sur les budgets des ménages en milieu rural 1968/69.

IUCN (International Union for Conservation of Nature). Survival Service Commission. 1969. The Red Book: Wildlife in Danger. Collins, London.

IUCN (International Union for the Conservation of Nature). 1972. Comptes Rendus de la Conférence Internationale sur la Conservation de la Nature et de ses Ressources à Madagascar. IUCN, Morges. 239 pp.

Jolly, A. 1964a. Choice of cue in prosimian learning. Animal Behaviour 12: 571–77.

_____. 1964b. Prosimians' manipulation of simple object problems. Animal Behaviour 12: 560–70.

_____. 1966a. Lemur Behavior. University of Chicago Press, Chicago. 187 pp.

_____. 1966b. Lemur social behavior and primate intelligence. Science 153: 501–06.

_____. 1972a. The Evolution of Primate Behavior. Macmillan, New York. 397 pp.

_____. 1972b. Hour of birth in primates and man. Folia primatol. 18: 108–21.

_____. 1972c. Troop continuity and Troop spacing in Propithecus verreauxi and Lemur catta at Berenty (Madagascar). Folia primatol. 17: 335–62.

_____. 1973. Primate Birth Hour. Int. Zoo. Yrbk. 13: 391–97.

_____; Gustafson, H.; Mertl, A.; and Ramanantsoa, G. (in press). Population, espace vital, et composition des groupes chez le maki (Lemur catta) et le sifaka (Propithecus verreauxi verreauxi) à Berenty, République Malagasy. Bull. Acad. Malg.

Jolly, C. J. 1970. Hadropithecus: a lemuroid small-object feeder. Man (new ser.) 5: 619–26.

Jolly, R., ed. 1978. Disarmament and World Development. Pergamon Press, Oxford and New York. 185 pp.

_____, and Raberinja, R. 1975. Système d'indicateurs socio-economique à Madagascar. Bureau du Plan, Tananarive.

Jungers, W. B. (in press). Craniometric corroboration of the specific status of Lepilemur septentrionalis, an endemic lemur from the north of Madagascar.

Juvik, J. O. 1975. The radiated tortoise of Madagascar. Oryx 13: 145–48.

Keiner, A. 1963. Poissons, Pêche et Pisciculture à Madagascar. Centre Technique Forestier Tropical, Nogent-sur-Marne. 403 pp.

_____, and Richard-Vindard, G. 1972. Fishes of the continental waters of Madagascar. In R. Battistini and G. Richard-Vindard, eds. Biogeography and Ecology of Madagascar. Junk, The Hague. 477–614.

Keith, G. C.; Forbes-Watson, A. D.; and Turner, D. A. 1974. The Madagascar crested ibis, a threatened species in an endemic and endangered avifauna. Wilson Bulletin 86: 197–320.

Kent, R. K. 1970. Early Kingdoms in Madagascar, 1500–1700. Holt, Rinehart & Winston, New York. 336 pp.

Koechlin, J. 1972. Flora and vegetation of Madagascar. In R. Battistini and G. Richard-Vindard, eds. Biogeography and Ecology of Madagascar. Junk, The Hague. 145–90

_____; Guillaumet, J. L.; and Morat, Ph. 1974. Flore et Végétation de Madagascar. J. Cramer, Vaduz, Germany. 687 pp.

Kolata, G. B. 1974. !Kung hunter-gatherers: feminism, diet, and birth control. Science 185: 932–34.

Kreig, M. B. 1965. Green Medicine. George G. Harrap, London. 462 pp.

Labatut, F., and Raharinarivonirina, R. 1969. Madagascar. Étude Historique. Nathan-Madagascar, Tananarive.

Lack, D. 1954. The Natural Regulation of Animal Numbers. Clarendon Press, Oxford.

Lamberton, C. 1934. Contribution à la connaissance de la faune subfossile à Madagascar. Lémuriens et Ratites: *Archéoindris, Chiromys, Megaladapis.* Mem. Acad. Malgache (new ser.) 17: 1–168.

Land, M. (in preparation). Structural basis of colour in the wings of *Chrysiridia* moths.

Le Bourdiec, F.; Battistini, R.; and le Bourdiec, P. 1969–1971. Atlas de Madagascar. Laboratoire de Géographie, Université Tananarive. 148 pp.

Le Bourdiec, P. 1972. Accelerated erosion and soil degradation. In R. Battistini and G. Richard-Vindard, eds. Biogeography and Ecology of Madagascar. Junk, The Hague. 227–60.

Leigh, E. G. 1975. Structure and climate in tropical rainforest. Ann. Rev. Ecol. Syst. 6: 67–85.

Lipton, Michael. 1977. Why Poor People Stay Poor: Urban Bias in World Development. Temple Smith, London. 467 pp.

Lovejoy, T. E. 1975. Bird diversity and abundance in Amazon Forest communities. Living Bird 13: 127–91.

MacArthur, R. H., and Wilson, E. O. 1967. The Theory of Island Biogeography. Princeton University Press, Princeton. 215 pp.

McGeorge, L. 1978. Influences on the structure of vocalizations in three Malagasy lemurs. In D. J. Chivers and K. A. Joysey, eds. Recent Advances in Primatology 3: 103–09. Academic Press, London.

McKenzie, D. P. 1972. Plate tectonics and sea-floor spreading. Amer. Sci. 60: 425–35.

———, and Sclater, J. G. 1973. The evolution of the Indian Ocean. Sci. Amer. 228(5): 62–72.

Mahé, J. 1972. The Malagasy subfossils. In R. Battistini and G. Richard-Vindard, eds. Biogeography and Ecology of Madagascar. Junk, The Hague. 339–66.

Martin, P. S., and Wright, H. E. eds. 1967. Pleistocene Extinctions. Yale University Press, New Haven and London.

Martin, R. D. 1972. A preliminary field-study of the lesser mouse lemur (*Microcebus murinus* J. F. Miller 1777). Zeitschrift Tierpsychologie suppl. 9: 43–89.

———. 1973. A review of the behaviour and ecology of the lesser mouse lemur (*Microcebus murinus* J. F. Miller 1777). In R. P. Michael and J. H. Crook, eds. Comparative Ecology and Behaviour of Primates. Academic Press, London. 1–68.

May, R. M. 1974. Stability in ecosystems, some comments. In Structure, Functioning and Management of Ecosystems. Centre for Agricultural Publications and Documents, Wageningen, Netherlands. 67.

———. 1975. Energy cost of food gathering. Nature 225: 669.

———. 1977. Thresholds and breakpoints in ecosystems with a multiplicity of stable states. Nature 269: 471–77.

———. 1978. Human reproduction reconsidered. Nature 272: 491–95.

Mayer, J. 1971. Riziculture Traditionnelle et Ameliorée. Société d'Aide et de Coopération, 110 rue de l'Université, Paris, 7e. I. La Plante, les Techniques culturelles; II. L'Opération "Productivité rizicole" à Madagascar; III. La Microhydraulique, applications à la riziculture.

Mertl, A. S. 1975. Discrimination of individuals by scent in a primate. Behav. Biol. 14: 505–09.

———. 1976. Olfactory and visual cues in social interactions of *Lemur catta.* Folia primatol. 26: 151–61.

———. 1977. Habituation to territorial scent marks in the field by *Lemur catta.* Behav. Biol. 21: 500–07.

Mertl-Millhollen, A. S.; Gustafson, H. L.; Budnitz, N.; Dainis, K.; and Jolly, A. 1979. Population and territory stability of the *Lemur catta* at Berenty, Madagascar. Folia primatol. 31: 106–22.

Millot, J. 1952. La faune malgache et le mythe gondwanien. Mem. Inst. Sci. Madag. A7: 1–36.

————. 1972. In conclusion. In R. Battistini and G. Richard-Vindard, eds. Biogeography and Ecology of Madagascar. Junk, The Hague. 741–54.

Milne-Edwards, A., and Grandidier, A. 1875, 1890–96. Histoire naturelle des mammiferes. In Histoire Physique, Naturelle et Politique de Madagascar. Paris. Vols. 6, 9, 10.

Milon, Ph.; Petter, J-J.; and Randrianasolo, G. 1973. Oiseaux Faune de Madagascar. 35. ORSTOM, Tananarive and CNRS, Paris. 263 pp.

Montgomery, G. G., and Sunquist, M. E. 1975. Impact of sloths on neotropical forest energy flow and nutrient cycling. In F. B. Golley and E. Medina, eds. Tropical Ecological Systems. In Ecological Studies 2. Springer-Verlag, New York. 69–111.

Moore, Jr., J. E. 1972. Palms in the tropical forest ecosystems of Africa and South America. In B. J. Meggers, E. S. Ayensu, and W. D. Duckworth, eds. Tropical Forest Ecosystems in Africa and South America: A Comparative Review. Smithsonian Institution Press, Washington DC. 63–88.

Moreau, R. E. 1966. The Bird Fauna of Africa and Its Islands. Academic Press, New York. 424 pp.

Moynihan, M. 1960. Some adaptations which help to promote gregariousness. From Proc. of the 12th Int. Ornith. Congr., Helsinki 1958. 523–41.

Nelson, H. D.; Dobert, M.; McDonald, G. C.; McLaughlin, J.; Marvin, B.; and Moeller, P. W. 1973. Area Handbook for the Malagasy Republic. U.S. Govt. Printing Office, Washington DC. 327 pp.

Odum, E. P. 1963. Ecology. Holt, Rinehart & Winston, New York.

————. 1969. The strategy of ecosystem development. Science 164: 262–70.

Pariente, G. 1974. Influence of light on activity rhythms of two Malagasy lemurs, *Phaner furcifer* and *Lepilemur mustelinus*. In R. D. Martin, G. A. Doyle, and A. C. Walker, eds. Prosimian Biology. Duckworth, London. 183–200.

Patterson, Bryan. 1975. The fossil aardvarks (Mammalia, Tubulidentata). Bull. Mus. Comp. Zool., Harvard 147: 185–237.

Paulien, R. 1951. Papillons communs de Madagascar. Publication de l'Institut de Recherche Scientifique, Tananarive. 90 pp.

————. 1961. La Zoogéographie de Madagascar et des Iles Voisins. Faune de Madagascar XIII. Tananarive, IRSM. 484 pp.

————. 1972. Some ecological and biogeographical problems of the entomofauna of Madagascar. In R. Battistini and G. Richard-Vindard, eds. Biogeography and Ecology of Madagascar. Junk, The Hague. 411–27.

Perrier de la Bathie, H. 1921. La Végétation Malgache. Extr. Ann. du Musée Coloniale de Marseille, 29e an., 3e ser., 9 vol. Challemel, Paris. 268 pp.

————. 1939–41. Orchidées. 49e Famille. Flore de Madagascar et des Comores. 2 vols. 477 and 387 pp.

Peterson, R. L. 1975. Searching for bats. Defenders Wildlife 50: 153–155.

Petter, F. 1972. The rodents of Madagascar: the seven genera of Malagasy rodents. In R. Battistini and G. Richard-Vindard, eds. Biogeography and Ecology of Madagascar. Junk, The Hague. 661–66.

Petter, J. J. 1962. Recherches sur l'écologie et l'ethologie des lémuriens malgaches. Mém. Mus. National d'Histoire Naturel. (new ser.) A: 27. 1–146.

————, and Peyriéras, A. 1970. Nouvelle contributions à l'étude d'un lémurien malgache, le aye-aye (*Daubentonia madagascariensis* E. Geoffrey). Mammalia 34: 167–93.

————; Schilling, A.; and Pariente, G. 1975. Observations on the behavior and ecology of *Phaner furcifer*. In I. Tattersall and R. W. Sussman, eds. Lemur Biology. Plenum Press, New York. 209–18.

Petter-Rousseaux, A. 1962. Recherches sur la biologie de la réproduction des primates inférieurs. Mammalia 26 (suppl.1): 1–88.

———. 1968. Cycles génitaux saisonniers des lémuriens malgaches. In R. Canivenc, ed. Cycles génitaux saisonniers de Mammifères sauvages. Masson, Paris. 11–22.

Peyriéras, A. 1976. Faune de Madagascar: Insectes Coléoptères, Carabidae, Scaritinae. 2: Biologie, vol. 41. Orstom, Paris. 220 pp.

Pollock, J. E. 1975. Field observations on *Indri indri:* a preliminary report. In I. Tattersall and R. W. Sussman, eds. Lemur Biology. Plenum, New York. 287–312.

———. 1977. The ecology and sociology of feeding in *Indri indri*. In T. H. Clutton-Brock, ed. Primate Ecology. Academic Press, London. 38–71.

Polo, M. 1295 (1875). The Book of Ser Marco Polo the Venetian concerning the Kingdoms and Marvels of the East. Trans. H. Yule. London, John Murray.

Prechtl, H. F. R., and Beintema, D. J. 1964. The Neurological Examination of the Full-Term Newborn Infant. Little Club Clinics in Dev. Mat. no.12. Heinemann, London.

Purchas, S. 1625. Haklytus Postumus, or Purchas his Pilgrims. London, vol. 2.

Rabearimanana, L. 1975. Mystique et sorcellerie dans le manuscrit de l'Ombiasy. 1. Le Tanguin. Omaly sy Anio (Hier et Audjourd'hui). Université de Madagascar, Dept. de l'Histoire, no. 1-2: 275–323.

Ramanantsoa, G. 1975. The sacred lemurs. Defenders Wildlife 50: 148–49.

Ratsiraka, D. 1975. Charte de la Révolution Socialiste Malagasy. Repoblika Malagasy, Tananarive. 106 pp.

Rauh, W. 1963. Didieréacées: 121ᵉ famille. Flore de Madagascar et des Comores. 37 pp.

Raven, P. H., and Axelrod, D. I. 1974. Angiosperm biogeography and past continental movements. Ann. Missouri Botan. Gard. 61: 539–673.

———. 1975. History of the fauna and flora of Latin America. Amer. Sci. 63: 420–29.

Raybaud, M. 1902. Les gisements fossilifères d'Ampasambazimba. Bull. Acad. Malgache (old ser.) 1: 64–66.

Razarihelisoa, M. 1973*a*. Contribution à l'étude des Batraciens de Madagascar. Ann. l'Univ. Madagascar. Sér. Sci. Nat. Math. 10: 103–25.

———. 1973*b*. Contribution à l'étude des Batraciens de Madagascar. Écologie et développement larvaire de *Mantidactylus brevipalmatus* Ahl., batracien des eaux courantes. Bull. Acad. Malg. 51: 129–42.

Richard, A. F. 1974*a*. Intra-specific variation in the social organization and ecology of *Propithecus verreauxi*. Folia primatol. 22: 178–207.

———. 1974*b*. Patterns of mating in *Propithecus verreauxi verreauxi*. In R. D. Martin, G. A. Doyle, and A. C. Walker, eds. Prosimian Biology. Duckworth, London. 49–74.

———. 1978. Behavioral Variation. Case Study of a Malagasy Lemur. Bucknell University Press, Lewisburg. 213 pp.

———, and Heimbuch, R. 1975. An analysis of the social behavior of three groups of *Propithecus verreauxi*. In I. Tattersall and R. W. Sussman, eds. Lemur Biology. Plenum, New York. 313–34.

Richards, P. W. 1972. Africa, the "Odd Man Out." In B. J. Meggers, E. S. Ayensu, and W. D. Duckworth, eds. Tropical Forest Ecosystems in Africa and South America: A Comparative Review. Smithsonian Institution Press, Washington, DC. 21–26.

Roederer, P. 1972. Les sols de Madagascar. In R. Battistini and G. Richard-Vindard, eds. Biogeography and Ecology of Madagascar. 201–26.

Rumpler, Y., and Albignac, R. 1978. Chromosome studies of the *Lepilemur*, an endemic Malagasy genus of Lemurs: contribution of cytogenetics to their taxonomy. J. Hum. Evol. 7: 191–96.

Russell, R. J. 1977. The behavior, ecology, and environmental physiology of a nocturnal primate,

Lepilemur mustelinus (Strepsirhini, Lemuriformes, Lepilemuridae). Thesis, Duke University, Durham, N.C.

Sauer, E. G. F., and Rothe, P. 1972. Ratite eggshells from Lanzarote, Canary Islands. Science 176: 43–45.

Sibree, J. 1880. The Great African Island. Trübner, London. 372 pp.

Smith, A. G., and Hallam, A. 1970. The fit of the southern continents. Nature 225: 139–44.

Smith, P. J. 1976a. Madagascar issue settled. Nature 259: 80.

———. 1976b. So Madagascar was to the north. Nature 263: 729–30.

Standing, H. F. 1908. On recently discovered subfossil primates from Madagascar. Trans. Zool. Soc. Lond. 18: 69–162.

Stearn, W. T. 1971. A survey of the tropical genera *Oplonia* and *Psilanthele* (Acanthaceae). Bulletin of the British Museum (Natural History). Botany 4: 261–323.

———. 1975. A synopsis of the genus *Catharanthus* (Apocynaceae). In W. I. Taylor and N. R. Farnsworth, eds. The Catharanthus Alkaloids. Marcel Dekker, New York. 9–44.

Stewart, J. 1975. Orchid safari. Defenders Wildlife 50: 136–40.

Sussman. R. W. 1975. A preliminary study of the behavior and ecology of *Lemur fulvus rufus* Audebert 1800. In I. Tattersall and R. W. Sussman, eds. Lemur Biology. Plenum, New York. 237–58.

———. 1977. Feeding behavior of *Lemur catta* and *Lemur fulvus.* In T. H. Clutton-Brock, ed. Primate Ecology. Academic Press, London. 1–37.

Svoboda, G. H., and Blake, D. A. 1975. The phytochemistry and pharmacology of *Catharanthus roseus* (L.) G. Don. In W. I. Taylor and N. R. Farnsworth, eds. The Catharanthus Alkaloids. Marcel Dekker, New York. 45–84.

Tattersall, I. 1972. The functional significance of airorhynchy in *Megaladapis*. Folia primatol. 18: 20–26.

———. 1973a. Cranial anatomy of the archaeolemurinae (Lemuroidea Primates). Anthropol. Papers Amer. Mus. Nat. Hist. 52: 1: 1–110.

———. 1973b. A note on the age of the subfossil site of Ampasambazimba, Miarinarivo Province, Malagasy Republic. Amer. Mus. Novitates. no. 2520: 1–6.

———, and Schwartz, J. H. 1974. Craniodental morphology and the systematics of the Malagasy lemurs (Primates, Prosimii). Anthropol. Papers Amer. Mus. Nat. Hist. 52: 141–92.

———, and Sussman, R. W. 1975. Observations on the ecology and behavior of the mongoose lemur *Lemur mongoz mongoz* Linnaeus (Primates, Lemuriformes) at Ampijoroa, Madagascar. Anthropol. Papers Amer. Mus. Nat. Hist. 52: 195–216.

Thorington, R. W. 1968. Observations of squirrel monkeys in a Colombian forest. In L. A. Rosenblum and R. W. Cooper, eds. The Squirrel Monkey. Academic Press, New York. 69–87.

Tin-Wa, M., and Farnsworth, N. R. 1975. The phytochemistry of minor Catharanthus species. In W. I. Taylor and N. R. Farnsworth, eds. The Catharanthus Alkaloids. Marcel Dekker, New York. 85–124.

Tronchon, J. 1974. L'Insurrection Malgache de 1947. François Maspero, Paris. 397 pp.

Swank, W. T., and Douglass, J. E. 1974. Streamflow greatly reduced by converting deciduous hardwood stands to pine. Science 185: 857–59.

Verin, P. 1971. Les anciens habitats de Rezoky et d'Asambalahy. Taloha, Revue la Musée d'Art d'Archéologie, Université Madagascar 4: 29–46.

Walker, A. 1967. Patterns of extinction among the subfossil Malagasy lemuroids. In P. S. Martin and H. E. Wright, Jr., eds. Pleistocene Extinctions. Yale University Press, New Haven and London. 425–32.

Walker, E. P.; Warnick, F.; Hamlet, S. E.; Lange, K. I.; Davis, M. A.; Vible, H. E.; and Wright, P. F. 1966. Mammals of the World. Johns Hopkins Press, Baltimore. 1,500 pp.

Ward, B. 1976. The Home of Man. Norton, New York. 297 pp.

———, and R. Dubos. 1972. Only One Earth. Penguin Books, Harmondsworth, Middlesex. 304 pp.

Warfield, R. K., and Bouck, G. B. 1974. Microtubule–macrotubule transitions: intermediates after exposure to the mitotic inhibitor vinblastine. Science 186: 1219–21.

Wegener, A. 1920. Die Entstehung der Continente und Ozeane. Vieweg, Braunschweig.

Whitmore, T. C. 1975. Tropical rainforests of the Far East. Clarendon Press, Oxford. 282 pp.

Whittaker, R. H. 1975. Communities and Ecosystems, 2d ed. Macmillan, New York.

Wilson, E. O. 1971. Competitive and agressive behavior. In J. F. Eisenberg and W. Dillon, eds. Man and Beast: Comparative Social Behavior. Smithsonian Institution Press, Washington, DC. 181–218.

Wilson, E. O. 1975. Sociobiology. Harvard University Press, Cambridge, Mass. 697 pp.

Zapfe, H. 1963. Lebensbild von *Megaladapis edwardsi* (Grandidier). Folia primatol. 1: 178–87.

Zavaboahary Malagasy. 1978. Dept. des Eaux et Forêts, Antananarive. 48 pp.

INDEX

267

Brickaville (town), 95
British influence in 19th century, 91, 113
Brookesia minima, 16, 17
Budnitz, N. (zoologist), 186
bug, colonial flattid, 206–07
bulbul: Madagascar, *Hypsipetes madagascariensis*, 44
butterflies, 216, 217; antenor swallowtail, *Papilio antenor*, 217
butter-gold tree: *Acridocarpus excelsus*, 209, 211

cactus: *Rhipsalis cassytha*, 15, 37; prickly pear, *Opuntia monacantha*, 180–83
Canal des Pangalanes, 94–97 passim
canoe. *See* pirogue
carnivores, xiii, 18, 19, 133, 169, 213, 237
Centella asiatica, 145
chadsia tree: *Chadsia grevei*, 214
chameleons, 16, 17, 237
Charaxes sp., butterfly, 216
Charles-Dominique, P. (zoologist), 218
cichlid fish, endemic, 16
climax communities, 50, 52
cloves, 26, 27, 232
coastal forest. *See* forest, coastal
cochineal bettle: *Dactylopius coccus*, 182–83
coffee, 36, 38, 39, 40, 232
Col des Tapia, 10
colea tree, 53
colonization. *See* France, colonial power
colubrid snakes, 16
commiphora bottle-tree: *Commiphora monstruosa*, 159
conservation policy, 6–9, 231–34. *See also* agriculture; education; employment; forestry service; trade
continental drift, 10–14
coral-billed nuthatch: *Hypositta corallirostris*, 31, 164
coua: blue, *Coua caerulea*, 28–29, 106; crested, *C. cristata*, 164; great ground, *C. gigas*, 198
coucal: Madagascar, *Centropus toulou*, 31, 106, 185
crab: fiddler, 74, 75; mangrove, *Scylla serrata*, 75–76
crocodile: *Crocodilus niloticus*, 119, 126, 129, 237, 238
cuckoo-falcon: Madagascar, *Aviceda madagascariensis*, 219
cuckoo-roller: Madagascar, *Leptosomus discolor*, 29
cycad: *Cycas thouarsi*, 95

daddy longlegs: cave-dwelling, *Decarynella gracilipes*, 114
Dainis, K. (zoologist), 186
Decary, R., (administrator), 114, 120, 175, 180, 182
deciduous woodland. *See* forest, deciduous
Defenders of Wildlife magazine, 67
de Gaulle, General, 93
de Guiteaud, plantation of, 219, 221
desert, spiny. *See* forest, spiny desert
Didiereaceae, xiii, 159. *See also* alluaudia; *Alluaudiopsis fiherenensis*; *Didierea trolli*
Didierea trolli, 16; *D. madagascariensis*, 204, 207
dô. *See* boa
Dox (poet), 125

duck: Bernier's, *Anas bernieri*, 16; red-billed, *A. erythrorhyncha*, 137; Meller's, *A. melleri*, 214
dugong: *Dugong dugon*, 71, 73
Du Pray, M. and Mme. (planters), 186

Eaux et Forêts. *See* forestry service
ebony: *Diospyros* spp., 16
education: and conservation, 6–7, 110, 114, 118–19, 228; pupil/teacher ratio, 35; and colonization, 93; and village, 213
egret: cattle, *Bubulculus ibis*, 219
elephant-birds: *Mullerornis* and *Aepyornis*, 11, 126, 128, 129
elephant's-foot tree: *Pachypodium lamerei*, 159, 162
Embleton, B. J. (geologist), 10
Emmanuel family, 34–40, 42–43, 232
employment, 26–28, 35–36; migrant labor, 174, 178, 183, 232
erosion, 32, 39–40, 79, 125, 210, 232
escarpment, 90, 91, 92, 95
eucalyptus, planted, 98–100
euphorbia: *Euphorbia laro*, 2, 159, 160; crown-of-thorns, *E. milii*, 151; *E. stenoclada*, 159
Eupleres goudotii, 18, 19
exhumation of the dead, 122–24

falcon, 21, 22; Madagascar cuckoo, *Aviceda madagascariensis*, 219
fanaloka: *Eupleres goudotii*, 18, 19
fern: bracket, *Asplenium nidas*, 52; *Cyathea* tree ferns, 52, 135; montane, 135
Fianarantsoa (town), 91
figs, 25, 53
filao: *Casuarina equisetifolia*, 95
fire: Great Fire, 33, 131; grass and forest, 208, 209, 226–28
fire-resistant tree, *Sclerocarya caffra*, 230
firewood: need of, 39–40; from reserve, 170
fish, endemic, 16
Flacourt, Sieur de, 129, 131, 138, 153–54
flamboyant tree: *Delonix regia*, xiii, 218
flame tree: Madagascar, *Hildegardia erythrosiphon*, 214
flycatcher: paradise, *Tchitrea mutata*, 198
flying foxes: *Pteropus rufus*, 193–94
forest: spiny desert, 3, 157–62, 170–72; reserves, protection, 7, 170, 233–34; rainforest, 25–26, 44–53, 102, 105–06; clearance, 26–28, 29, 30, 33–34, 170–72, 177; area remaining, 33; savoka, 33, 38; firewood, 39–40, 98; coastal, 95; planted softwoods, 99–100; montane, 134–35; western slope transitional, 156–57; gallery 185–86; deciduous, 208–11, 213–18. *See also* savanna
forestry service, 6–9, 93–100, 170, 233–34
Fort Dauphin (town), 138, 153
fossa: *Cryptoprochta ferox*, xiii, 19, 169, 213
fossils, giant sub-, 126–134
France: forest area 33; colonial power, 64, 91–94, 180; early settlement, 153–54, 180
frogs, 16; Antongil scarlet, *Discophus antongili*, 40; tree, 54, 55; burrowing, *Pletodontohyla tuberata*, 135; sarobakaka, *Rhacophorus goudoti*, 135; torrent, *Man-*